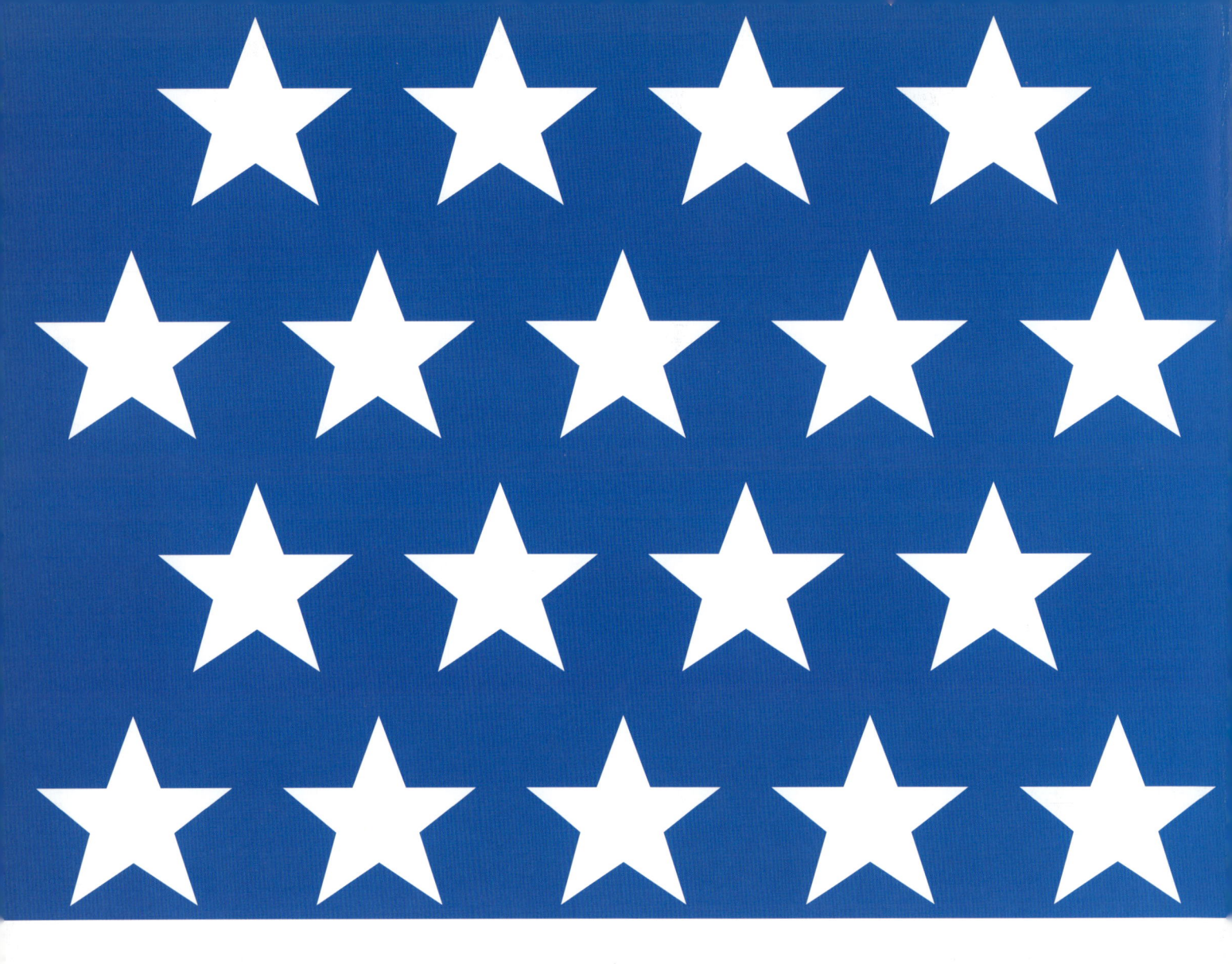

PORTRAITS OF CITIES

To Helena, my dear wife,
without whom this book would have never been written.

Published by 22nd. Century Film Corp., New York
21 West 58th Street, New York, New York 10019, U.S.A.

Copyright © Dong Kingman, 1997

All rights reserved. No part of this publication may be
reproduced, stored in a retrieval system, or transmitted,
in any form or by any means, electronic, mechanical,
photocopying, recording, or otherwise, without the prior
written permission of the publishers.

Library of Congress Catalog Card Number 97-60668
ISBN 0-9658333-5-6

Printed in Hong Kong
By South China Printing Co. (1988) Ltd.

CONTENTS

1 FOREWORD:
KINGMAN'S MANY COLORED CHAOS BOX
by Alexander Eliot Excerpt from Time Magazine

8 MUSEUMS AND PERMANENT COLLECTIONS

26 HONOURS AND AWARDS

46 I TAUGHT MYSELF TO PAINT (WITH PICTURE)
by Dong Kingman

48 FIRST REVIEW IN SAN FRANCISCO NEWS, 1936

50 PICTURES

66 CABLE CARS

74 PORTRAITS OF CITIES
by Dong Kingman

76 EXCERPTS FROM THE LIFE MAGAZINE

84 THE EYE AND HAND OF DONG KINGMAN
by William Saroyan

88 MY ART IN FILMS
by Dong Kingman

95 EXCERPTS FROM AMERICAN ARTIST MAGAZINE:
DONG KINGMAN PAINTS PEKING IN SPAIN
ON AN INDIVIDUAL APPROACH TO WATERCOLOR
AN INTERVIEW, by Ernest W. Watson
THE INTIMATE WORLD OF DONG KINGMAN, by Eugene M. Ettenberg

118 STAGING BRILLIANT WATERCOLORS
by Dong Kingman (Appearing in American Artist magazine 4-6-1995)

122 MAGAZINE ASSIGNMENTS

126 PAN-AMERICAN AIRWAYS 1ST CLASS MENU COVERS

130 THE LIFE OF A MURAL
by Dong Kingman

132 ALL ABOUT DONG KINGMAN
by Herb Caen and Helena kingman

PREFACE

  I am a painter of portraits - not of human faces, but of faces of cities permeated with interminable human spirits.
  I have always lived in cities. Born in Oakland, California, I have lived in San Francisco, HongKong, and New York City.
  In this book, you will see many more portraits of cities than the ones mentioned above. Between teaching and painting assignments, I have been around the world many times, everywhere I went, I would sit down somewhere to paint on locations. Some of the finished products became prize-winning pictures, others found their way into museum and permanent private collections.
  Through the years, magazines like <u>Time</u>,<u>Life</u>, and the <u>American Artist</u> have reported on my continuous search for the human heart and soul in cities.
  Fascinating the task continues to be! A search that never ends.

Kingman's Many Colored Chaos Box

Foreword By Alexander Eliot

Alexander Eliot, former Art Editor for Time Magazine, has written many stories about me and my exhibitions from the 1940s to the 1960s.

During the early 20th century, the major American watercolorists were Winslow Homer and John Singer Sargent. At mid-century, they were John Marin and Charles Burchfield. Today it's Dong Kingman, who combines the observation of Homer, the suavity of Sargent, the dynamism of Marin, and the lyricism of Burchfield. To top it all off, Kingman projects a breezy, gently fantastical wit that's all his own. With self-effacing sympathy, spontaneity, and butterfly-grace, he plays at creating evocative revisions of the world about us. Kingman reminds me of Cook Ting in the old Chinese legend, whose cleaver sliced everything and made, all clear—with just a zip and a zoop.

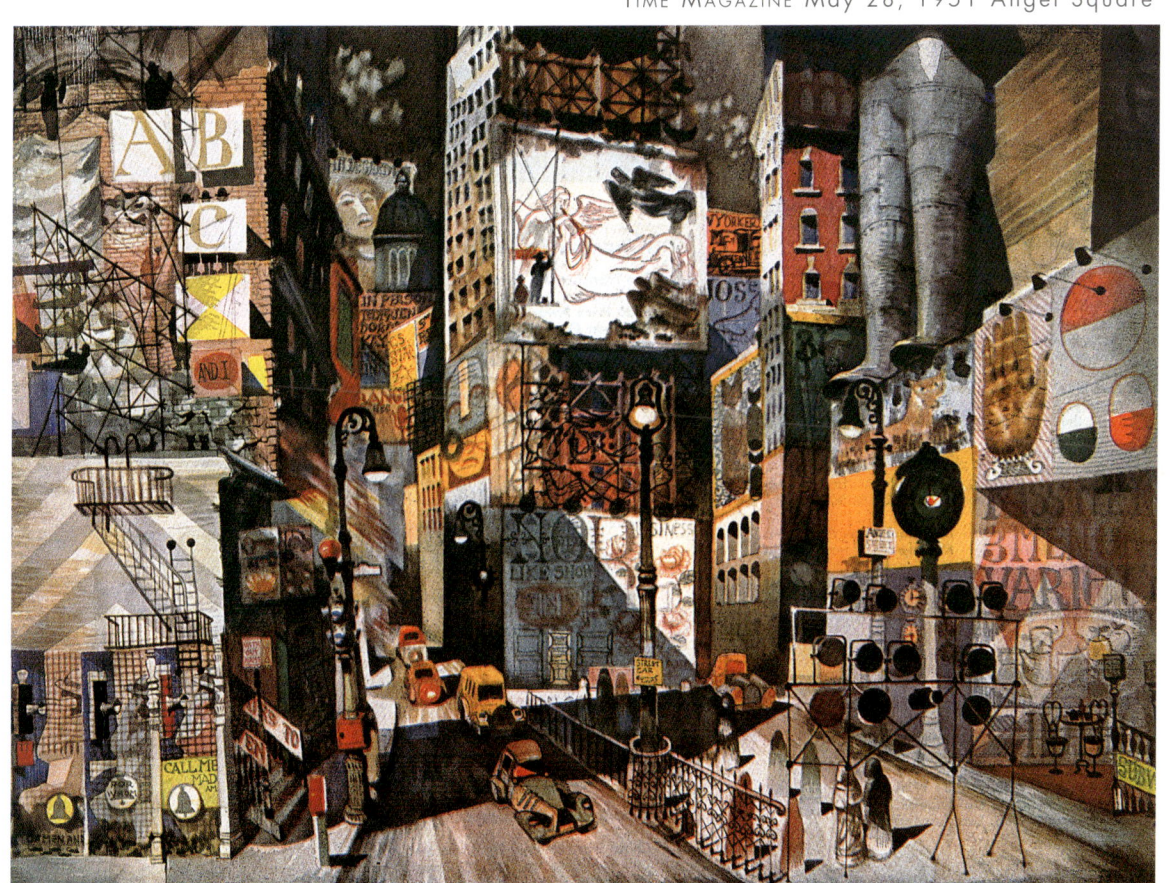

TIME MAGAZINE May 28, 1951 Angel Square

Chinese Firecrackers in Manhattan

A more complicated subject than Times Square would have been hard for a painter to find, but bouncy, bucktoothed Dong Kingman found it right up his alley. The result is as tasty as spice cake—with a frosted title, Angel Square, which is a fair sample of Kingman's wit. What holds his picture together is worsted-tight composition, plus an extremely subtle use of bright and dull colors to give it dramatic height and depth.

At 40, Kingman is one of the world's best watercolorists. A ten-year retrospective show of his work, at a Manhattan gallery this month, is topped by *Angel Square*, to which he devoted much of the last two years. His other new paintings of Manhattan street and subway scenes have the same cheerful quality of spluttering Chinese firecrackers.

"If people take my work too seriously," Kingman told me once, "I'm disappointed. I mean, the signs say "Go Here, Go There", when you don't really have to. And on Sundays, when there's no traffic, the stoplights keep blinking as if they were crazy. Don't you feel that way?"

True artists set themselves to actively observe, delineate, and finally re-image aspects of this mixed-up world for us. What gets them started on such a lonely and incredibly difficult mission? Kingman's initiation as an artist was the earliest I've ever come across. When he was only five, his family traveled eastward from San Francisco to Hong Kong (he would make the return journey at 18). That childhood, 35-day voyage was in steerage class. The crowding, discomfort, the near-immobilization amid ever-changing immensities, with no place to play, cannot have been easy. Plus, the first world war was in progress and German torpedoes an ever-present danger. "I could sense the excitement on people's faces," Kingman remembers, "and observe fascinating responses. There were many interesting characters aboard, so I began to sketch them day after day."

Subsequently, a Hong Kong artist named Szetu Wei undertook Kingman's instruction. His "good spirit and human understanding" were crucial , Kingman acknowledges, "but I believe the best teacher is yourself."

In the tradition of Master Szetu, Kingman too has taken pains to help thousands of his own students get started. The man's quick, alert, laughing and ever-sympathetic presence is in itself encouraging to others. Looking back on his long career he remembers even the hard times with gratitude. "Whenever I felt discouraged," he recalls, "I would stop and think something had always come along which enabled me to continue learning."

Master Kingman keeps learning, on painting trips around the globe, with all his characteristic butterfly-grace and tact. "There are many things in my art which I'm not satisfied," he remarks. "It may take only a day to learn how to use your tools and your medium, but it takes more than a lifetime to become any good,"

The most important cultural development during the past half-century has been the interflowing of East and West. Kingman has faced the challenge, willed the mission, and finally fulfilled his destiny of creative participation in this interflow. Thus, when interviewed by his brilliant partner Helena Kuo some years ago, Kingman confessed: In my early days as an artist I had a difficult time finding myself and trying to reconcile my Chinese heritage with my American thinking... Today, however, I no longer worry about these distinctions. For me, there is no such thing as Oriental or Occidental."

Kingman follows the Western and the Eastern ways, both at once. As a Chinese American citizen of the world. he's devoted his long life to pulling reason and intuition together for the purposes of art. Result: watercolors that display balanced complexity, aesthetic intensity, and intuitive wholeness, all three! His best pictures energize the heart and calm the mind. Each one is itself a clutch of vivid immediacy.

"I have great respect for the Chinese masters who worked from memory," Kingman says. "However, I try to take their techniques one step further by combining Eastern and Western painting methods. That is, I usually start my watercolor on location and finish it in the studio by recalling the scene and using my imagination to develop it... I might paint a park scene—people sipping tea or coffee in an outdoor cafe, a sunny sky with kites flying, birds singing on tree branches, a lake with colorful sails and whales swimming around, or every window of a building filled with faces looking out, or linking with a rainbow of colors in red, yellow, blue, green. orange. and purple!"

Anyone familiar with the roots of Taoism will recognize in Kingman a modern reflection of the legendary Chinese "Gourd Masters" who employed calabash bottles or sometimes "chaos boxes" to re-arrange reality through sorcery. Instead of a calabash bottle, Kingman uses an instant-coffee jar (containing two ounces of water) for his painting expeditions. And in place of a "chaos box" he goes equipped with a light paintbox and a folding stool. 'I believe you should carry whatever you feel you need for painting outdoors." he says with his quick smile, "But most important of all, you should always remember to take your inspiration with you."

Why work in watercolor? "Choosing a medium is like selecting an instrument for a musician,' Kingman explains. "I find watercolor best for my temperament. It's a quick-drying medium and you must think fast. I can create light sensitive tones on my paper as well as rich, dark colors—yet watercolor always retains its transparent quality... To me, the white of the paper is most valuable." This reminds me of a classic tale by Chuang Tzu. Once upon a time the Emperor of the South Sea was called Shu (Brief), and the Emperor of the North Sea was called Hu (Sudden). They both loved visiting the hospitable Emperor of the Central Region, who was called Hun-tun (Chaos). In so doing they inadvertently destroyed their friend! Kingman's quick wet strokes never do that to the mirror-white paper, the primordial "Central Region" of his ever-delicate play.

Way back in the 1940's, when I was Time Magazine's art critic, I practice of interviewing artists at fancy restaurants—on Time of course—because I loved to eat and drink. At my first meeting with Kingman, he suggested I order for myself and when I'd done so he ordered a glass of water! Nothing else. Producing his ever-present pen and sketchpad, he proceeded to sketch me. I blushingly stuffed myself! By the time I'd reached the bottom of my second glass of wine, I realized this diminutive artist was using vast power to overturn the big fat critic in me. I mean the power of water, which always seeks the lowest place and yet wears down mountains. We've been friends ever since.

One more story, and I'll call it a day. There was a man named Chuang Chou, who dreamt he was a butterfly happily fluttering around, doing as he pleased. Upon waking, he found himself to be solidly and unmistakably Chuang Chou. Then a thought struck him. Was he the man who had just dreamt of being a butterfly, or was he really a butterfly who now dreamt of being Chuang Chou?

I think, myself, that human consciousness is a dreamy state; most of us seem only half-awake. Not so Dong Kingman; he keeps his eyes open. That's what makes him such good company, and such a great artist.

Alexander Eliot

TIME MAGAZINE September 3, 1945

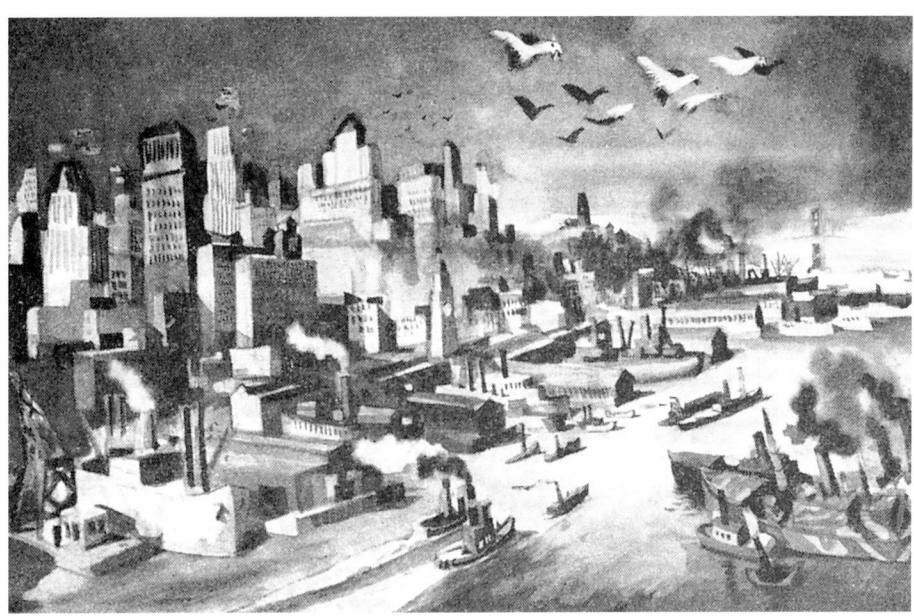

Midtown Galleries

DONG KINGMAN'S SAN FRANCISCO,
OCCIDENTAL REPORTAGE WITH ORIENTAL OVERTONES

DASHING REALIST

Bouncy, buck-toothed little Dong Kingman, a California born Chinese, bas meandered over much of the U.S., recording in bright, breezy brush strokes the look of the land. In the course of his visual reporting he has whipped out about 30 pictures a year. and sold most of them at an average of $250 a piece.

Last week, at San Francisco's M. H. de Young Memorial Museum, his home town got a look at 64 deftly. slapdash Dong watercolors. One standout was a gay gull's-eye view of San Francisco's war-crowded harbor (see cut). To get a proper perch. to paint it from ~ Dong pitched a pup tent dizzily atop the Bay Bridge. It was a long way up from the narrow obscurity of San Francisco's Chinatown where he began.

Sidewalk started when Dong was five years old, his American-born father got tired of running a band laundry, moved the family to Hong Kong. There be ran a successful department store while Dong chalked his early works on sidewalk out front. They looked good to his father, who packed Dong off to Hong Kong's Lingnan Academy to learn about art. The head-master. who had studied in Paris, took Dong under his wide-sleeved wing, taught him oriental Hsieh-yi ("to draw, a conception") and occidental Hsieh-cheng ("to draw reality"). Dong inclined toward Hsieh-cheng.

At 18, he returned to the U.S., worked two years in an overall factory, sank $75 in a restaurant which flopped because he spent more time painting than cooking. In 1936, after a spell as a houseboy, be began painting on a $94-a-month WPA grant.

All-American. Critics who look for oriental innuendoes in Dong's bright colors and brash brushwork can trace his work back to China's 1,400-year-old tradition of sacrificing detail to get the "rhythmic vitality" of a scene. But Dong is, and counts himself, All-American. Since April, as an Army private, he has been doing secret plainclothes work for the cloak-&-dagger. Office of the Strategic Services. On furloughs he returns to his apartment just off Nob Hill and his pretty Chinese-American wife. He sometimes wears a blue mandarin coat but also. likes loud sports jackets.

His free way of painting what he sees, Dong has a characteristic explanation: "Nature is very messy, it is the artist's job to straighten it out."

TIME, September 3, 1945

TIME MAGAZINE April 18, 1949

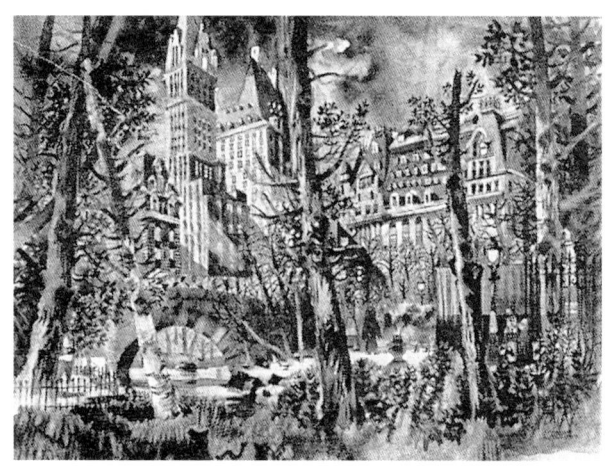 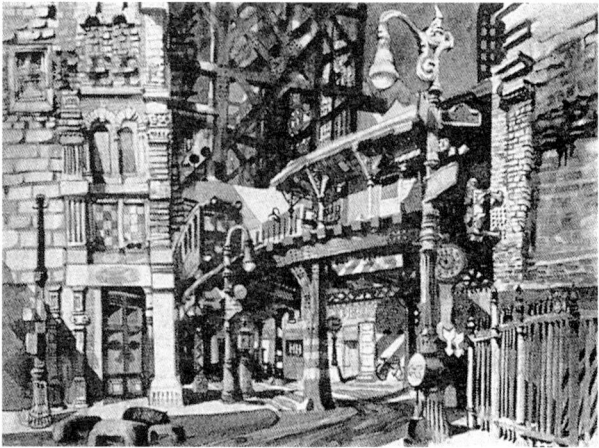

Midtown Galleries
A Day In Central Park, (left) & Franklin Square (right). *If a crowd gather, sing in Chinese.*

MEETING OF EAST & WEST

Manhattan gallerygoers were treated to some surprising new views of their city last week. In an exhibition of brush drawings and watercolors by a bouncy little Chinese-American artist named Dong Kingman, they found a strange but somehow convincing version of the place. Kingman had painted bits of the town from Central Park to the Battery, making most of his sketches on Sundays and working from half-concealed positions behind garbage cans and in doorways so as not to attract attention. "Sometimes a crowd would gather anyway," Kingman says, "and I'd have to drive them away by singing Chinese songs—very hard on the ears."

Born in the U.S., Kingman was taken to Hong Kong at the age of five, returned at 18 and went to work in a California overall factory. When the overall business palled, he did a hitch as a houseboy and another in a Chinese restaurant. Finally the WPA came along and gave him a chance to paint full-time, started him toward becoming a bang-up success with his brush (Time, Sept. 3, 1945). Since his discharge from the Army, where he served as a private in the OSS in Washington, he has been living in Brooklyn and teaching at Columbia and Hunter College.

One Way Up. His new paintings are his best yet. Kingman composed each one as elaborately as a Chinese puzzle, lit them with hectic dabs and flashes of bright color, and peopled them with wistful or sometimes sinister figures that seemed to hover uncertainly about the edges of his pictures, like the onlookers that interrupted his work. The paintings are crammed with signs reading Coffee Coffee Coffee, Goat, or ABCDEFGHIJK, and with crooked street lamps, unlikely stoplights, and one-way signs that often as not point straight up or down. "I put all that in for fun," Kingman explains. "If people take my work too seriously, I'm disappointed. Of course, my pictures are sarcastic too. I mean, the signs say 'Go Here, Go There' when you don't really have to, and on Sundays, when there's no traffic, the stoplights keep on blinking as if they were crazy. Don't you feel that way?"

Halfway Back The sarcasm is more friendly than biting, for Kingman takes a naive delight in U.S.ways. He keeps the radio in his studio going constantly ("It softens my mind and helps me paint. know all about Luncheon at Sardi's and Heigh-ho, Silver!"), and all through dinner he watches television programs with his wife and two children. "To Chinese people," he says, "football is very queer, but I like to go and see the games. Also, play bridge once a week."

At 38, Kingman's thoughts are turning eastward again. "Everyone writes that my work is half East and half West," he says, "that I'm in between. I don't know, I just want to be myself. Sometimes I dream I'm in Hong Kong; I want to go see if the dream is right."

TIME MAGAZINE January 25, 1960

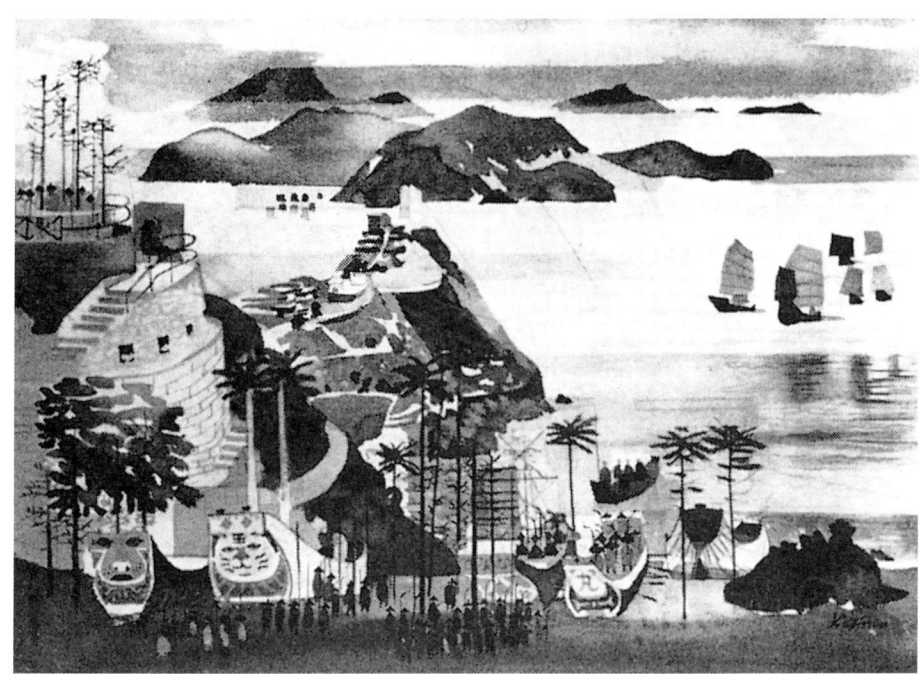

"200 Fisherman at South Bay" (Hong Kong)

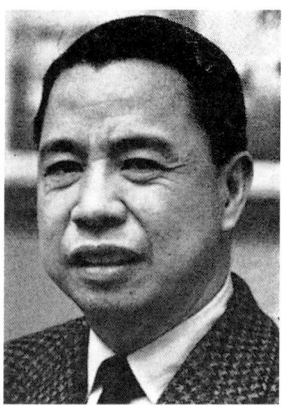

Below, Dong Kingman

SIDEWALK SUPERINTENDENT

Eleven years ago Dong Kingman confessed that he often dreamed of Hong Kong, his boyhood home, and that he would like to go back and "see if the dream is right." An around-the-world lecture tour sponsored by the State Department gave Artist Kingman his first opportunity, and increasing financial success has enabled him to repeat parts of the trip each year with his pretty wife. While his wife saw the sights, Kingman sat painting waterfronts in Hong Kong, sidewalk scenes in Rome, Paris and London. The fruits of his fun, on view at Manhattan's Wildenstein Gallery this week, were very like happy dreams: luminous, lighthearted, and full of surprising juxtapositions.

Even in a boom season, Kingman's success is phenomenal. A London exhibition last fall delighted the critics, and a Paris show is planned for the spring. With works in 30-odd American museums and a minimum guarantee from his gallery, Kingman sits on top of the world. Capping his pleasure is the fact that there have been times when the world seemed to be sitting on top of him. The son of a Chinese store owner, he studied painting in Hong Kong, moved to the U.S. at 18, worked as a houseboy, cook and factory hand. The WPA art program started him on his long, steep climb from the gaudy obscurity of San Francisco's Chinatown. Passionately fond of city life, Kingman now lives in the heart of Manhattan, constantly prowls its streets with sketch pad in hand. "I feel I am learning to draw," he says with his habitual smile of polite delight. "Maybe when I get to be old and can't get around well, I'll be able to do more things from imagination." Actually, Kingman uses his imagination to people his real scenes with creatures never seen on land or sea, some grass-high and others building-high. "A big man," says Kingman, who is 5 ft. 1 in., "perhaps doesn't notice so much difference between large and small. I like to paint people at different levels, and sometimes with wheels under them so they can move about more quickly." He also uses giant faces, single eyes, fantastic animals, and meaningless signs to fill odd corners of his designs with elusive life. This week's show offered, amidst a host of similar fantasies, people on unicycles carrying dumbbells, That Kingman airily explained, "give weight to my painting." Turning serious, he added: "I'm disappointed when people take my work too seriously."

Museums:
Private and Permanent Collections

In 1936 when I began to work as a full-time watercolor painter, Mr. Albert Bender of San Francisco, an art collector, kept buying my pictures to give to museums for their permanent collections of nearly every major museum in the U.S. Following is a partial list:

Adelphi University, Garden City, New York

Addison Gallery of American Art, Andover, Massachuetts

Art Institute of Chicago, Chicago, Illinois

Atlanta Art Association, Atlanta, Georgia 1947

Brooklyn Museum of Art, Brooklyn, New York

Boston Museum of Art, Boston, Massachusetts

Bloomington Art Association, Bloomington, Indiana

Butler Art Institute, Youngstown, Ohio

Columbus Museum of Arts & Crafts, Columbus, Georgia

Cranbrook Academy of Art, Bloomfield Hills, Michigan

Davenport Municipal Art Gallery, Davenport, Iowa

Dartmouth College, Hanover, New Hampshire

De Young Museum of Art, San Francisco, California

Des Moines Art Center, Des Moines, Iowa

Evansville Museum of Art & Science, Evansville, Indiana

Fine Arts Gallery of San Diego, San Diego, California

Fort Wayne Art Institute, Fort Wayne, Indiana

Charles & Emma Frye Art Museum, Seattle, Washington

Honolulu Academy of Art, Honolulu, Hawaii

Hirschhorn Museum, Washington D.C.

Joslyn Art Museum, Omaha, Nebraska

University of Kansas Museum of Art, Lawrence, Kansas (1973)

Los Angeles County Fair Association, Los Angeles, California

Mills College, Oakland, California

University of Minnesota, Duluth, Minnesota (1957)

Munson-Williams-Proctor Institute, Utica, New York

New Britain Museum of American Art, New Britain, Connecticut

National Academy of Design, New York, N.Y.

Museum of Modern Art, New York, N.Y.

Pennsylvania State College, University Park, Pennsylvania

Pennsylvania Academy of Fine Arts, Philadelphia, Pennsylvania (1956)

Pioneer Museum & Haggin Galleries, Stockton, Califronia (1954)

Pomona College, Pomona, California (1941)

San Francisco Museum of Art, San Francisco, California

San Francisco Art Association, San Francisco, California

State University College, Oswego, New York

Springfield Art Association, Springfield, Illinois

Toledo Museum of Art, Toledo, Ohio

Tweed Gallery, University of Minnesota, Duluth, Minnesota

TIME magazine collection, New York, N.Y.

Wadsworth Atheneum, Hartford, Connecticut

The Wisconsin Union, University of Wisconsin, Madison, Wisconsin (1945)

Witte Memorial Museum, San Antonio, Texas

Whitney Museum of Art, New York, New York

Wilmington Society of Fine Arts, Wilmington, Delaware

Sheldon Memorial Art Gallery, Lincoln, Nebraska

Museums: Private and Permanent Collections

Metropolitan Museum of Art, New York, New York

AUL Headquarters, Indianapolis, Indiana

Historical Society of San Diego, San Diego, California

Campbell Historical Museum, Campbell, California

Springfield Art Museum, Springfield, Missouri, South Ferry House

Delaware Art Museum, Wilmington, Delaware, Railroad Oakland

MacNider Museum, Mason City, Iowa

International House, World Trade Center, New Orleans, Louisiana

Chamber of Commerce, Salt Lake City, Utah

Lousiville Museum of Natural History, Louisville, Kentucky

City Hall, Honolulu, Hawaii

City hall, San Francisco, California

City Hall, Atlanta, Georgia

Official Residence of American Ambassador, Beijing, China

Official Residence of American Consul-General, Guangzhou, China

Pan-American Airways Collection

Hyatt Regency Hotels, Hawaii

Mural in Lincoln Savings Bank, New York, New York

Mural in Boca Raton Hotel & Tower, Boca Raton, Florida

official Residence of American Ambassador, Moscow, USSR

Official Residence of American Ambassador, Prague, Czechoslovakia

Benihana collection

American Tourister International collection

Stonepine Resorts collection

Stage Delicatessen collection

On the following pages are some fo the paintings in collections

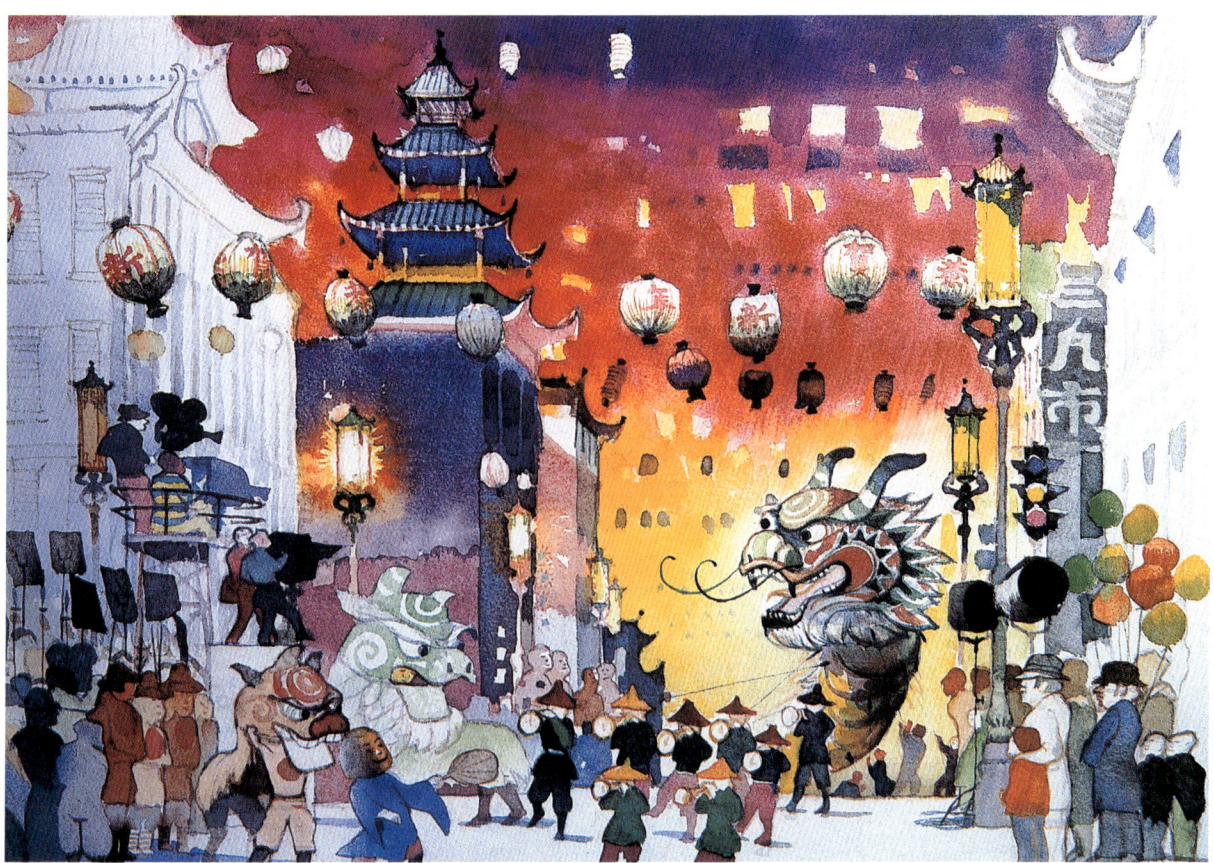

San Francisco's Festival, collection of Charles & Emma Frye Art Museum ~ Seattle, Washington

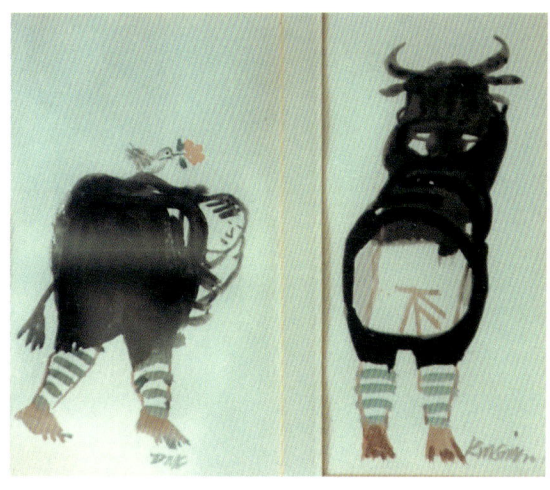

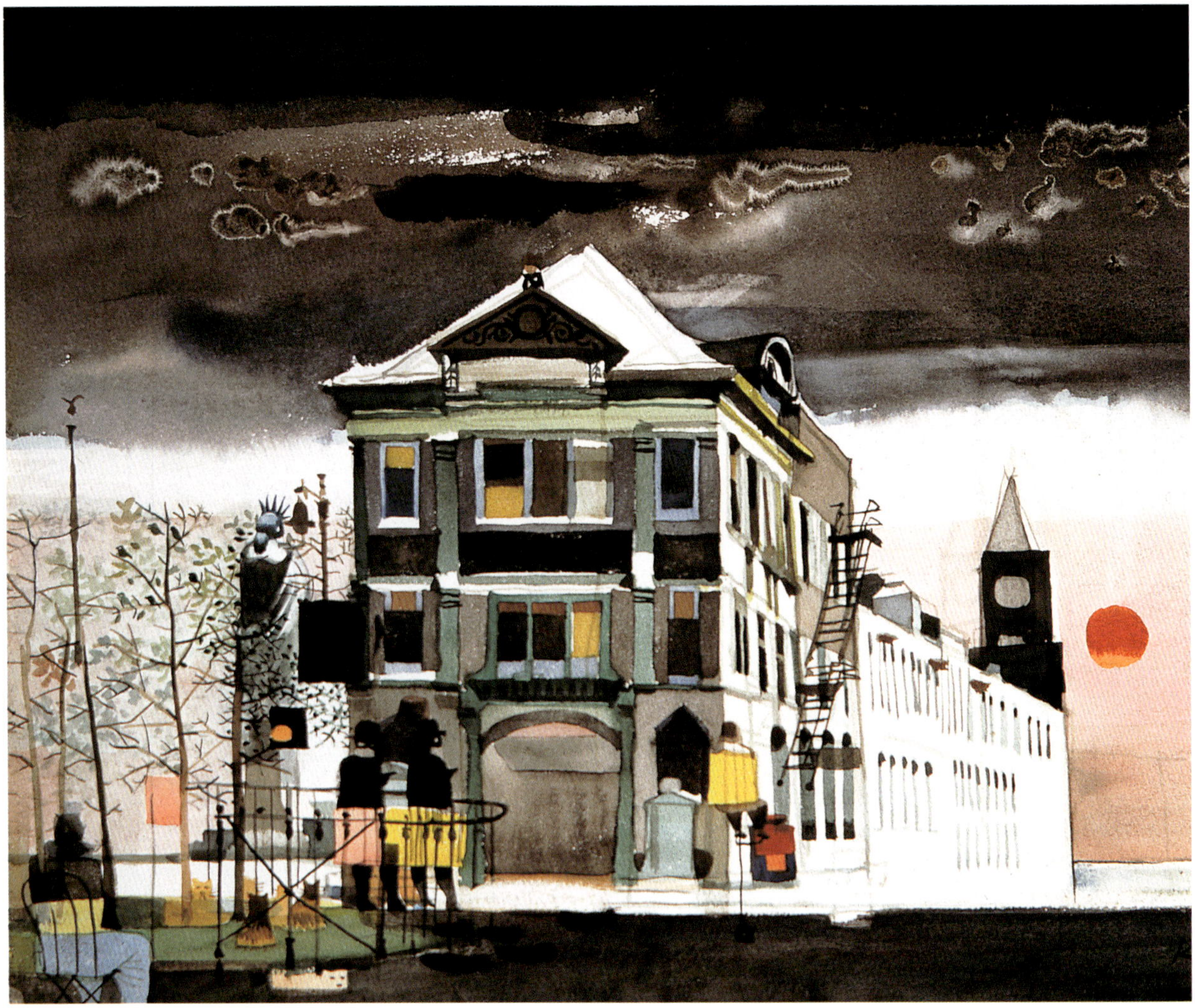

MUSEUMS: PRIVATE AND PERMANENT COLLECTIONS

South Ferry Building, Springfield Art Museum, Springfield, Missouri.

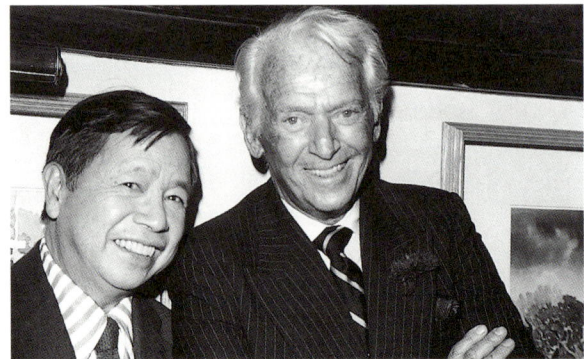

Douglas Fairbanks, Jr.

Philadelphia, Hood Museum of Art, Dartmouth College, Hanover, N.H.

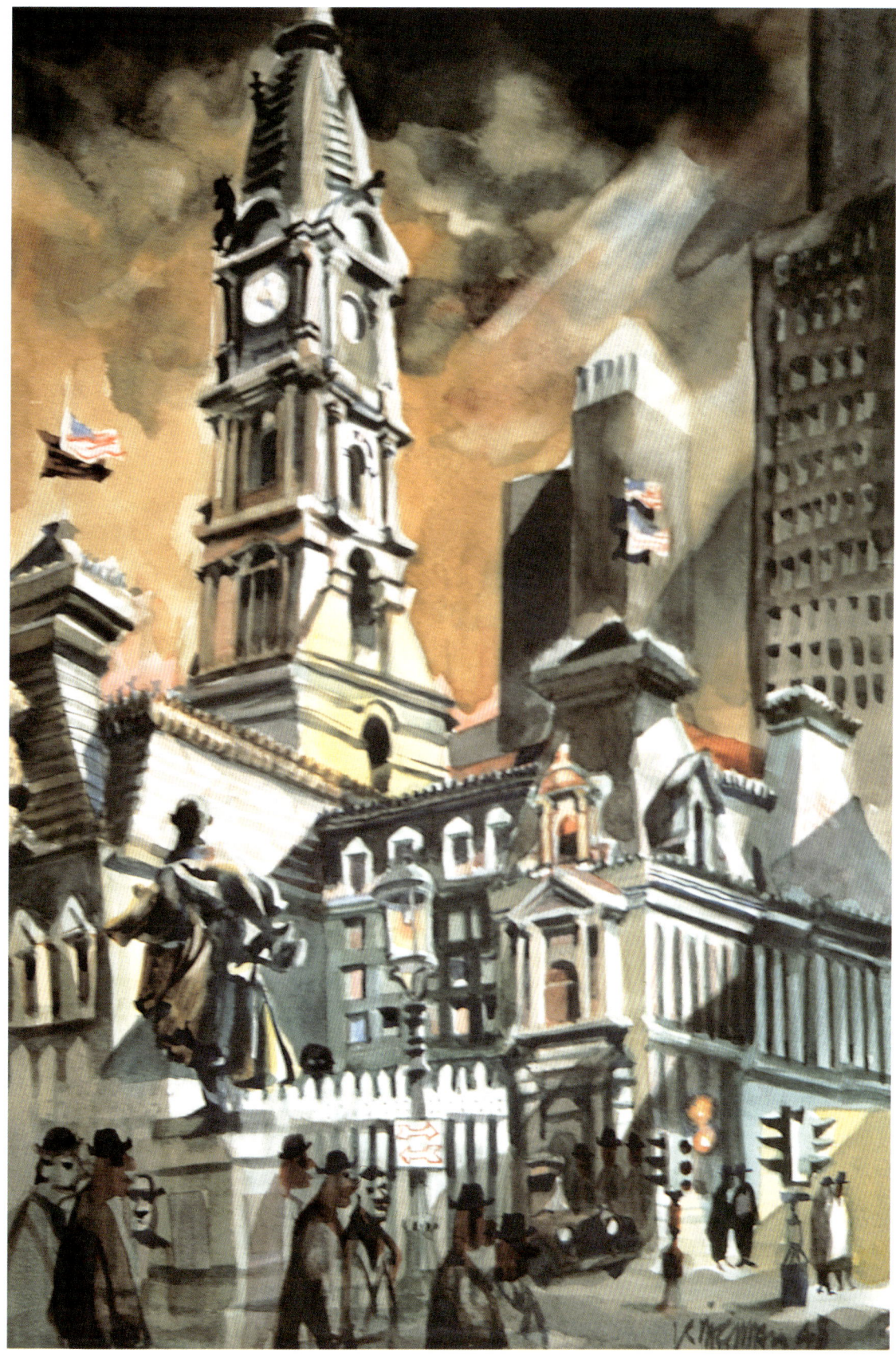

13

Museums: Private and Permanent Collections

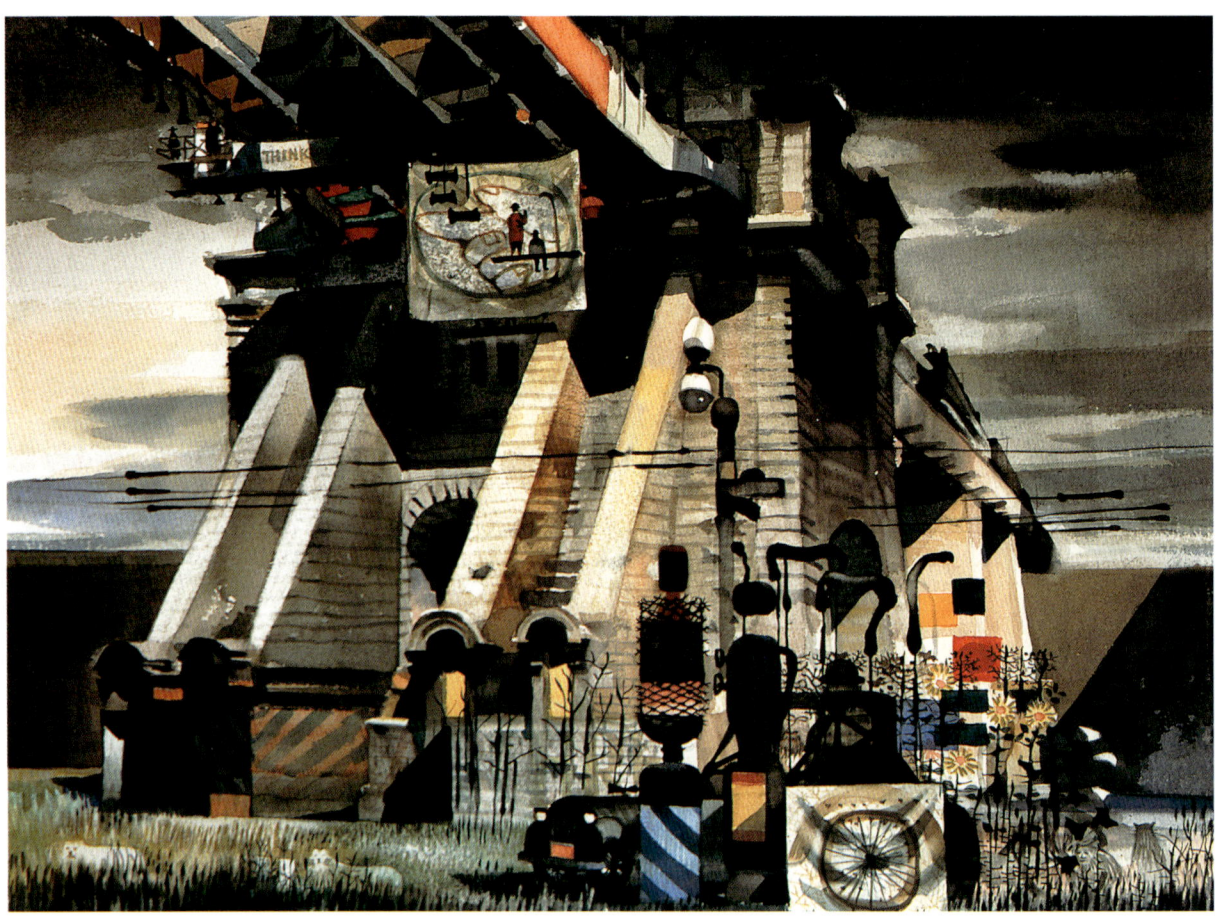

Bridge and Gas Station, Des Moines Art Center, Des Moines, Iowa.

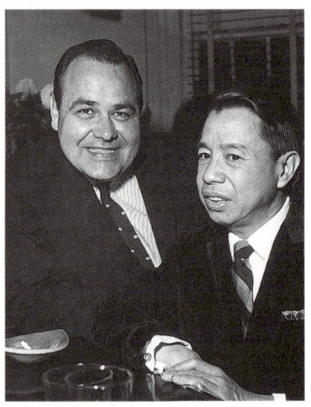

Jonathan Winter

642 Webster Street, Oakland, California

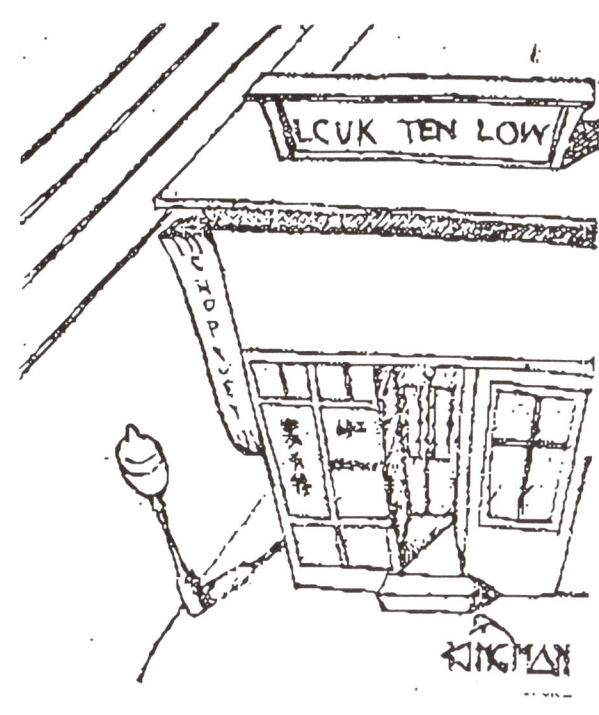

Coming to Omaha, Joslyn Art Museum, Omaha, Neb

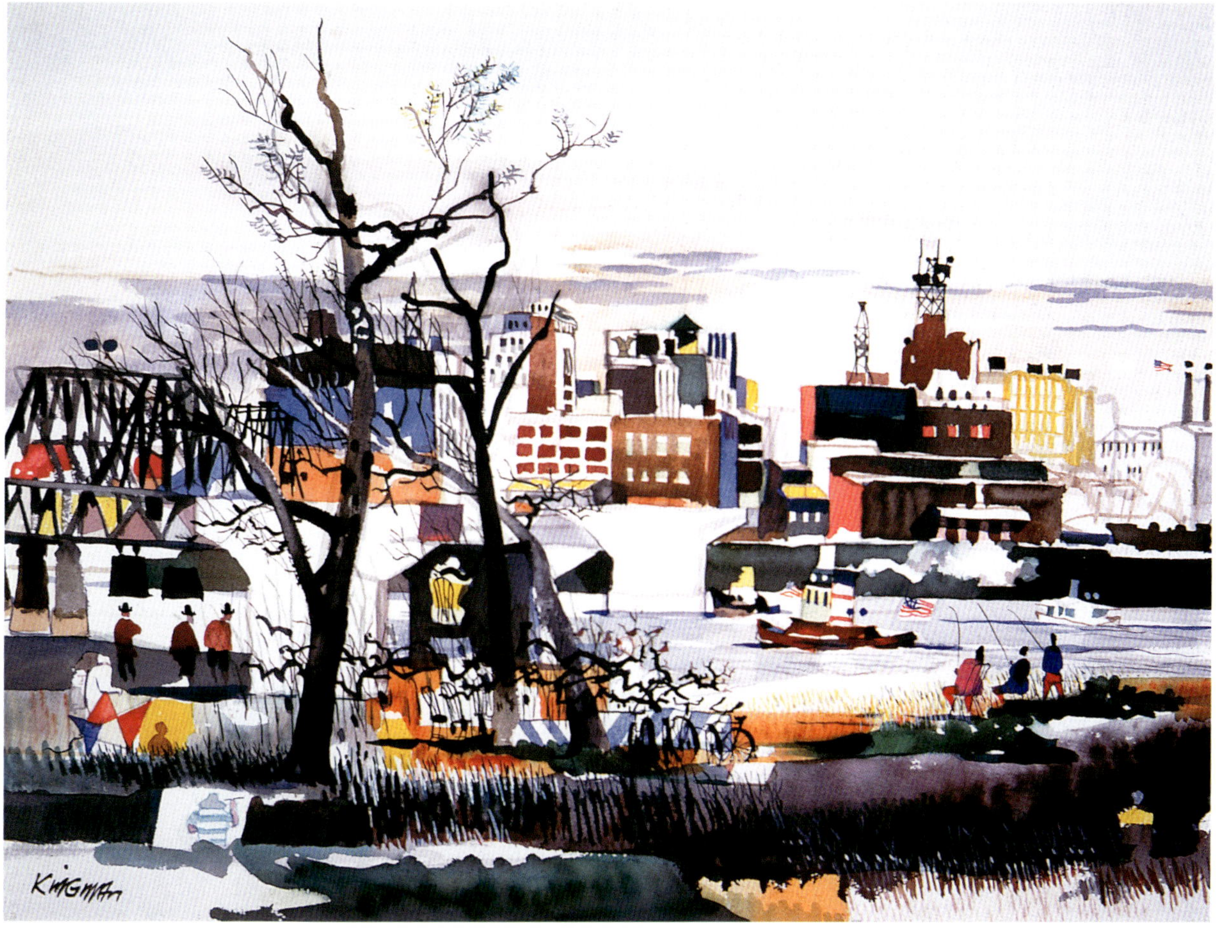

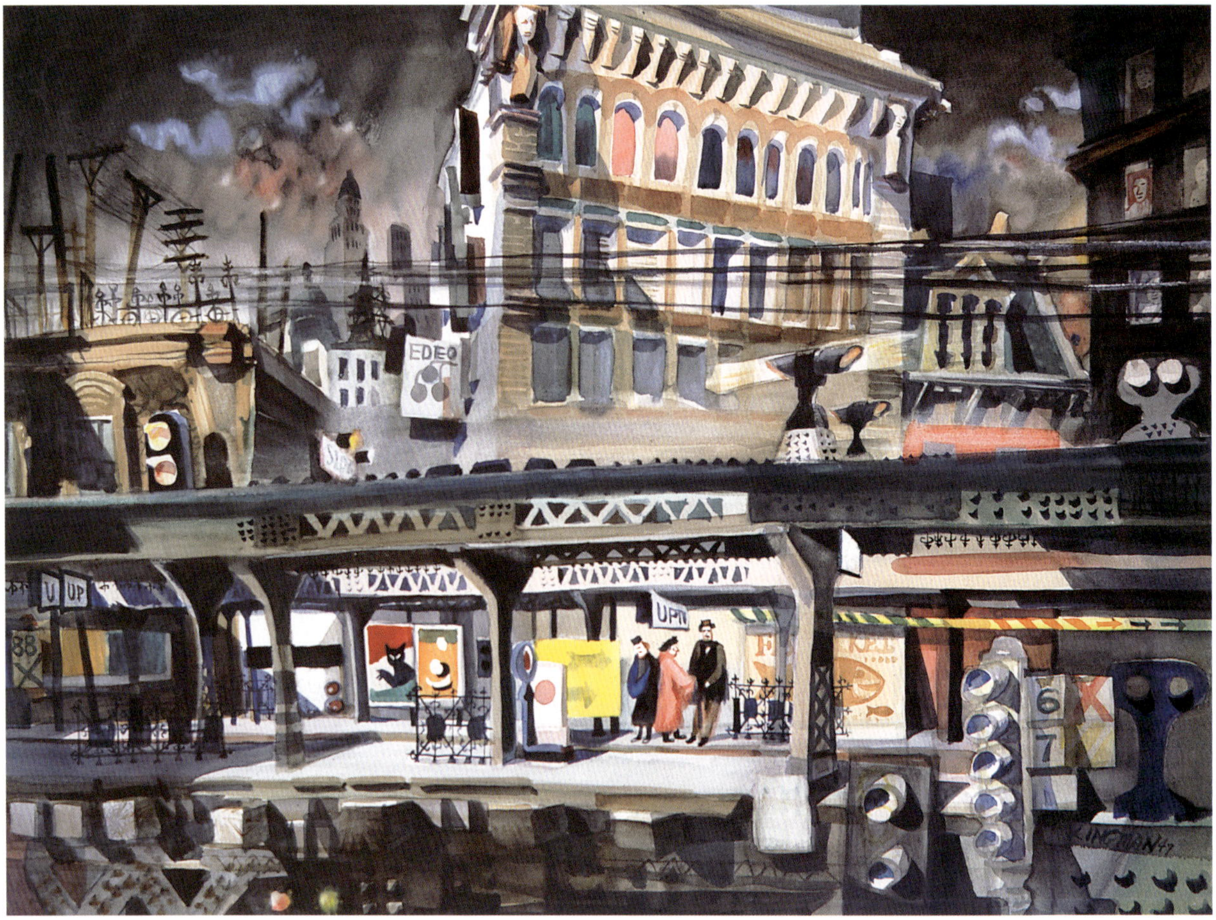

Museums: Private and Permanent Collections

Munson-Williams, Proctor Institute, Utica, NY

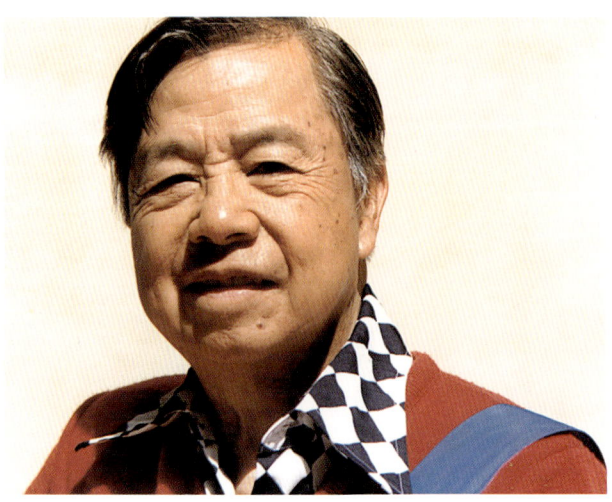

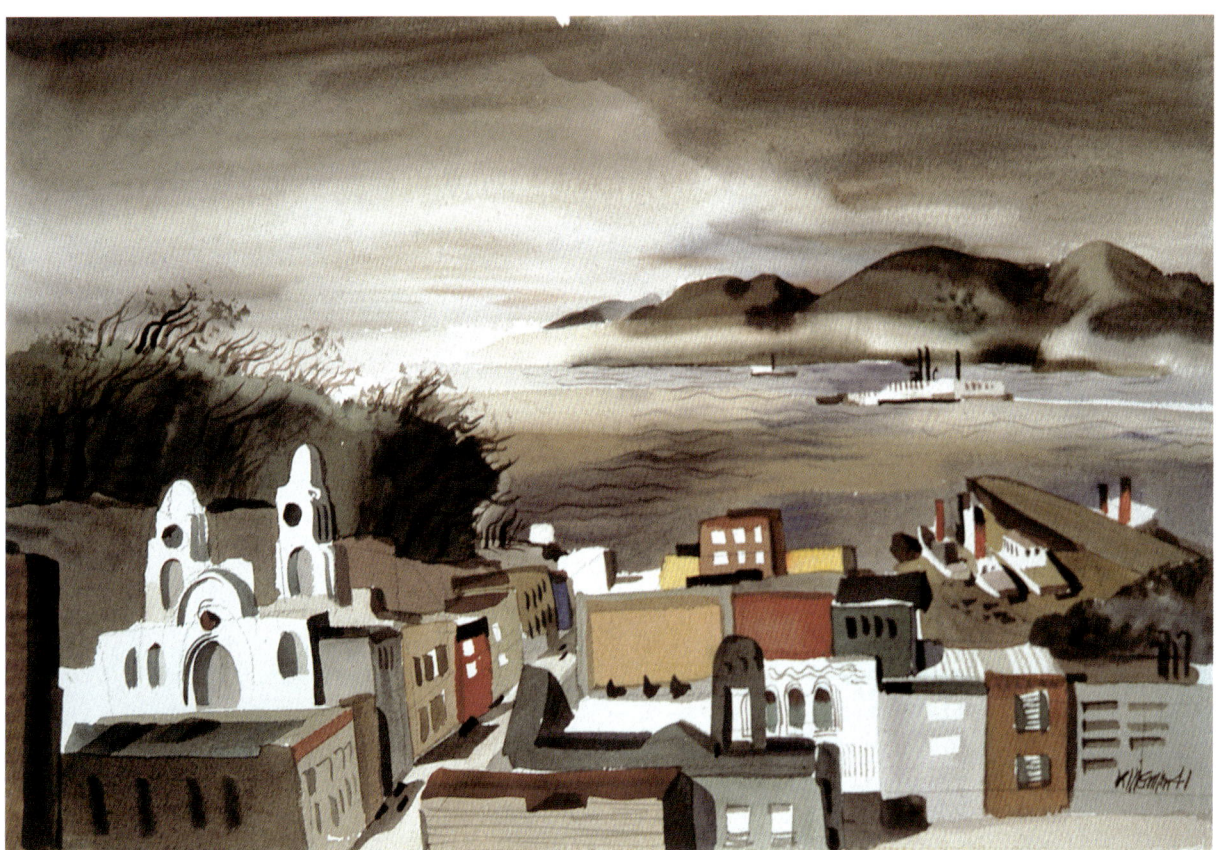
From My Roof, Museum of Modern Art, New York, N.Y.

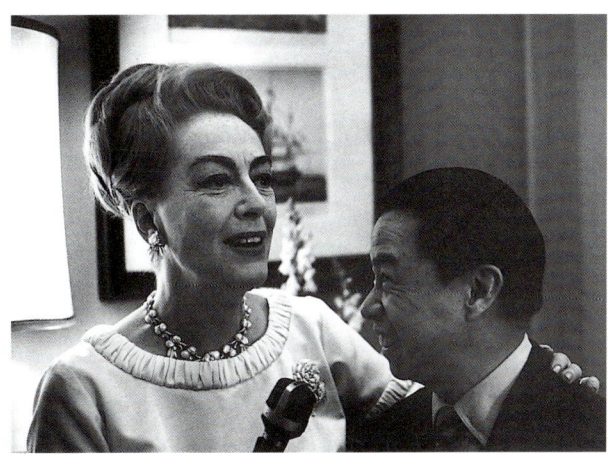
Joan Crawford

Museums: Private and Permanent Collections

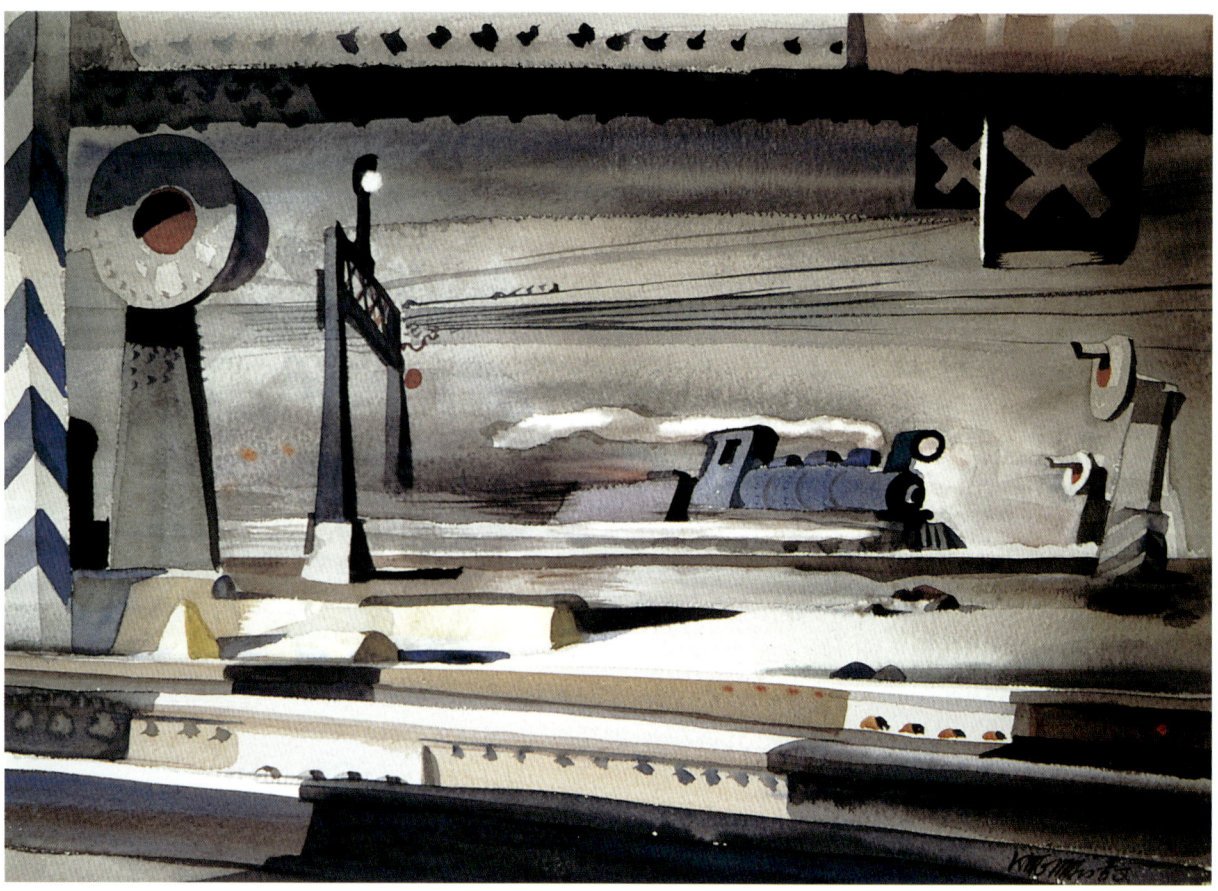

Chicago, Art Institute of Chicago

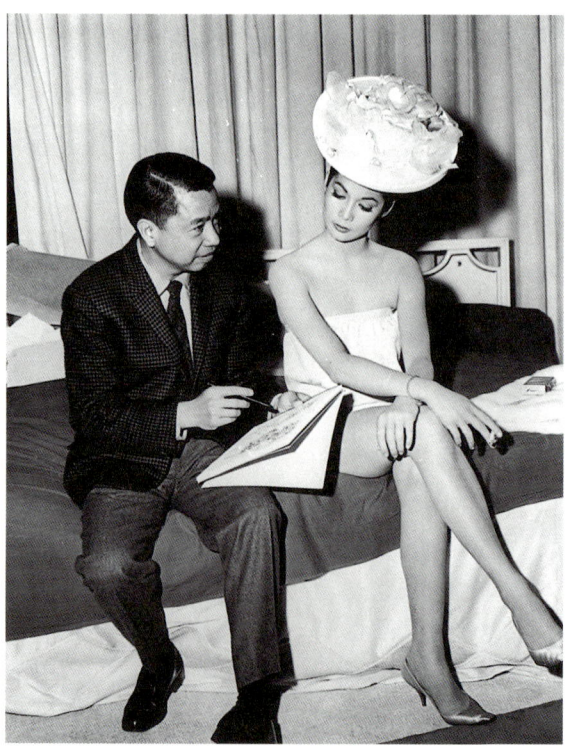

Nancy Kwan

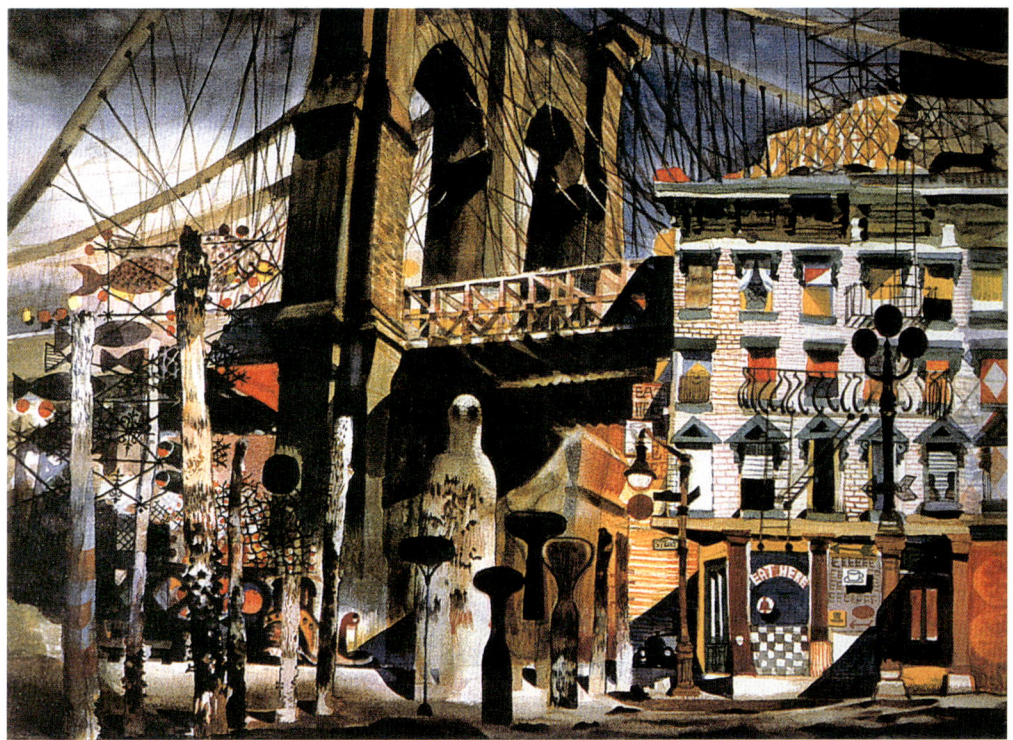
Bridge and White Building, collection of MacNiden Museum, Mason City, Iowa

Old Logs, collection of Brooklyn Museum, New York
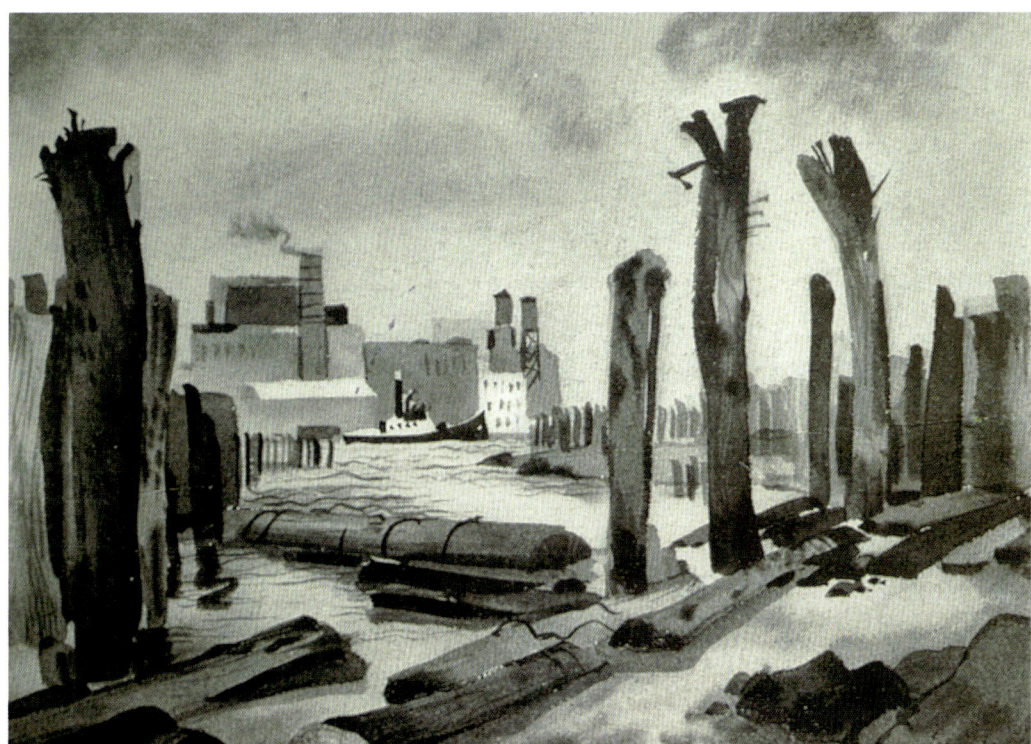

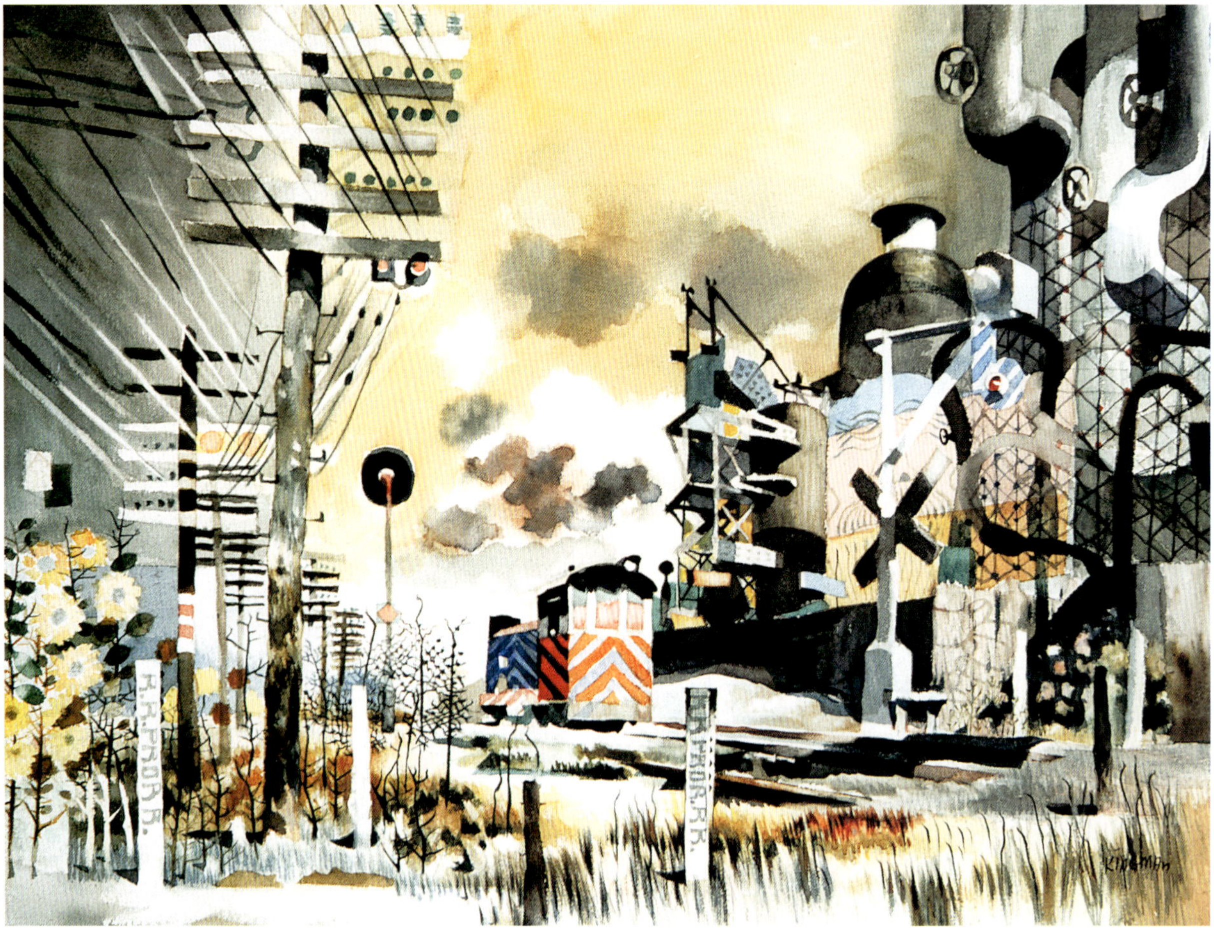

Museums: Private and Permanent Collections

Railroad Oakland, Delaware Art Museum, Wilmington, Delaware

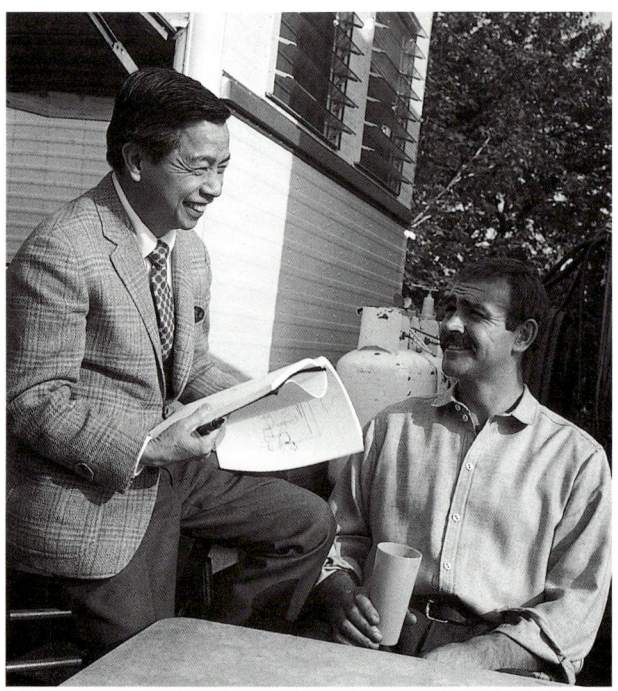

Sean Connery

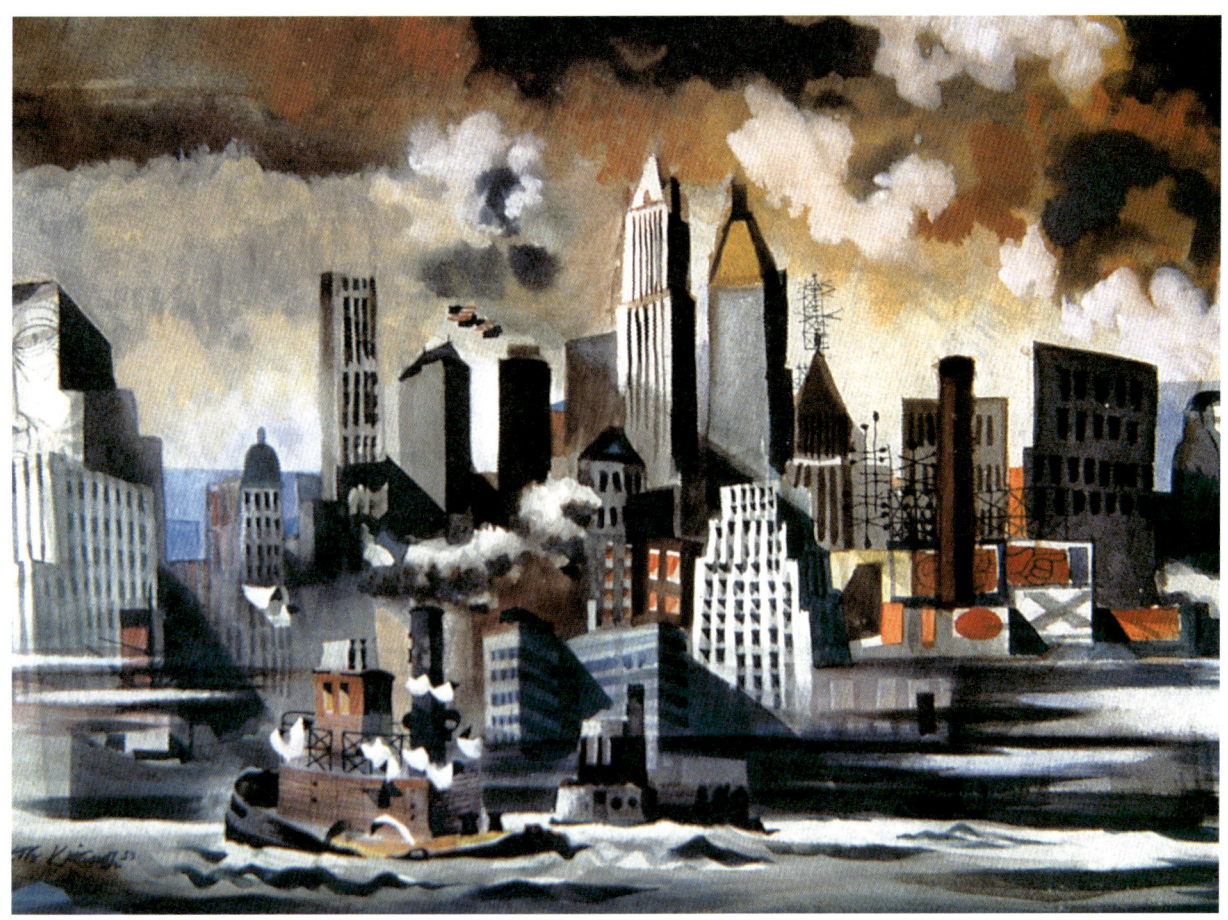

New York Harbour, Toledo Museum of Art, Toledo, Ohio

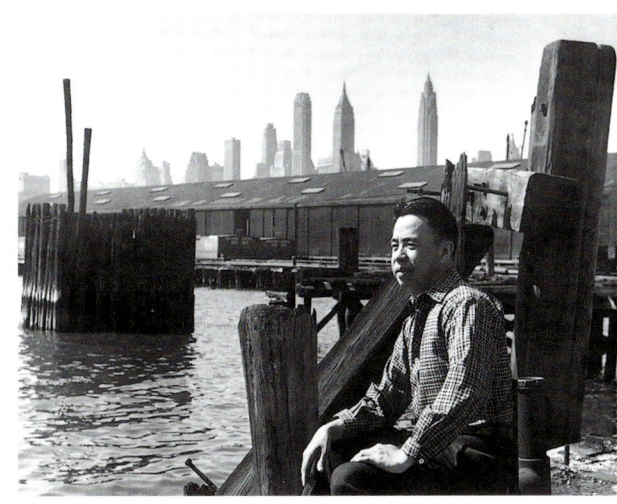

Museums: Private and Permanent Collections

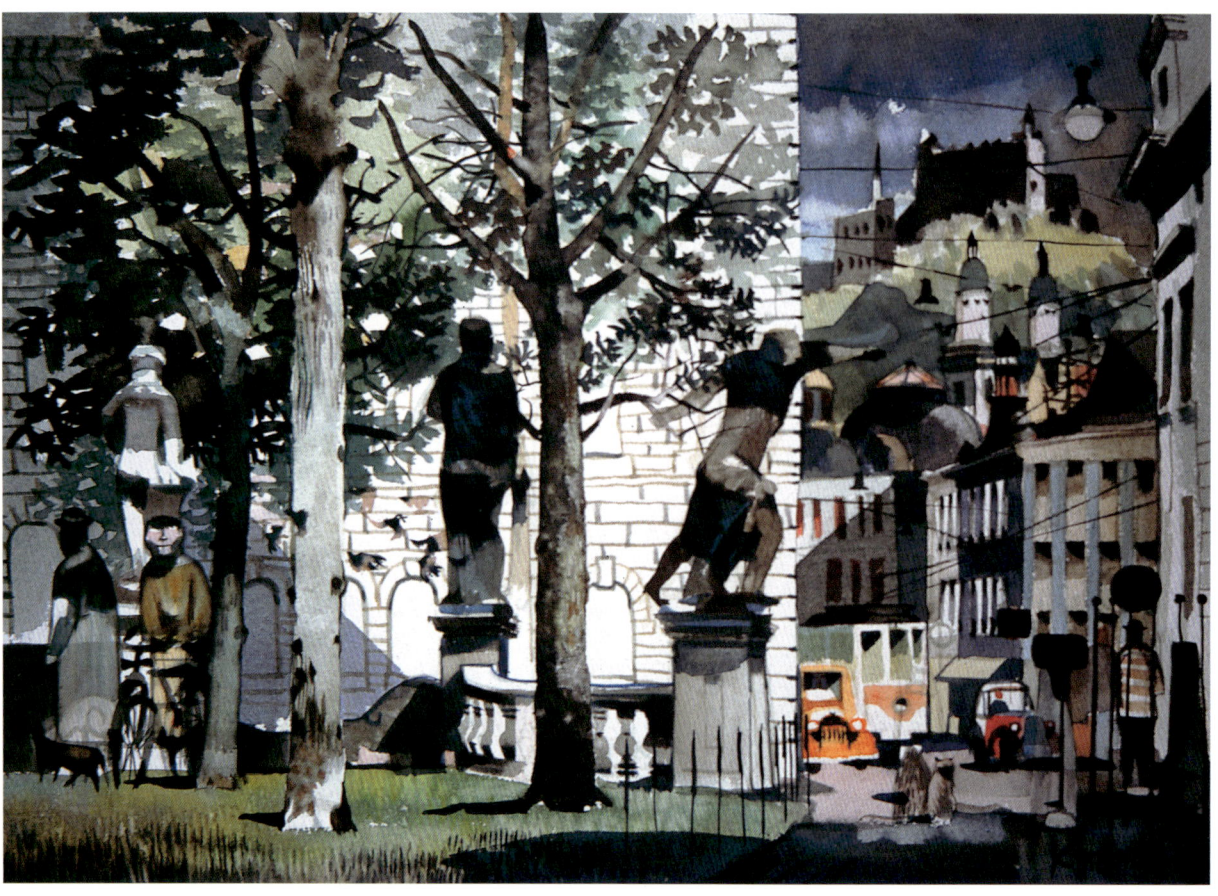

The Statues, Pennsylvania Academy of Fine Arts, Philadelphia, Pa.

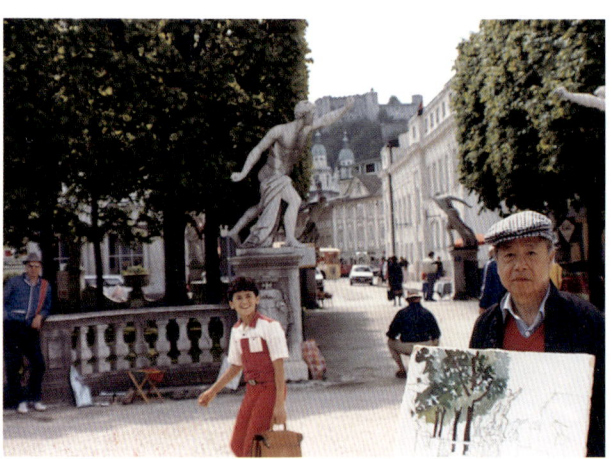

Salzberg

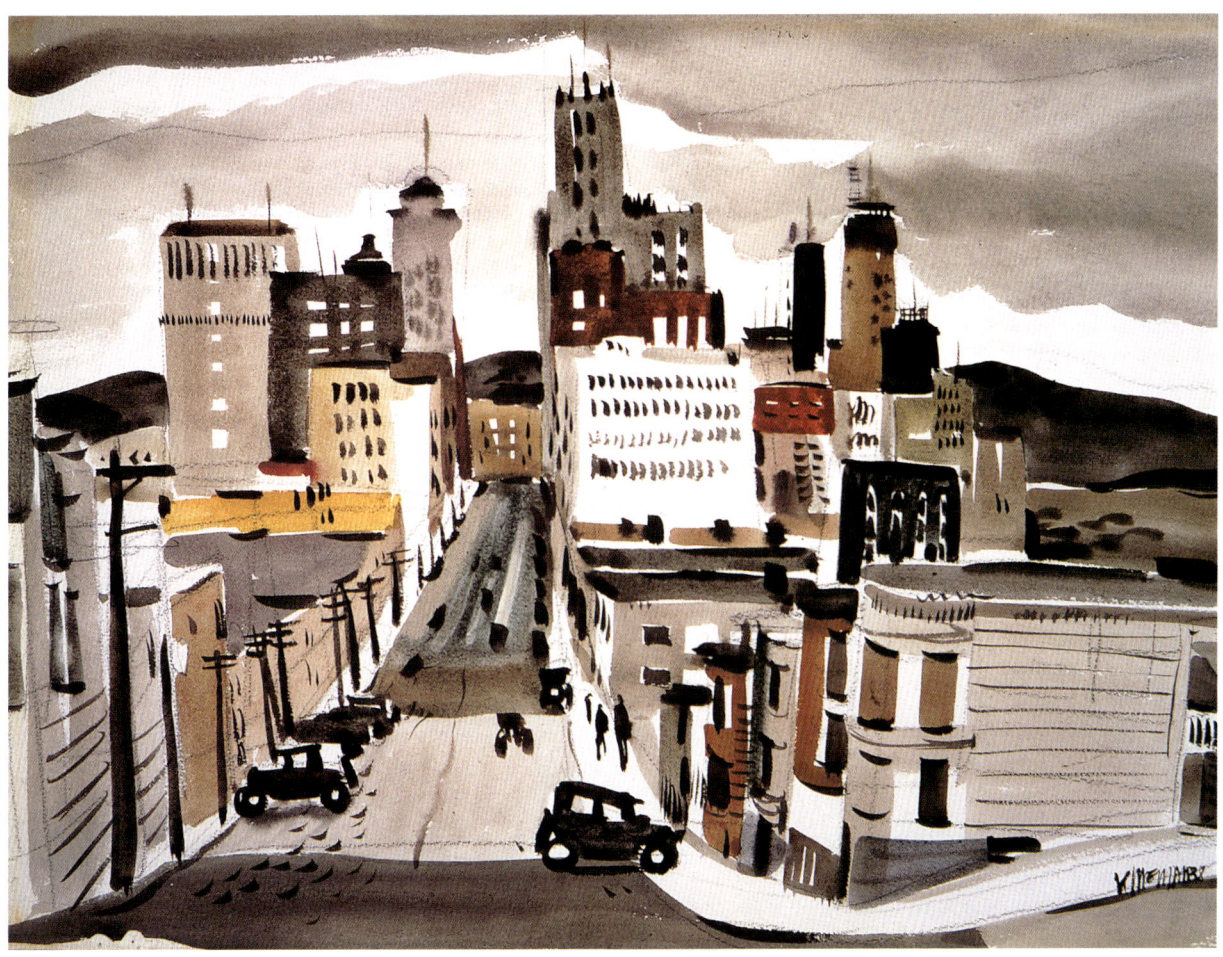
Montgomery Street, San Francisco Museum of Art, San Francisco, CA

Museums: Private and Permanent Collections

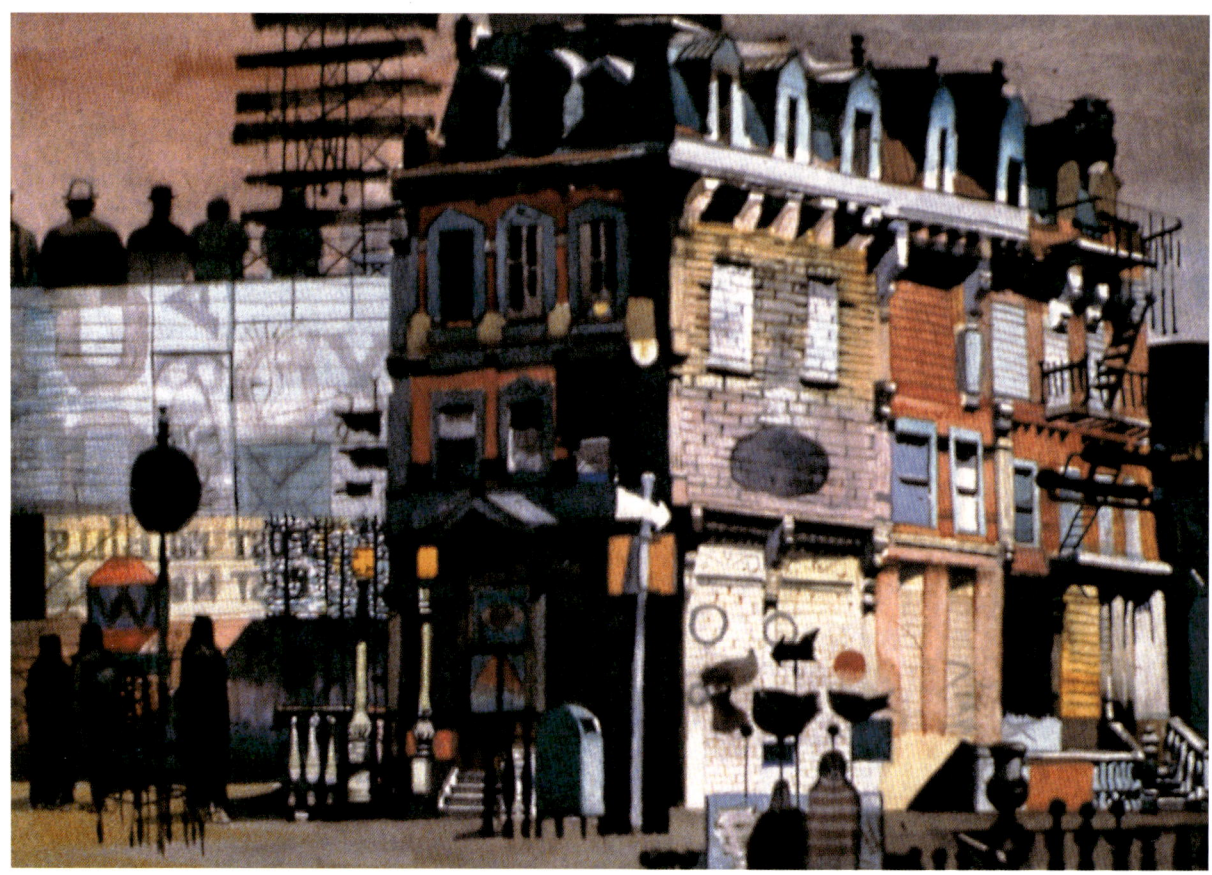

The Building, Columbus Museum of Arts and Craft, Columbus, Ga

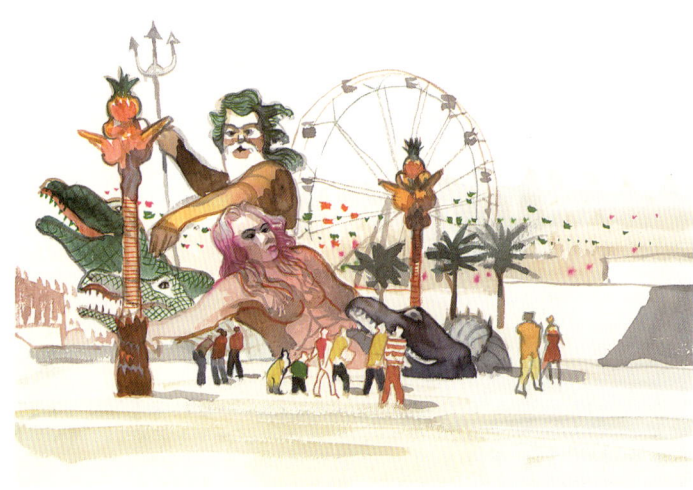

New Orleans World Fair

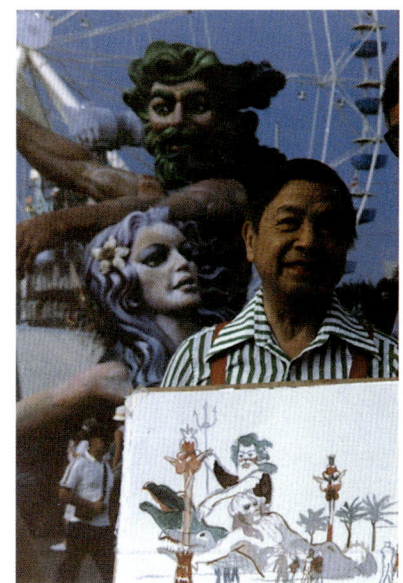

New Orleans World Fair

EL and Snow, Whitney Museum of Art, New York, NY

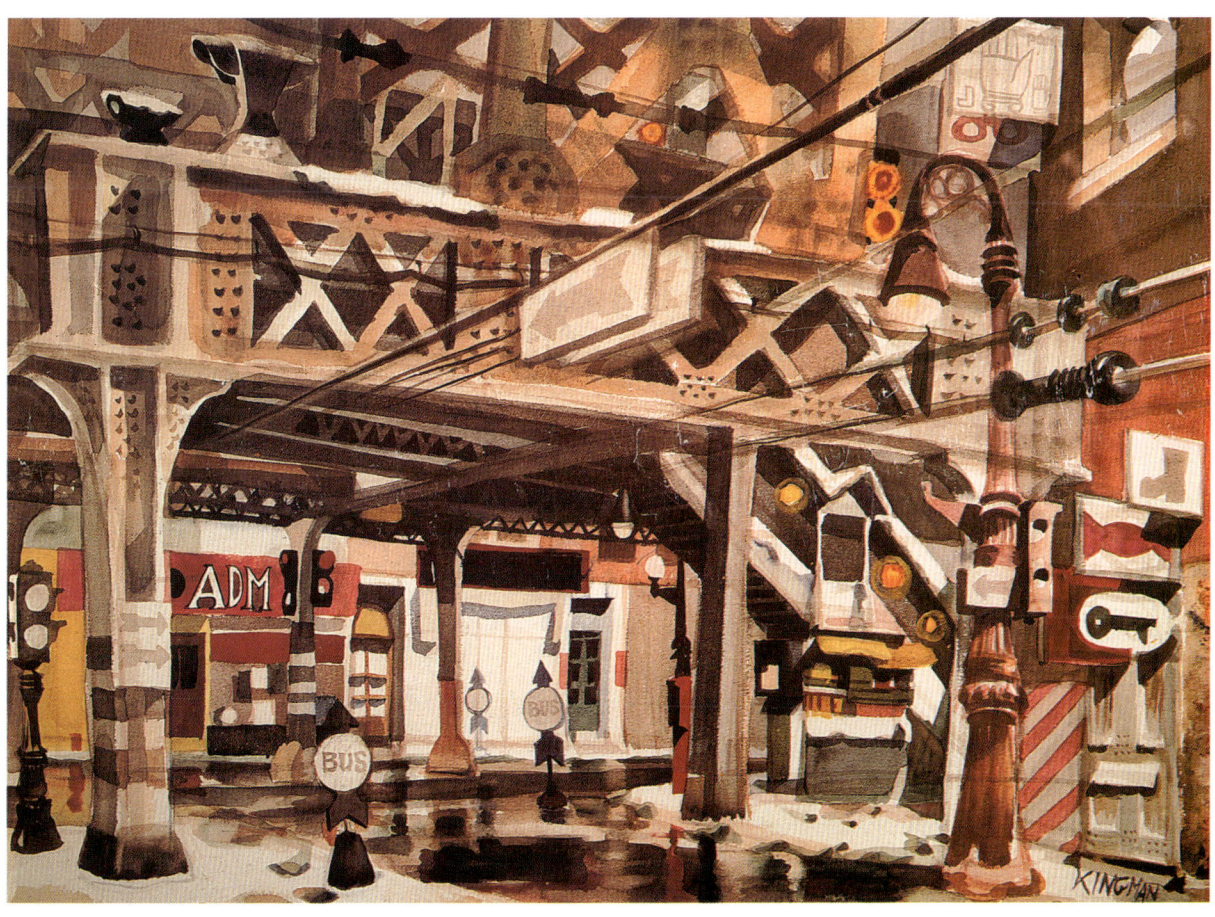

Honours And Awards

When I started out as a watercolor painter, I sent my pictures to many of the watercolor annual shows, but we were always rejected In 1936, to my surprise my picture was not only accepted but won the First Purchase Prize from the San Francisco Art Association. I have, to date, won many honors, prizes, and awards, as follows:

San Francisco Art Association, First Purchase Prize, 1936

Chicago Art Institute, International Watercolor Exhibition Award. 1941

Guggenheim Fellowship, 1942

Guggenheim Fellowship, 1943

Oakland Art Gallery Award, 1943

Audubon Artists Medal of Honor, 1946

Philadelphia Watercolor Club, Joseph Pennel Memorial Medal, 1950

Metropolitan Museum of Art, $500 Award for "Moon & Locomotive".

Pennsylvania Academy of Art, Philadelphia Watercolor Prize, 1953

American Watercolor Society Award, 1956

Audubon Artists Award, 1958

American Watercolor Society, Silver Award 1960

American Watercolor Society, $200 Award for "Square Near Big Ben", London. 1962

National Academy of Design Award, 1963

American Watercolor Society Award, 1964

American Watercolor Society Award, 1965

American Watercolor Society Award for "Demonstration in Park", 1967

San Diego Art Gallery Award, 1968

Philadelphia Watercolor Club Award for Advancement of Watercolor Art, 1968

National Academy of Design, Walter Bigg Memorial Award for "Junks Near Farm", 1971

American Watercolor Society, Lena Newcastle Memorial Award for "Times Square",1972

US Department of State, Round the World Cultural Exchange, 1954

Detroit Museum Award

American Watercolor Society, High Winds Medal Award for "Waterfront Symphonette" 1973

National Academy of Design, 150th Anniversary Gold Medal Award, 1975

American Watercolor Society, V. K. McCracken Award for "Hongkong by the Bay" 1976

National Academy of Design, Walter Bigg Memorial Award, 1977

American Watercolor Society, Ford-Times Award for "Paris A.M." 1977

Artists in Watercolor Competition, 4th prize $350 "Artists At Work", Paris 1979

American Watercolor Society Barse Miller Memorial Award, $400 "Plaza Sitters", 1979

Honorable "ADMIRAL" of' the Navy, Omaha, Nebraska, 1979

Key to the City of Omaha, Nebraska, 1979

Key to the City of Cincinnati, Ohio, 1980

Honorable "Citizen" of Louisville, Kentucky, 1980

Honours And Awards

Honorable *"Captain"* of Belle of Louisville, Kentucky, 1980

"Man of the Year", Chinatown Planning Council, New York, NY. Feb, 1981

San Diego Watercolor Society prize *"13 Men Under A Tree"*, 1983

"Man of the Year", Chinese Community Council, Oakland, California, 1985

American Watercolor Society, High Winds Medal Award, $900 for 13 Men Under A Tree, 1986.

Honorable Recipient of DOLPHIN MEDAL AWARD, highest honor awarded by the American Watercolor Society for *"Yellow Cab"*, 1987.

Honorary Doctorate degree for Humane Letters, Academy of Art College, San Francisco, California, 1987

"Man of the Year", Variety Club of New York, 1991

American Watercolor Society, Elizabeth Calian Award, $300 for *"One Tree and 6 Locomotives"*.

American Watercolor Society, Paul Remmey Award, $300 for *"Tienanmen is Near"* 1990

"Man of the Year", Rotary Club of Chinatown, New York, NY 1991

American Watercolor Society, Mary Pleisner Award $500 for *"Mount Rushmore"*, 1991

American Watercolor Society, H. Gramatky Award, *"Four Men On A Bicycle"* 1989.

American Watercolor Society, Edgar A. Whitney Award for *"Red Sails on East Wind"*, 1993

American Watercolor Society, Anne Williams Glushein Award for *"Hongkong 1997"*, 1995.

And others

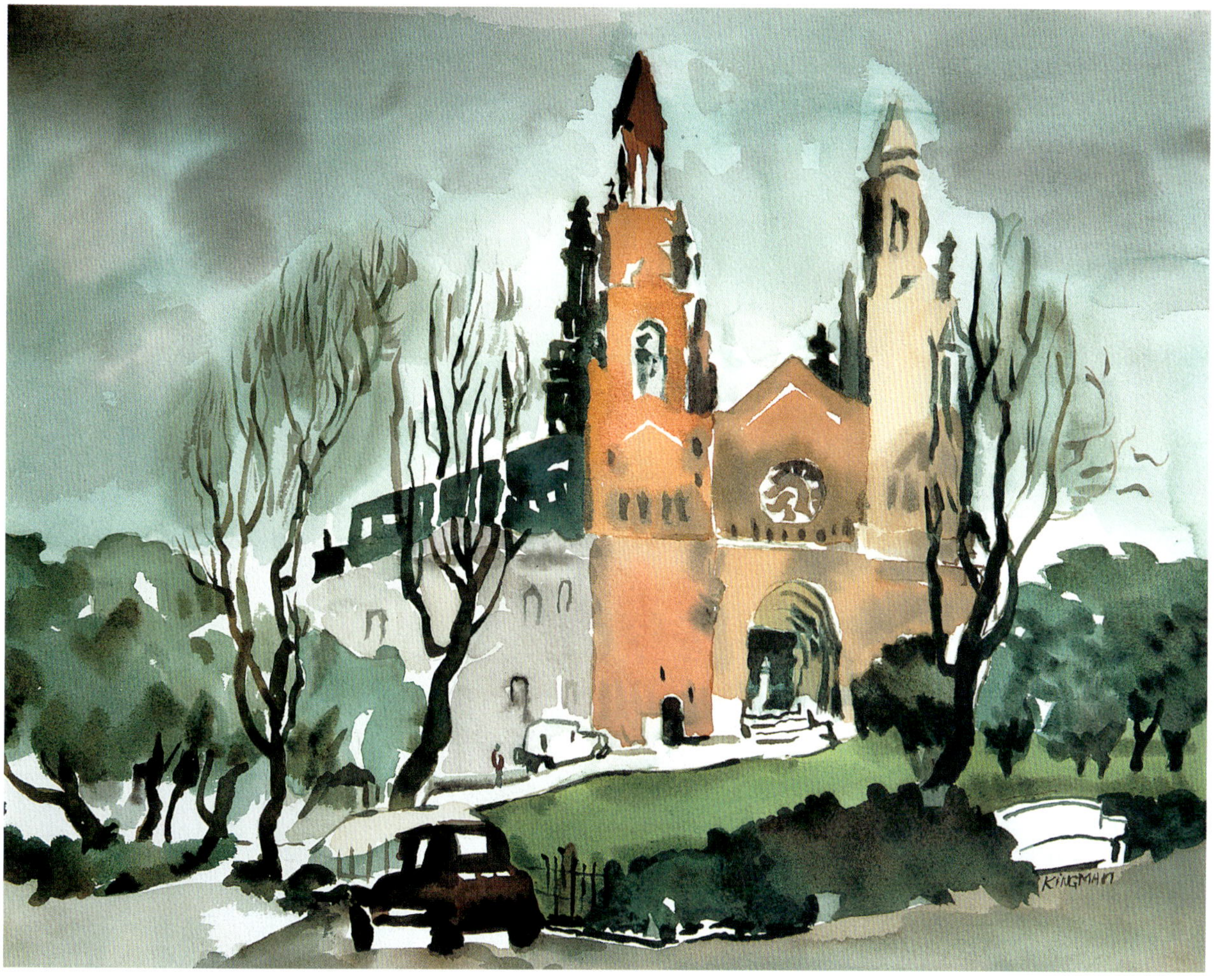

Church #One, San Francisco Art Association, First Purchase Prize 1936

CHURCH # ONE
I painted this on location at Union & Green Streets in the Italian Section of San Francisco. This was a triangle area where people sit waiting for buses. I saw and painted the Church between trees while sitting there, working away as I always did. Little did I know I would win a prize for this.

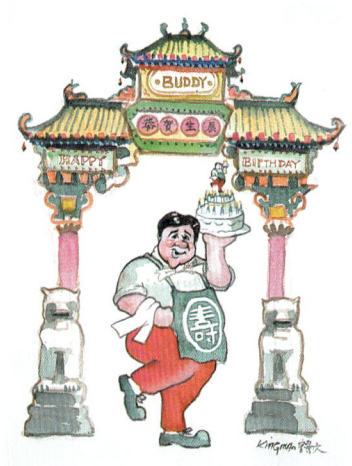

Buddy Hackett

Honours And Awards

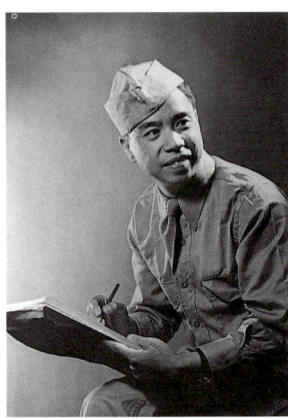

In the Army O.S.S.

DEMONSTRATION IN THE PARK
This was my impression of people going on demonstrations or strikes protesting complaining what they should have and have not got. They would demonstrate what they thought was important at the time for dogs, cats, elephants, lions, tigers, the water they drink, or the air they breathe.

Demonstration in Park, American Watercolor Society Award 1967

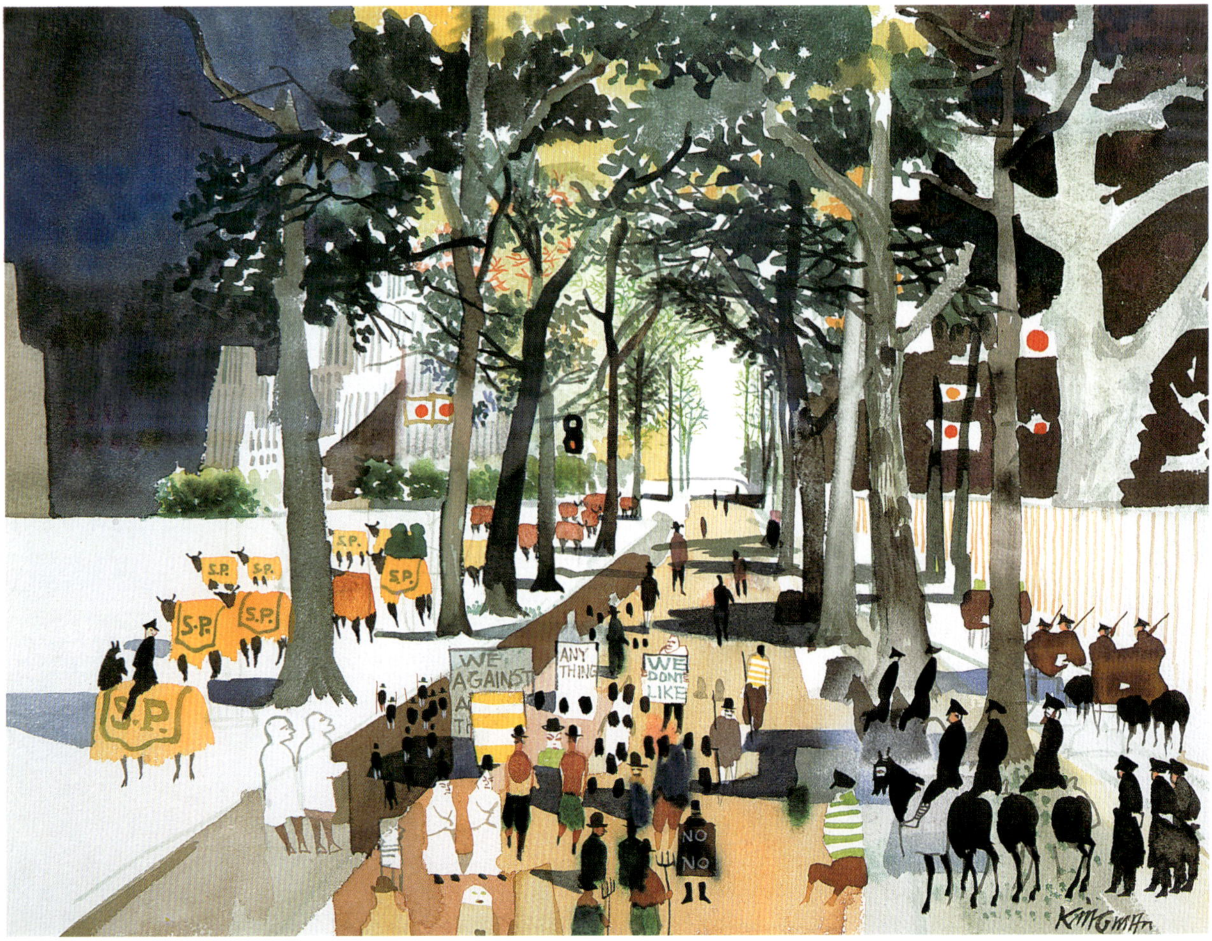

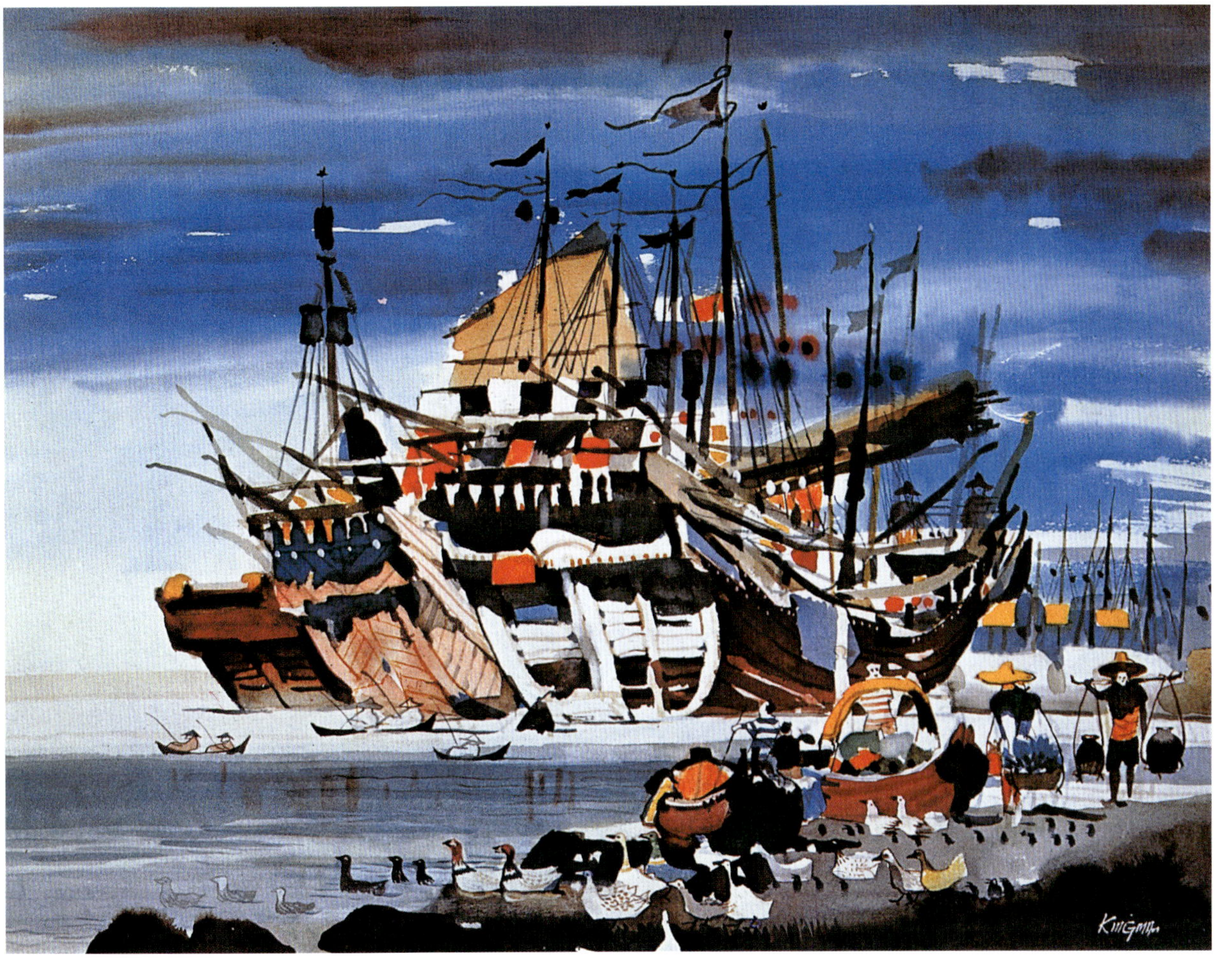

Junks near Duckfarm, Natio er Bigg Memorial Award, 1971

I started this picture with Junks in Aberdeen Hong Kong. When I came back to the studies, I added ducks and chickens to make it look nothing like it was before.

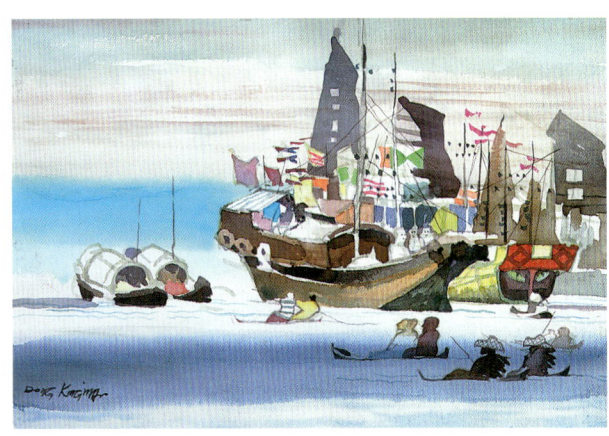

Yul Brynner

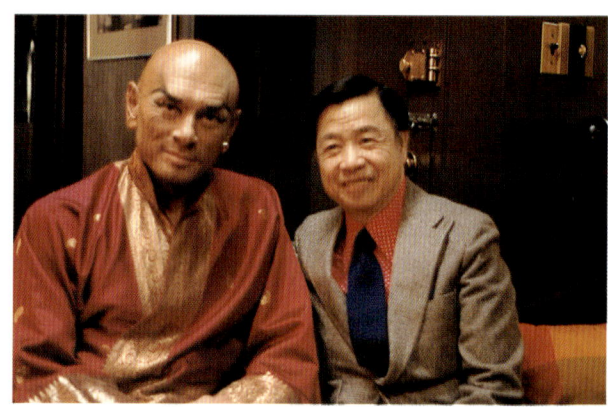

ARTIST AT WORK, PARIS
There was a place called Sacre Coeur in Paris which I very much wanted to paint. When my wife and I went back the next morning, the place was aleadf full of 20 or so artists who had the same idea – sitting around painting from the same angle. I looked around, and found many more standing up easels with artists in front. Later on, I found out that they were not artists at all. They just set up shop to look like artists to sell pictures to tourists.

Artist At Work, Paris. Artist in Watercolour Competition, 1979

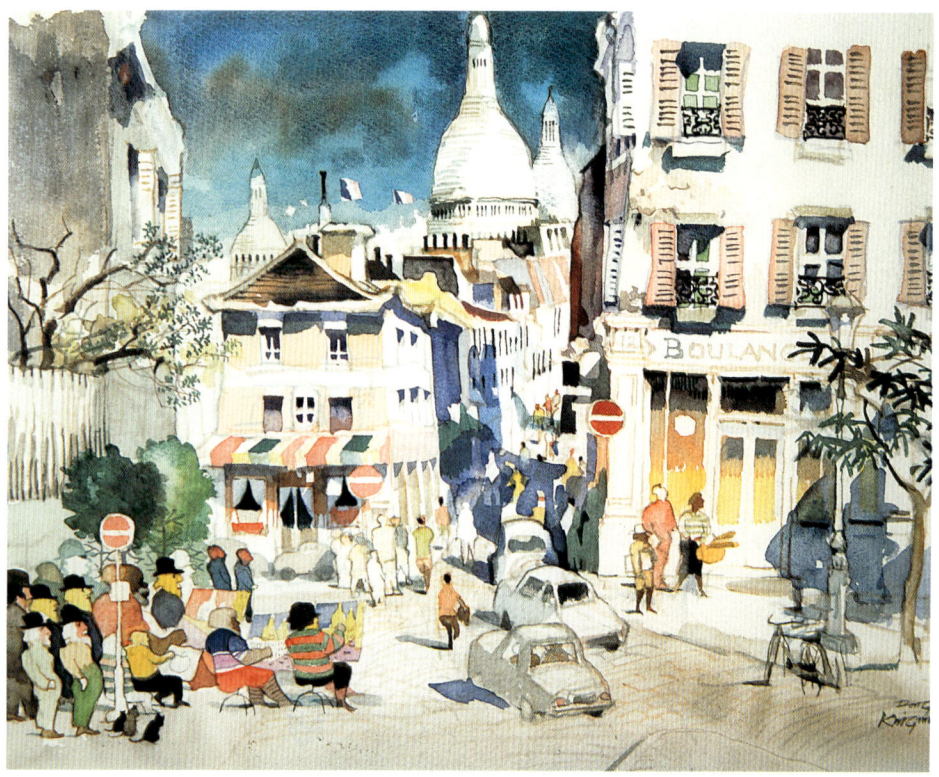

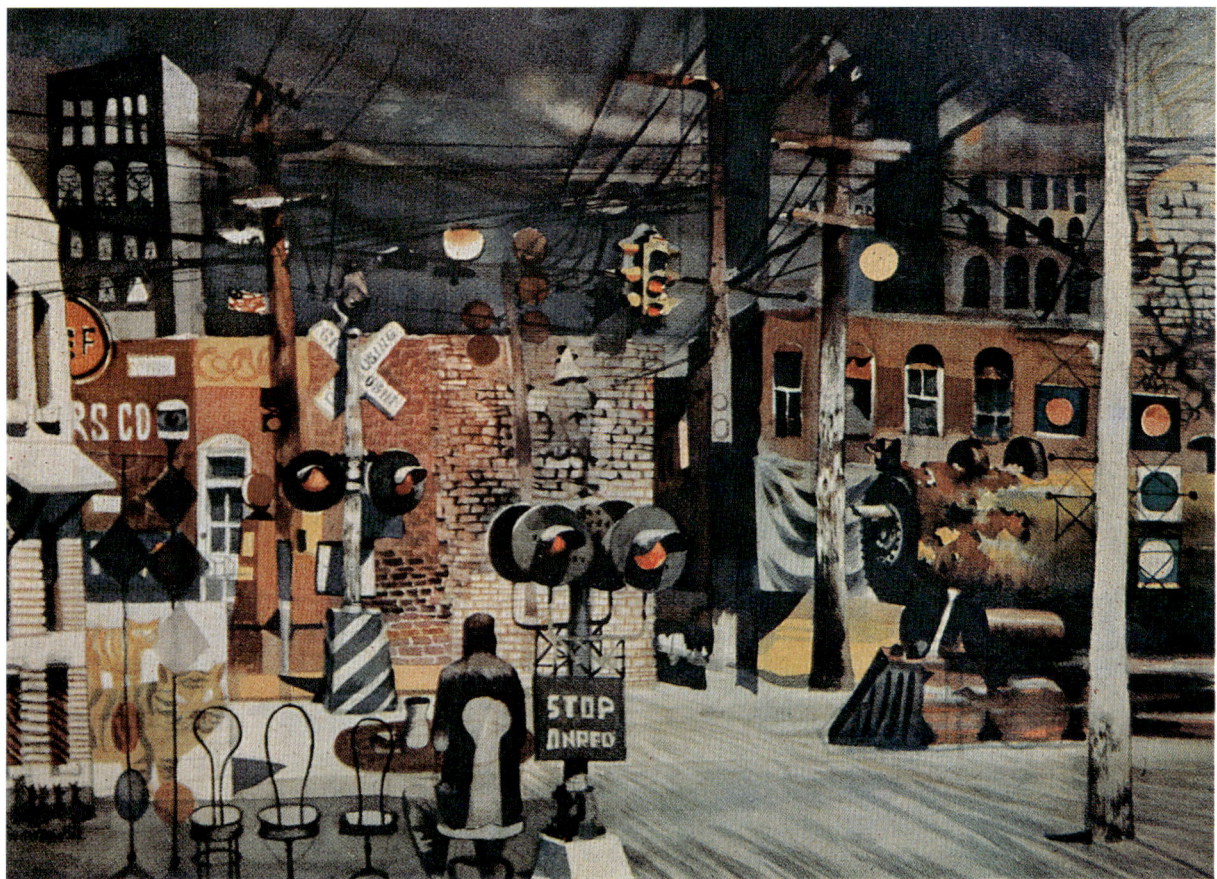

Moon & Locomotive, Metropolitan Museum of Art, $500 Award

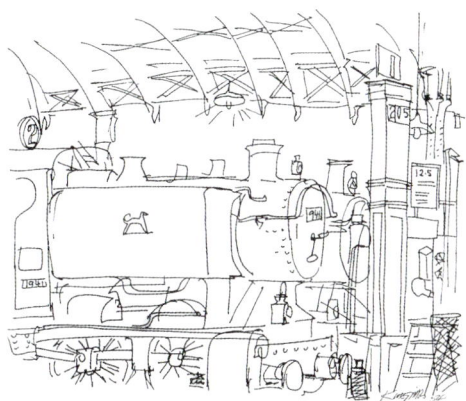

Saturday Night, Paddington Station", Pen and Ink drawing, 9.11.1954

MOON & LOCOMOTIVE
My Uncle took me to visit our ancestral home in the village when I was 8 years old. I was standing on the railroad platform when I saw a big black locomotive looking like a giant dark ugly dragon charging towards me, ready to eat me up. Then it made a loud screeching noise, blowing out steams all over, and stopped in front of me. In this picture, I tried to create a man waiting for the locomotive like the man in the play *Waiting For Godot* - it is coming, but getting nowhere.

Honours And Awards

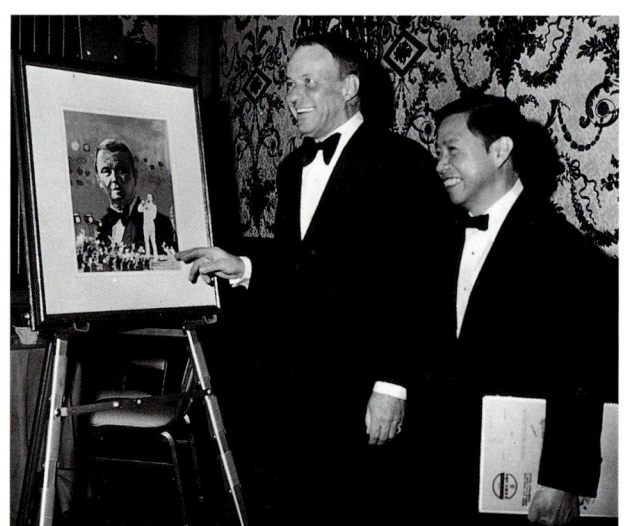

Frank Sinatra

Golden Gate Scenario, San Diego Watercolor Society Prize, 1968

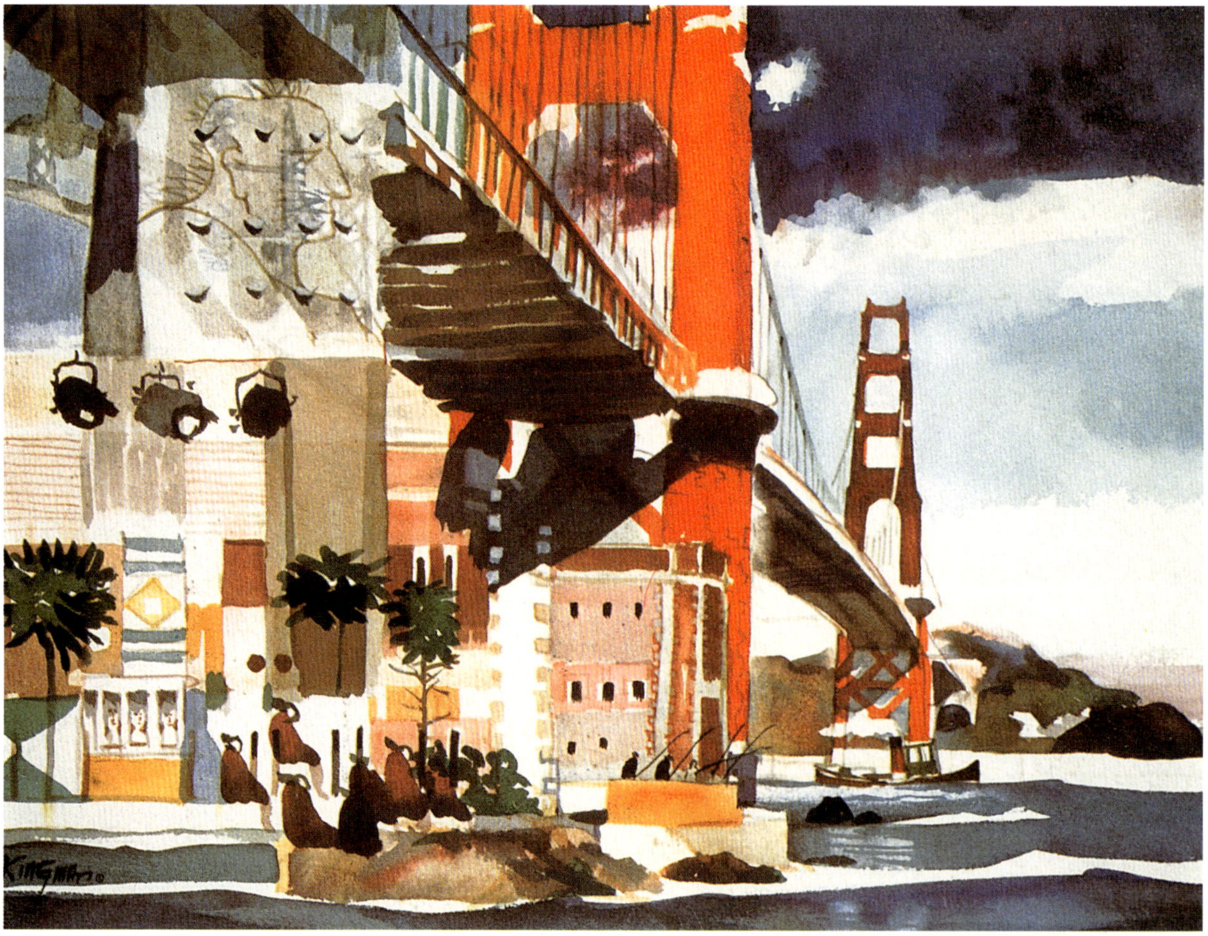

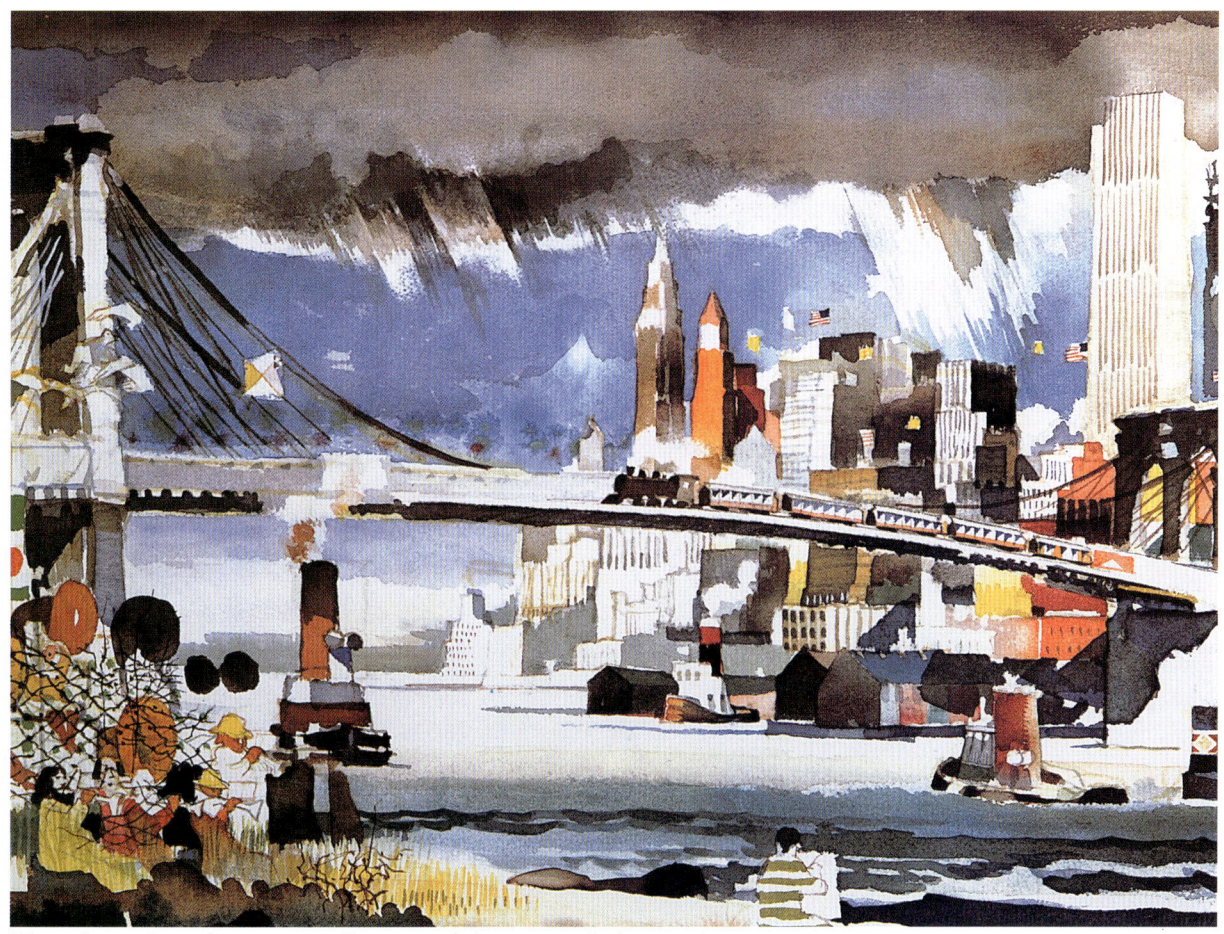

Waterfront Symphonette, collection of American Embassy, Beijing
American Watercolor Society, High Winds Medal Award, 1973

When I got out of the Army, I moved my whole family from San Francisco to Brooklyn Heights where I bought a house within walking distance to the waterfront near the Brooklyn Heights Concourse. From there, I painted many pictures of the Brooklyn Bridge and the Manhattan Bridge from many different angles. I started most of these pictures on location, and finished them in the studio. The title of this picture called Waterfront Symphonette won the High Winds Medal Award at the American Watercolor Society in 1974, is now in the permanent collection of the Ambassador's Residence in Beijing, China.

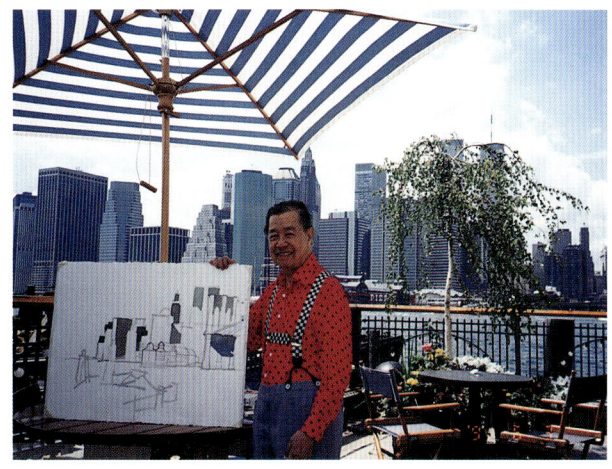

Honours And Awards

Paris A.M.

When I was looking for subject to paint outside the Louvre Museum in Paris, I asked my wife to go inside to look at the art collections. An hour or so later, she came out to tell me what fabulous objects she saw in the Louvre, when I had just finished my painting ready to go back with her to the hotel. This is what I call "Killing two birds with one stone".

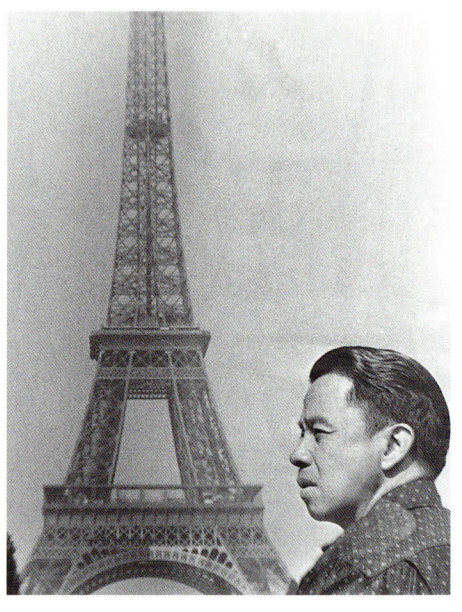

Paris A.M, collection of Mr. & Mrs. Dong Kingman, Jr.
American Watercolor Society, Ford-Times Award, 1977

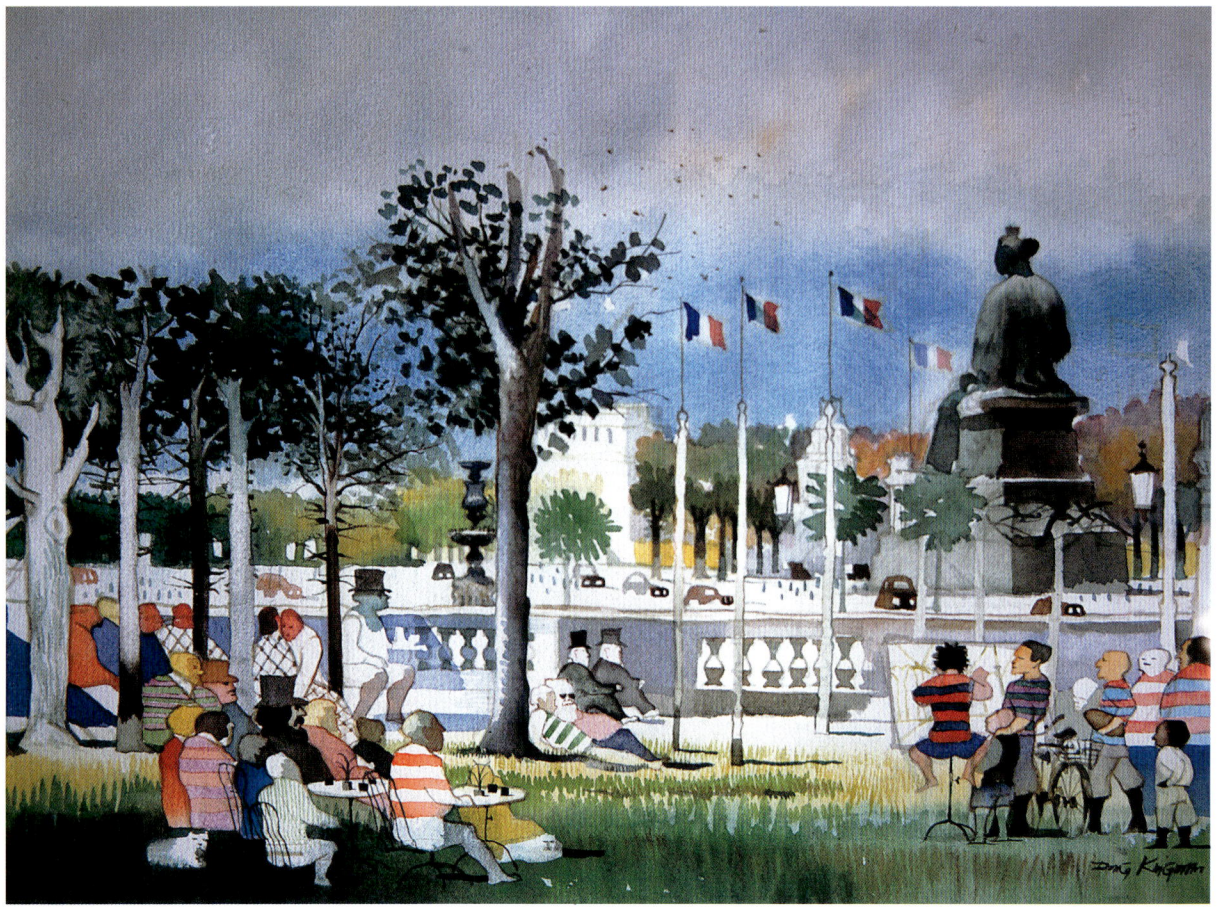

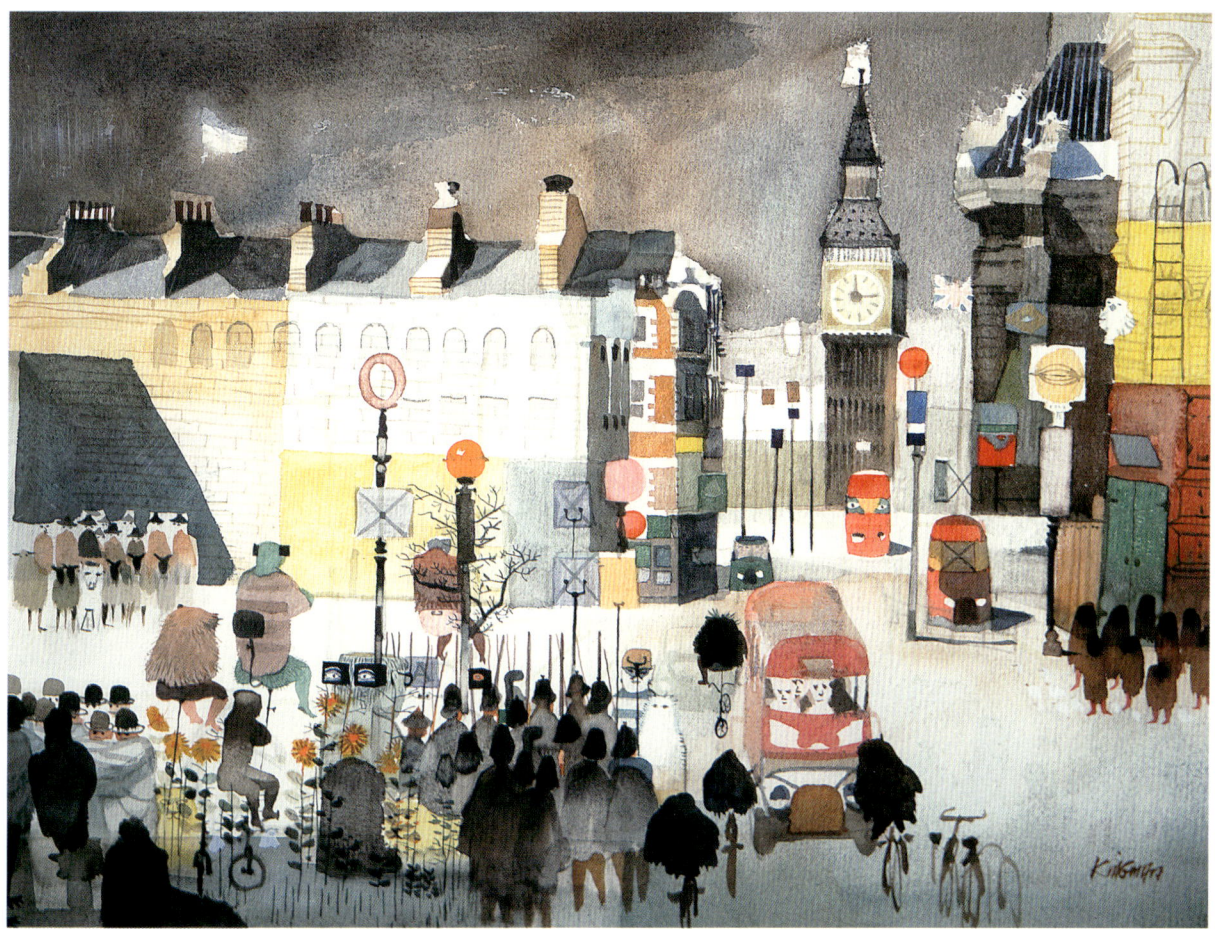

Square near Big Ben, London, American Watercolor Society, $200 award.

BIG BEN

I started this picture on location in London, then added some people and a few other things when I got back to the studio. The people look like Bobbies, the London police, some on tricycles, in buses, or just standing around. They give me the feeling of a typical London street scene with strong sunlight and shadow.

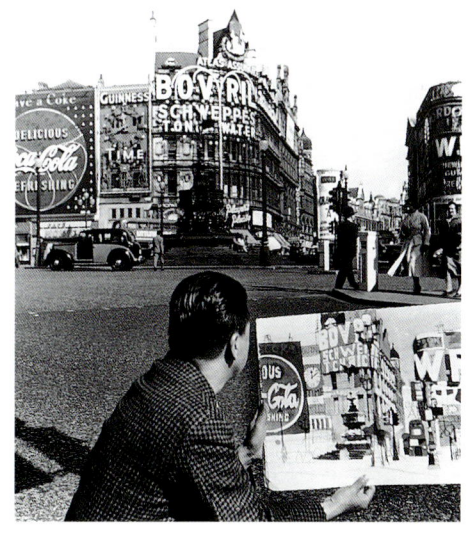

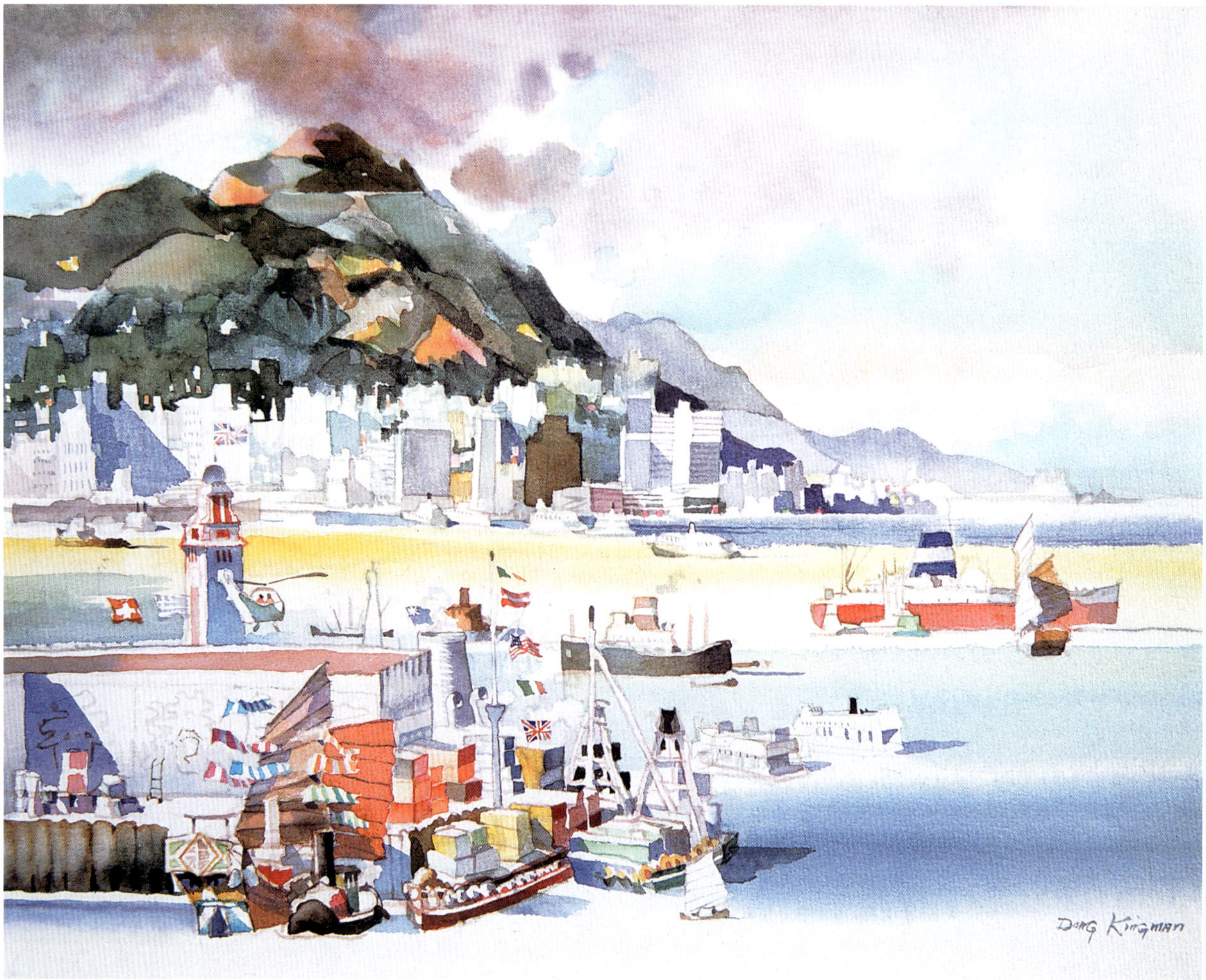

HONOURS AND AWARDS

Hong Kong By the Bay, American Watercolor Society, 1976

HONG KONG BY THE BAY
This picture was painted from the window of my hotel in Kowloon. You can see heaving men loading heavy cargos into ship's hold, and small junks hovering like ants around big vessels. The Victoria Mountain provides strong feeling in the background.

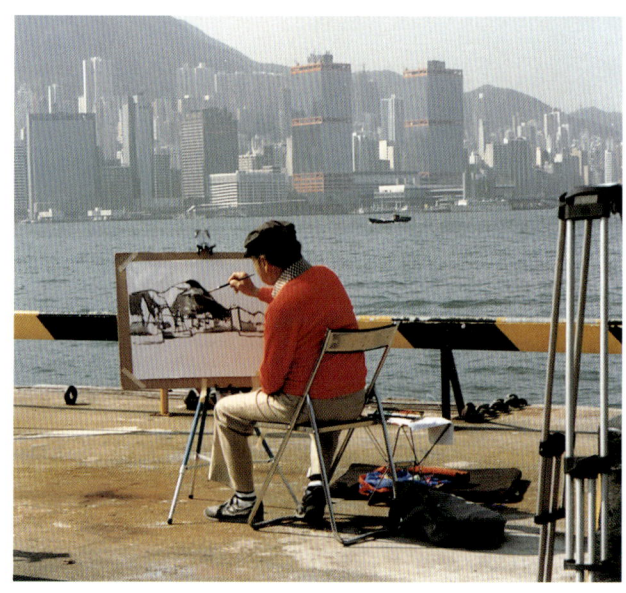

THIRTEEN MEN UNDER A TREE
I started this picture with thirteen men, but composition was unbalanced. So I added five cows, three ships, and one tugboat to give it a good balance.

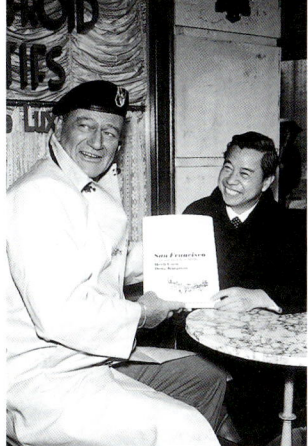

John Wayne

Thirteen Men Under A Tree, American Watercolor Society, High Winds Medal Award, 1986

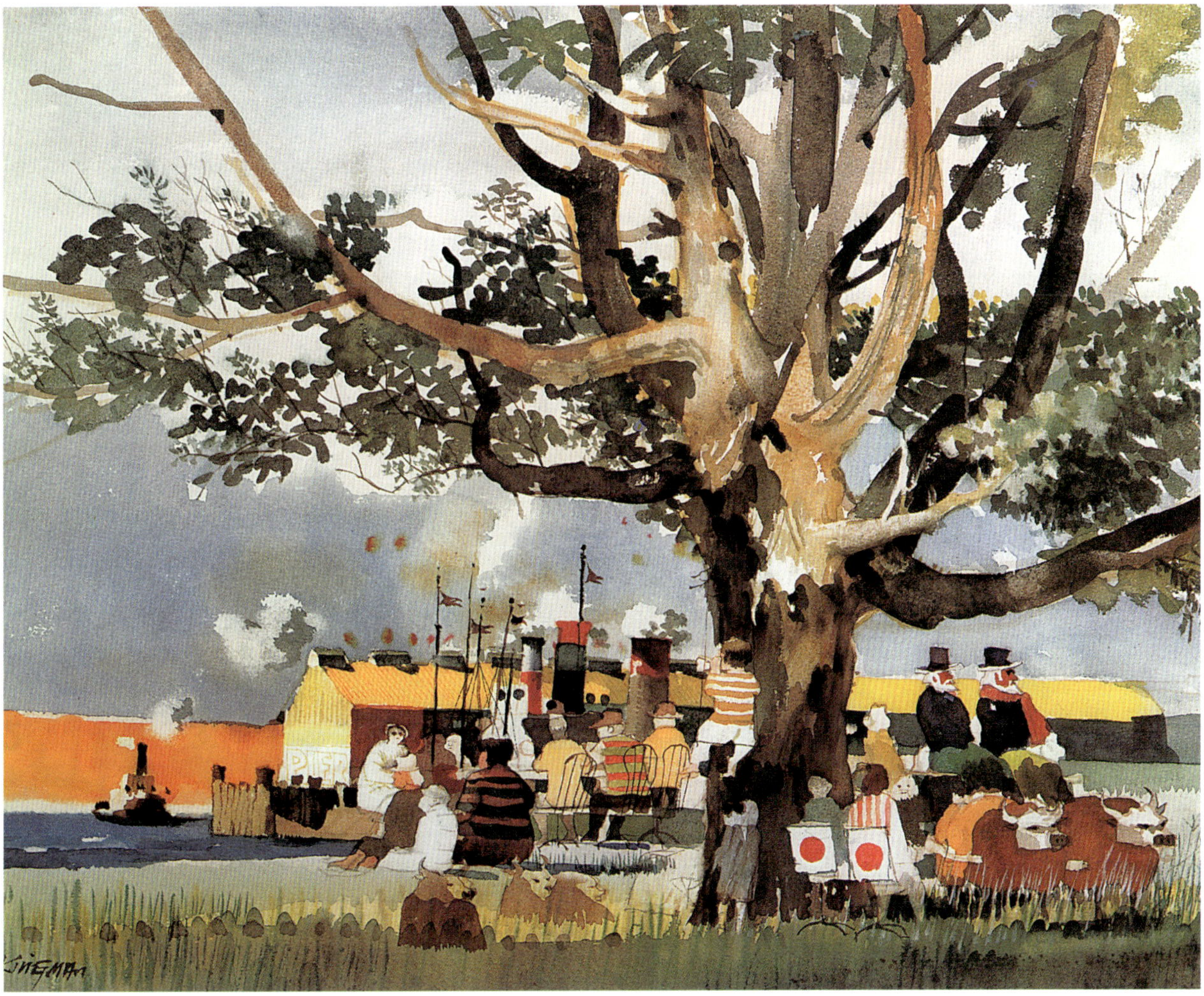

HONOURS AND AWARDS

TIENANMEN IS NEAR
Here, I tried to relate the story of the student's uprising in Tienanmen in 1989. Men against steel — no way to win a losing war.

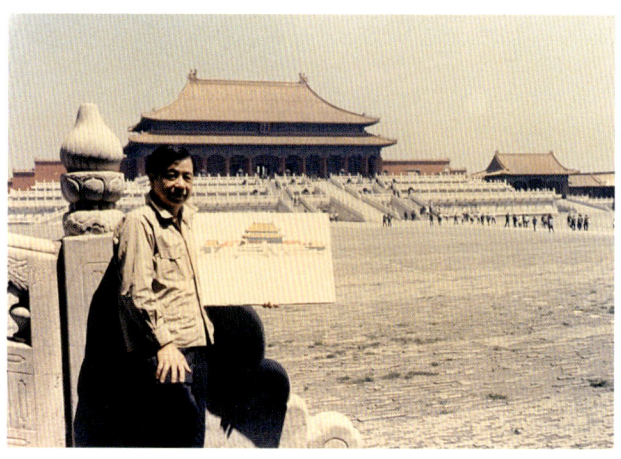

Tienanmen is Near, American Watercolor Society, Paul Renney Award, 1990

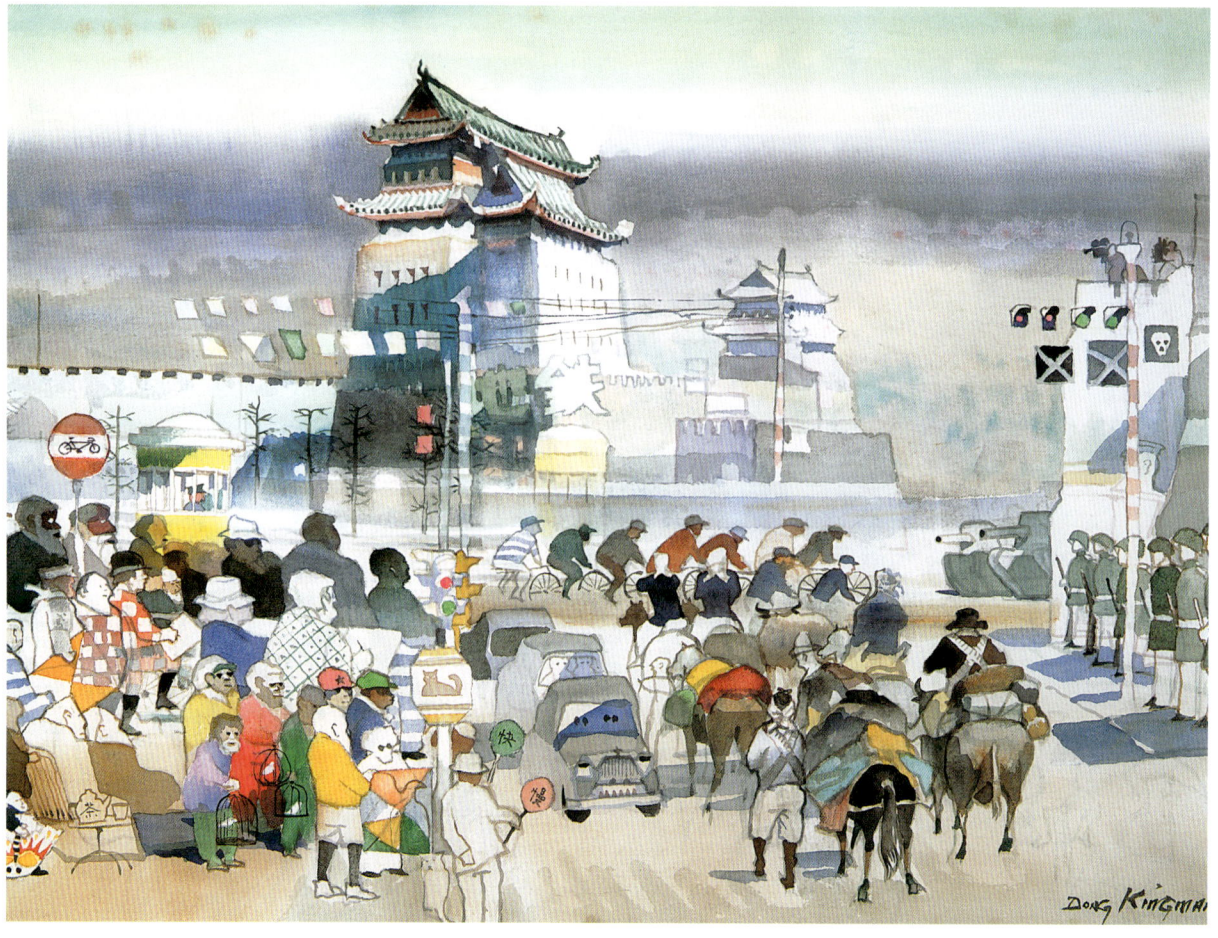

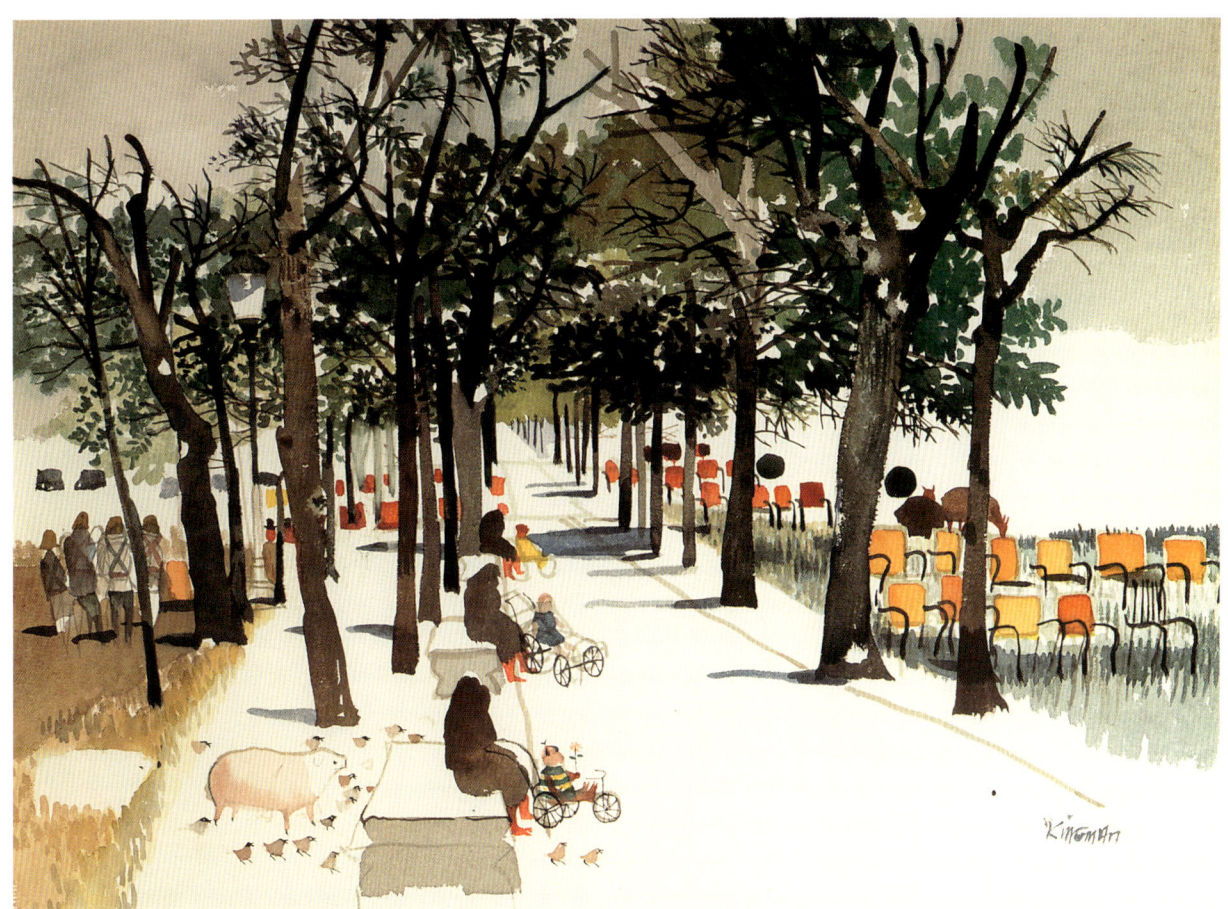

American Watercolor Society Award, 1964

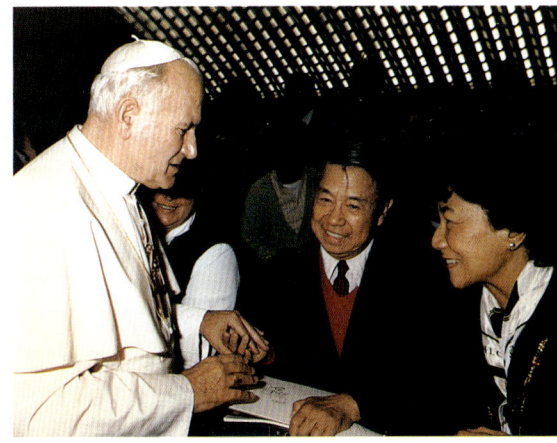

Pope John, Helena and I

Honours And Awards

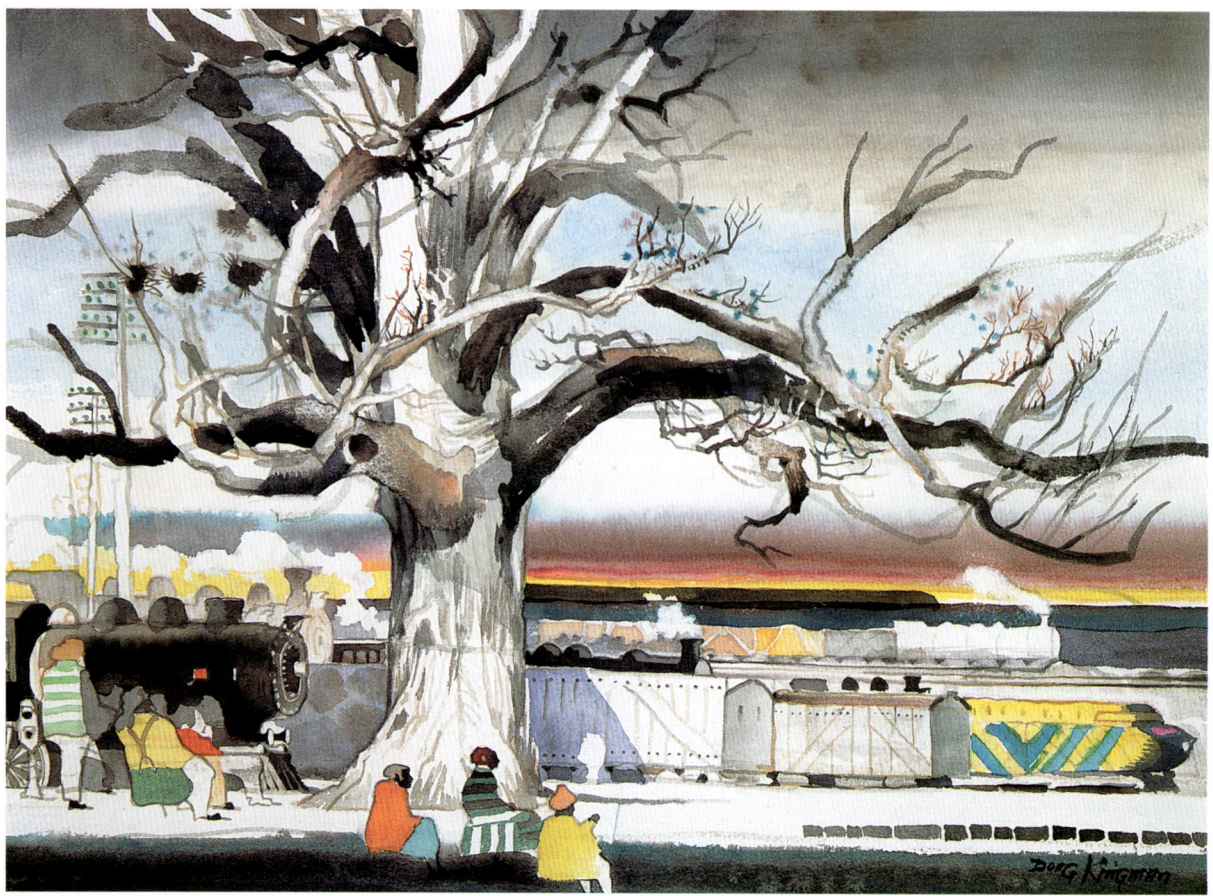

One Tree And Six Locomotives, American Watercolor Society, Elizabeth Callar Award, 1988

ONE TREE AND SIX LOCOMOTIVES
I painted a tree on location. When I came back to the studio, I added on one locomotive, and two people. Later, I added more locomotives, and more people to give the picture a more interesting composition, with placement of light and dark value.

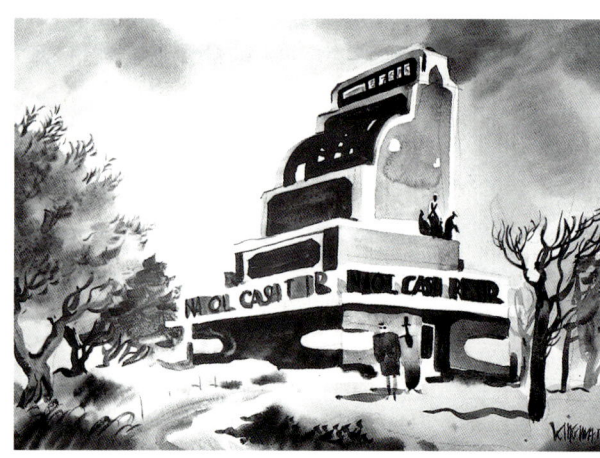

World's Fair 1940, San Francisco

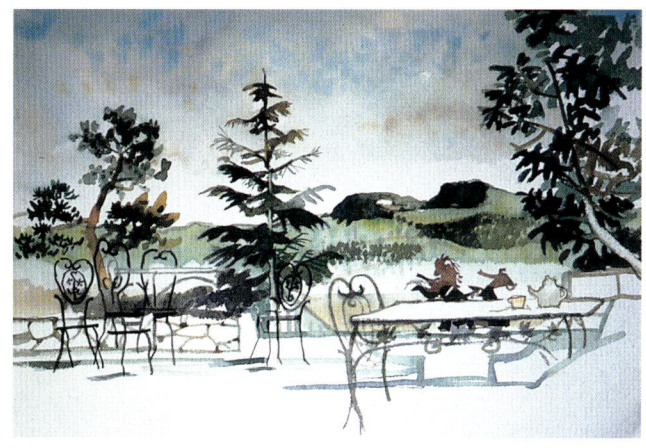
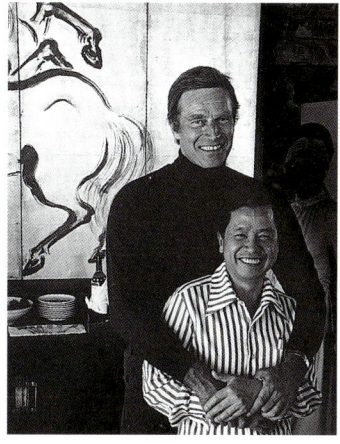

Heston's gardenCharlton Heston

Hong Kong 1997, American Watercolor Society Award, collection of Mr. & Mrs. Charlton Heston

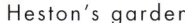

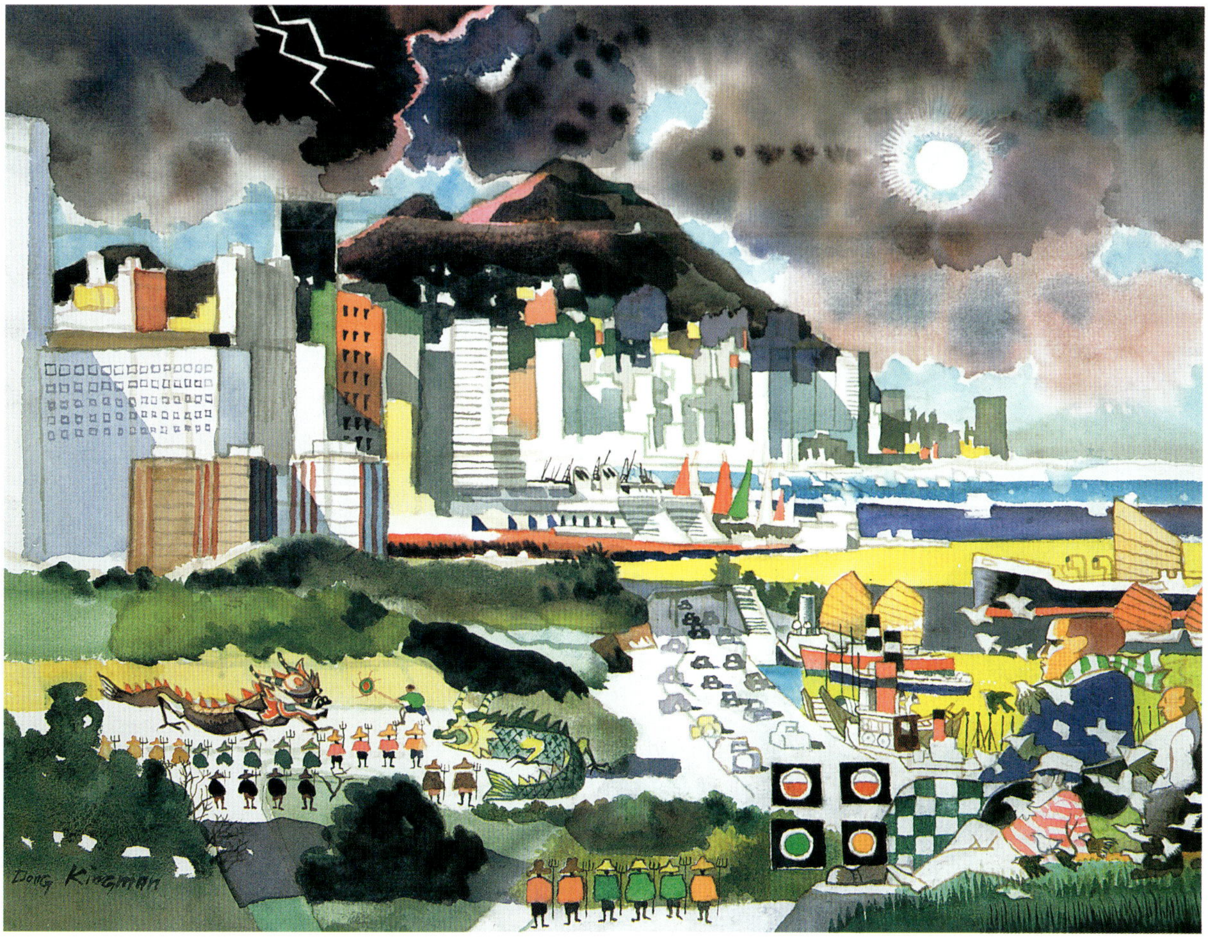

Honours And Awards

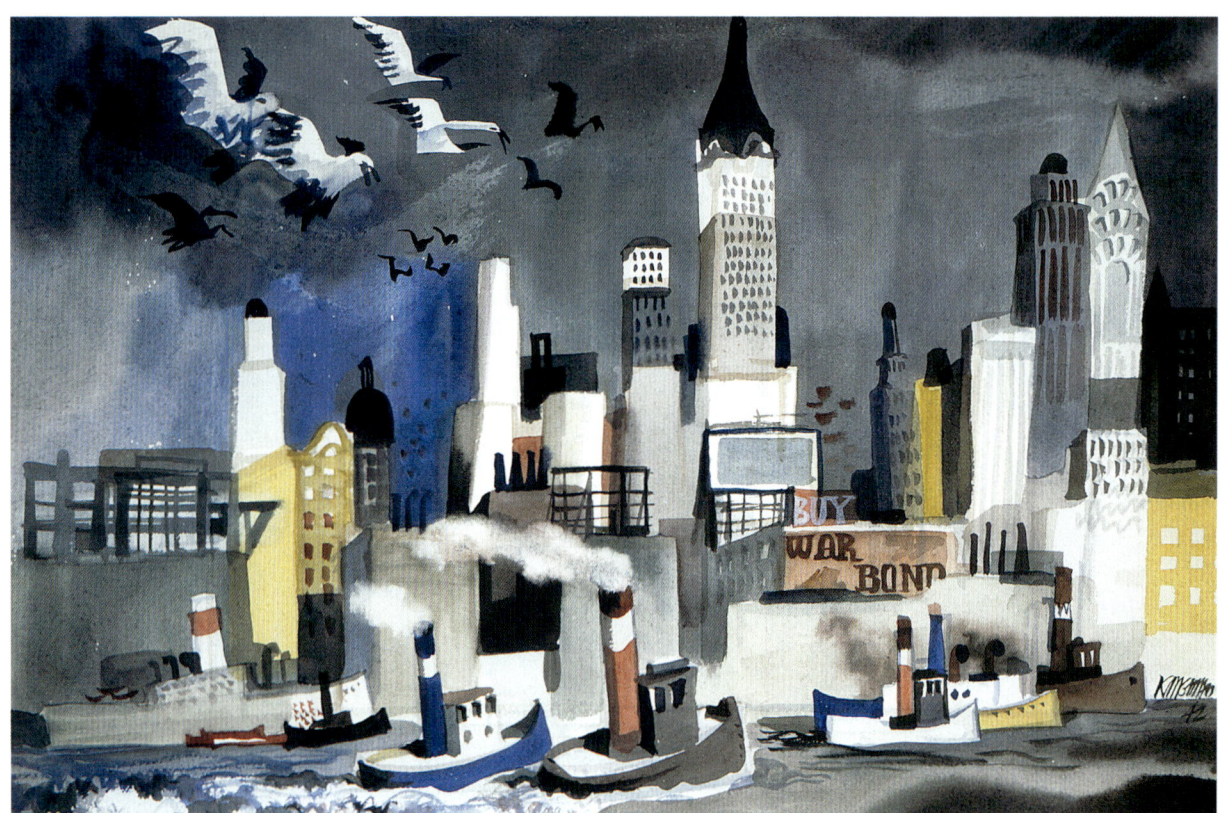

New York After Storm, Sheldon Memorial Art Gallery, Lincoln, Neb

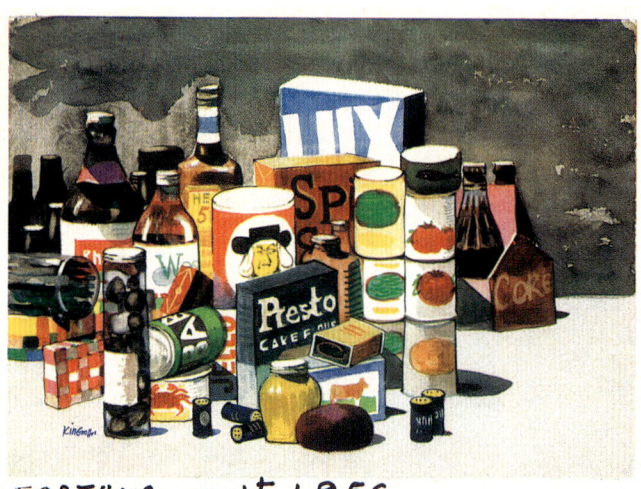

Fortune Magazine Sept 1956

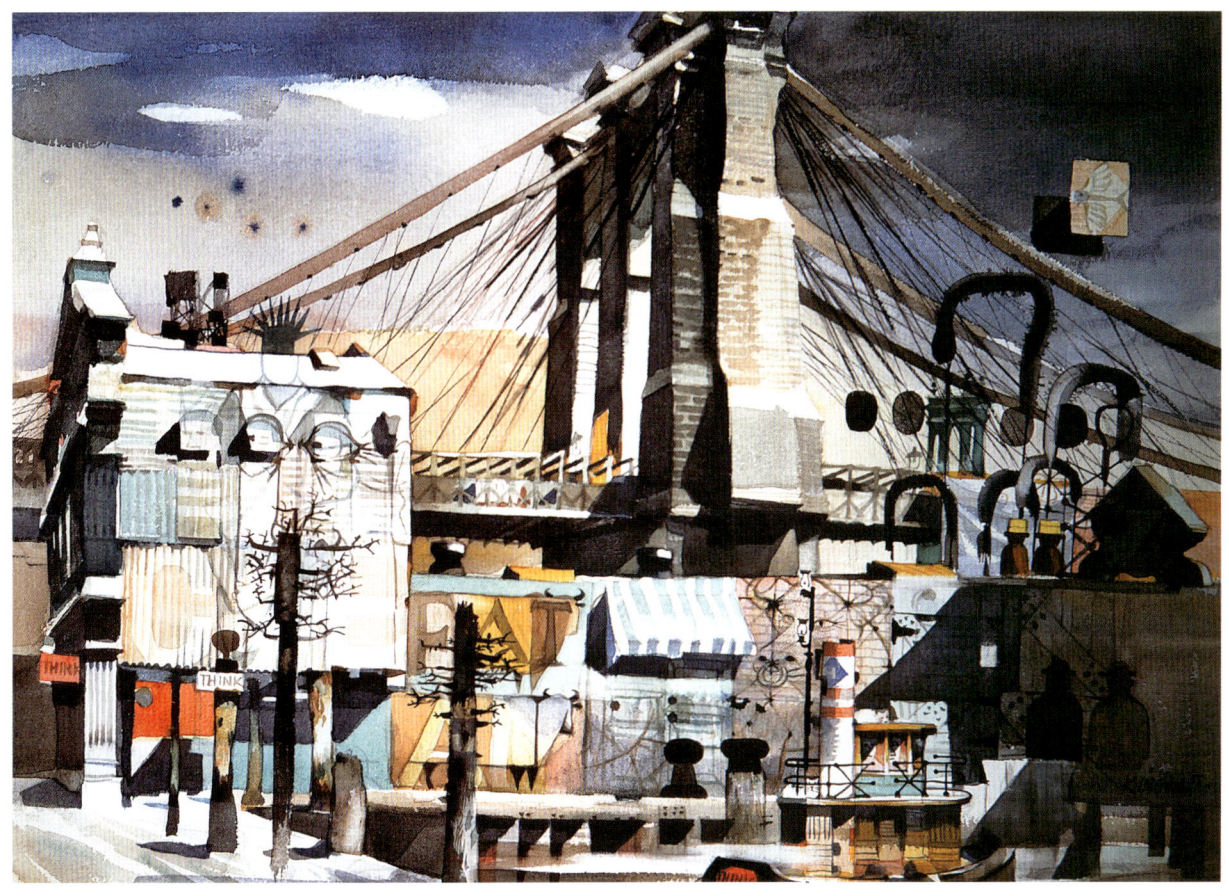

South Street Bridg, Metropolitan Museum of Art, New York, NY

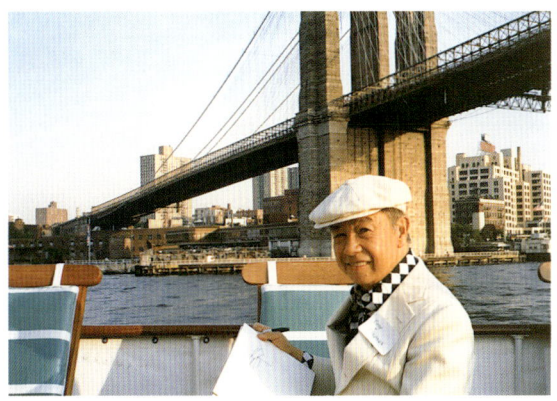

I Taught Myself To Paint

I had wanted to be a painter since I was five years old. I participated in art contests and won prizes when I was in Grammar School in HongKong. When I went to the American missionary Lingnan School, the Principal and my teacher and mentor Mr. Ssetu Wei was very enthusiastic about my art work. I returned to the US in 1929 during the deep Depression. I worked as a waiter and a dishwasher. In 1931, I bought a restaurant for $75. When I was not busy at the restaurant in the afternoon, I went to study art at then nearby Fox & Morgan Art School in Oakland. I was so happy and enthusiastic to finally have a chance to learn to paint. Happily, weeks went by, following students doing oil painting outdoors every Friday. Five weeks later, my teacher Mr. Fox called me into his office and told me, "You know nothing about painting… You better go back to work in your chop-suey house. You'll never make it as an artist."

These words hurt me more than anything I could remember. I still wanted to paint. One day, it dawned on me to put away all my oil painting supply and equipment and concentrate on watercolor painting which was my native heritage.

Not long after that, the roof of my restaurant caved in after a torrential California rain storm. There was no business. I packed up and took my wife and baby to leave Oakland for San Francisco to stay away from my bill collectors.

In San Francisco, an art school called Academy of Advertising Art which had a long flight of stairs outside going from the street floor to the fifth floor on Grant Avenue. The sign of the School stirred my interest in studying art every time I walked pass the long flight of stairs. One day, I decided to register in that school to satisfy my yearning to learn to paint. Half way up, Mr. Fox's words kept ringing in my ears, "You'll never make it as an artist." Immediately, I turned around to run down the stairs without registering.

I had no money to feed my wife, baby, myself, and a cat, least of all to study art in a school. I found a small job working as a houseboy six-and-half days a week for the Drew family. On Sunday mornings, my only half day off, I would go out to paint different San Francisco scenes in the streets. I taught myself to paint as I went along. There were many group shows and annual exhibitions given by local artists in the Bay area. I sent in my work, but was rejected every time.

In about a year I had accumulated many paintings from my Sunday morning's outdoor sketchings. There was an art center gallery, specializing in helping up-and-coming young artists by giving them exhibitions. The exhibition they offered me was a half-man show. The other half show I shared with a lady artist.

On April 4, 1936, a day I will long remember, an art critic wrote a rave review about my art work in a San Francisco newspaper. I did not know much English at that time. I was serving dinner at the table for the Drew family. I was surprised to find they were reading their newspapers instead of eating.

They told me later that their houseboy is now a famous artist!

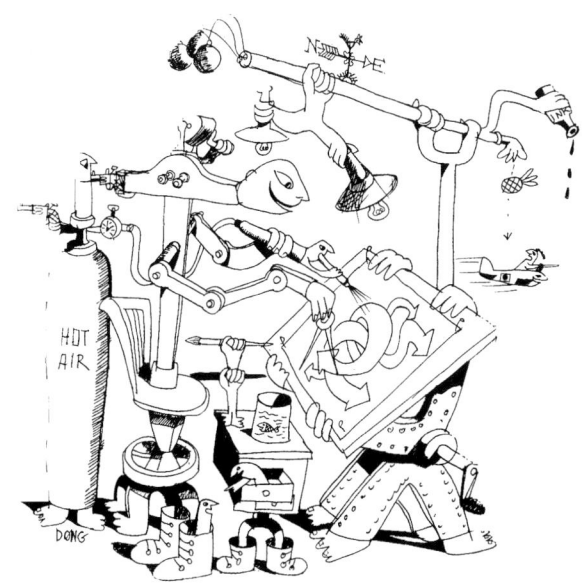

Saturday, April 4, 1936 — THE SAN FRANCISCO NEWS

FRESHNESS APPARENT IN 20 WATER COLORS BY DONG KINGMAN

IN SHOW AT ART CENTER

One-Man Exhibition Indicates That Young Chinese Has Found Unusual Style of Expression

BY JUNIUS CRAVENS

ONCE in a while one unexpectedly happens upon a one-man show which should step out in front of the line, as it were, to have honors pinned on it. Such an exhibition, it seems to me, is Dong Kingman's, at the Art Center, 730 Montgomery-st. That young Chinese artist is showing 20 of the freshest, most satisfying water colors that have been seen hereabouts in many a day. Though Kingman may be comparatively unknown, his name is not entirely new to local gallery visitors. Isolated examples of his work have appeared from time to time in group exhibitions.

The answer probably is that Kingman already has developed that universal quality which may place a sincere artist's work above the limitations of either racial characteristics or "schools." Kingman's art belongs to the world-at-large of today.

● ● ●

KINGMAN'S name may seem as bafflingly Western as his painting, but that is because he has turned it wrong end to. His given name is Kingman; Dong is his family name.

But this is Kingman's first attempt to stand alone, so to speak, and the result more than justifies the venture. By their one-man exhibitions shall ye know them.

There is nothing in Kingman's painting which betrays the Oriental. On the other hand, while his approach is that of a Westerner, there is nothing in the result which hints at an attempt on the part of the artist to imitate anything that is foreign to him.

Though Kingman was born in Oakland, his family moved back to China while he was still a child, and he spent 14 of his formative years there.

The native drawing master at the Hongkong school which he attended had studied art in Paris. That teacher, as is an old Oriental custom, took two or three of his outstanding pupils to the country during the summer vacation periods for a serious study of art, Kingman among them. He seems to have been an excellent teacher.

So, when Kingman returned to San Francisco, seven or eight years ago, he already had a pretty solid foundation in Western methods. Since that time he wisely has been self-taught. He now seems to be fairly well started along the road toward individual expression.

Landscapes and San Francisco street scenes in which human figures appear incidentally, predominate in Kingman's exhibition. He handles his color fluently, in broad, telling masses. He is never finicky. He is completely sincere and never superficial. Here is a real water color painter.

● ● ●

Pictures

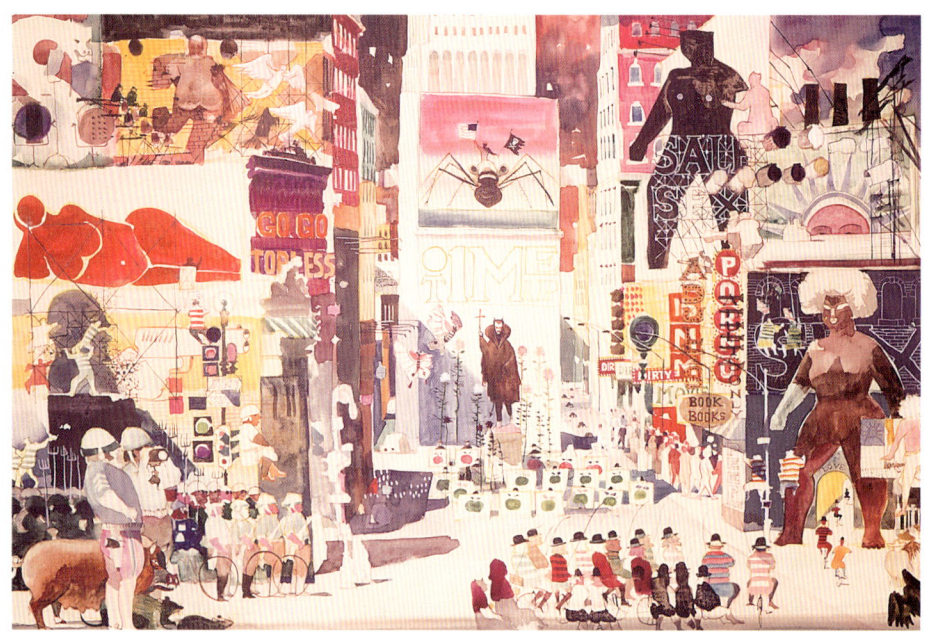

Sex in Times Square, collection of Mr. & Mrs. Bill Cosby

I found this Indian Temple in midst of Chinatown in the heart of Singapore

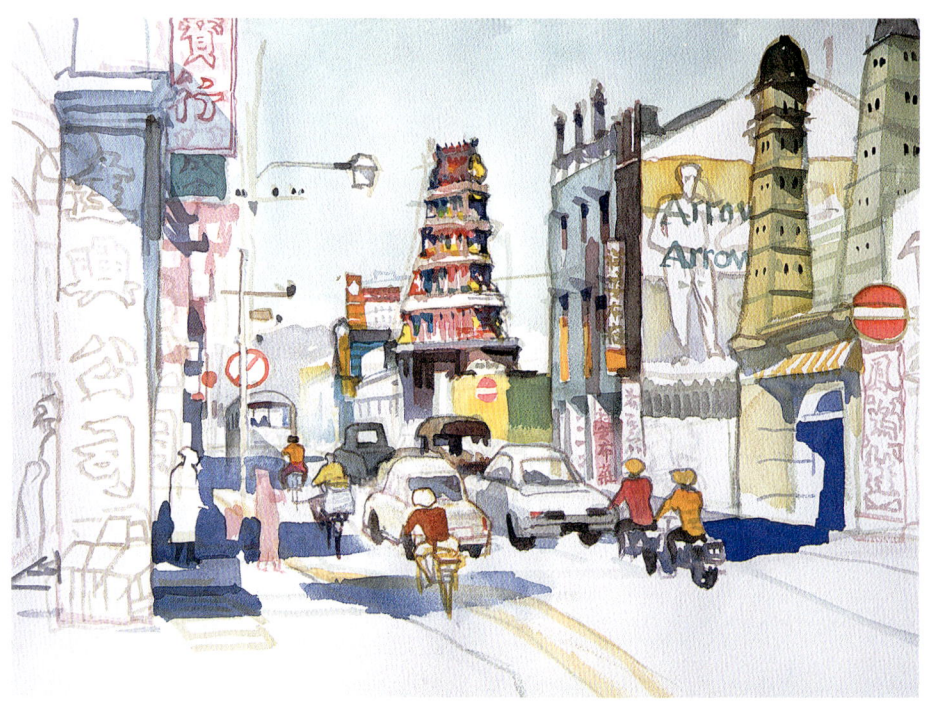

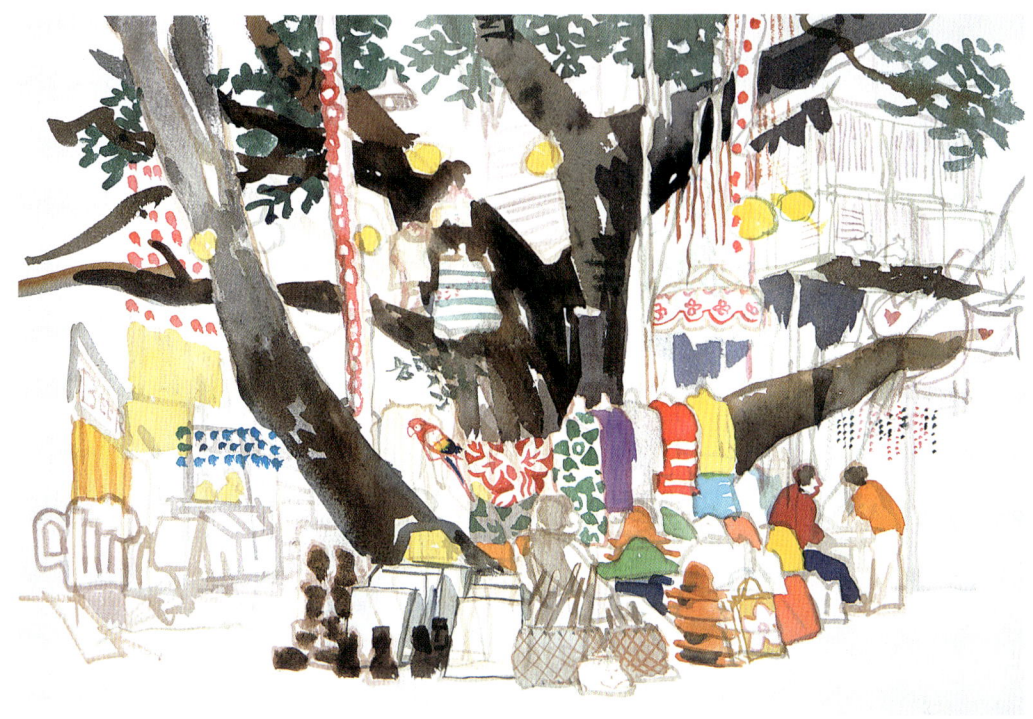

International market, collection of Mr. and Mrs. Dwight Strong

Storm Over Summer Palace, collection of Mr. & Mrs. Y.S. Lim

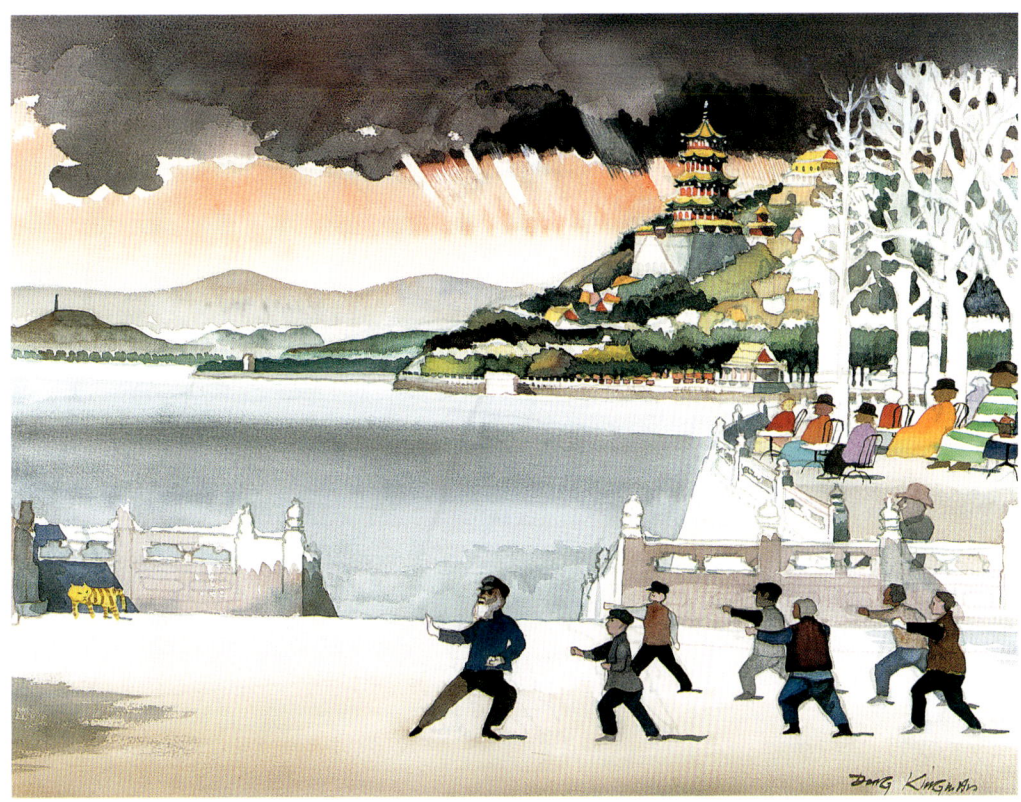

Taj Mahal

In 1954, I was invited to go around the world as a Goodwill Ambassador for the U.S. Department of State. One of my first stops was New Delhi, India. But I did not get to go to Taj Mahal which I was so anxious to see. In 1960, I received an assignment from Pan-Am Airways to paint one of the most famous places in India - the Taj Mahal. My wife Helena and I left New York for HongKong to New Delhi to take a taxi to Taj Mahal, arriving at midnight in a full moon in September. I could not see the Taj in bright electric light from the hotel window. Wtih help of Helena, I painted the Taj with candlelight. I found the painting terrible when I saw it the next morning. But I had an idea when I returned to the studio in New York. I would create the Taj in three levels: the middle level would be where the Taj was; the lower level would be busy people, vendors and elephants; and the top level would be a night scene with the romantic round yellow moon peeping through the dark skies. Pan-American Airways used this picture in every way they could and would for their First Class menu cover, in their Clipper Magazine, etc.

Yellow Moon, **Taj Mahal**

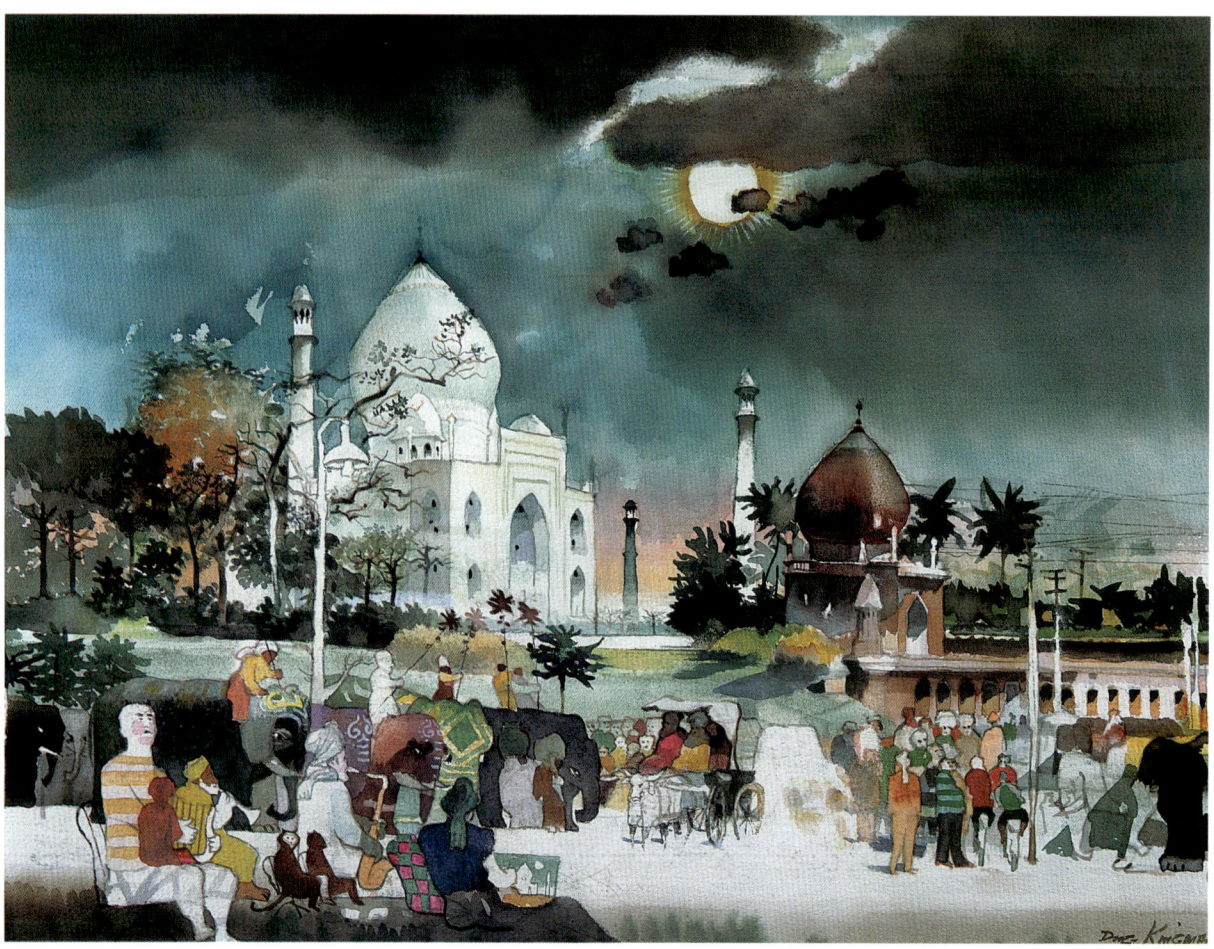

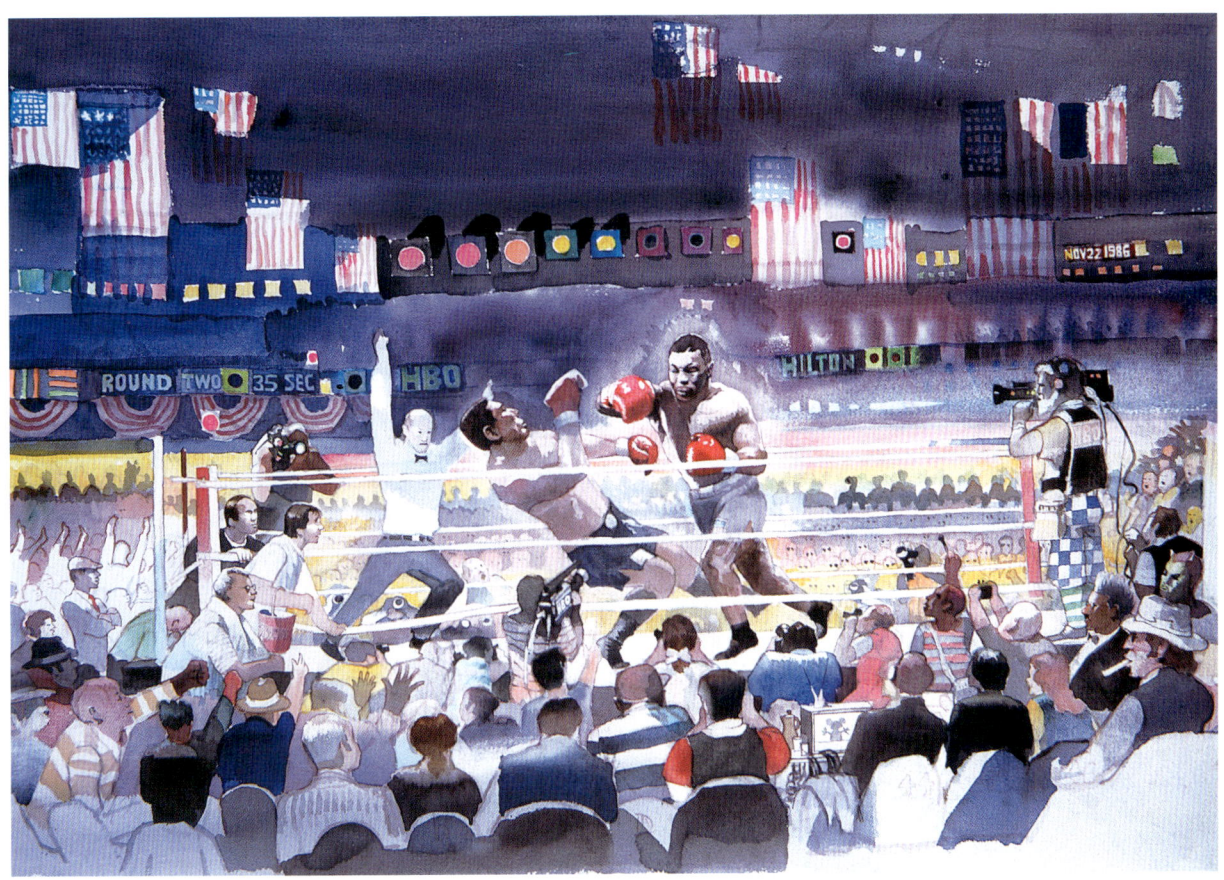
War of Dragons, A Knockout, collection of Mrs. Jim Jacobs

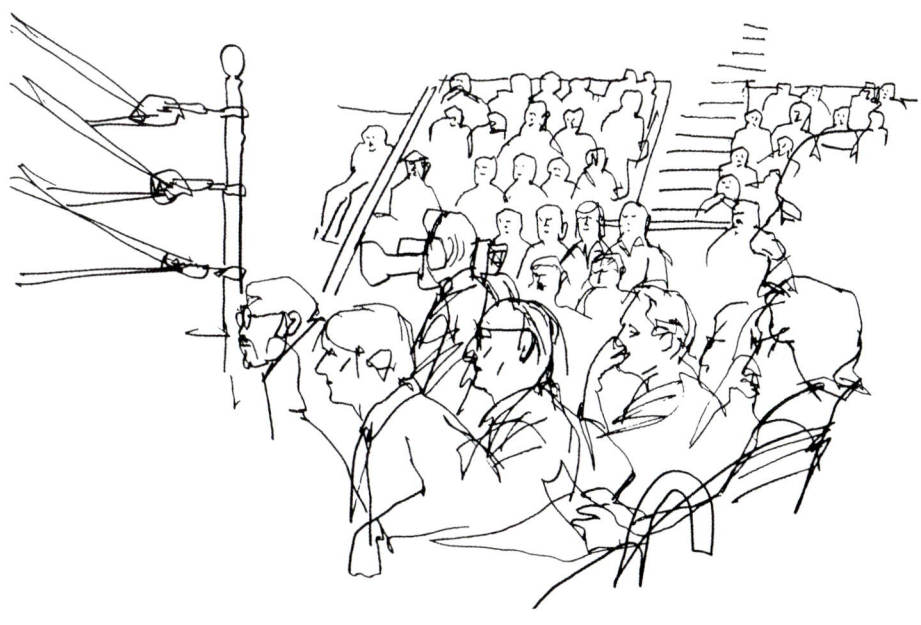

PICTURES

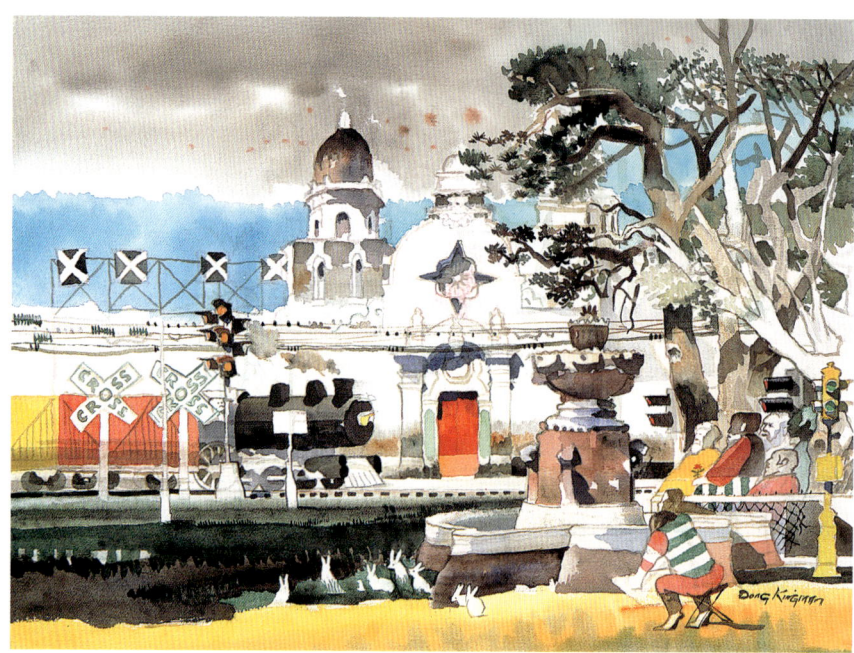

Old Mission Station

Venice, Italy, collection of Mr. and Mrs. Hank Ketcham

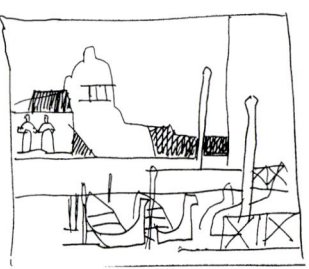
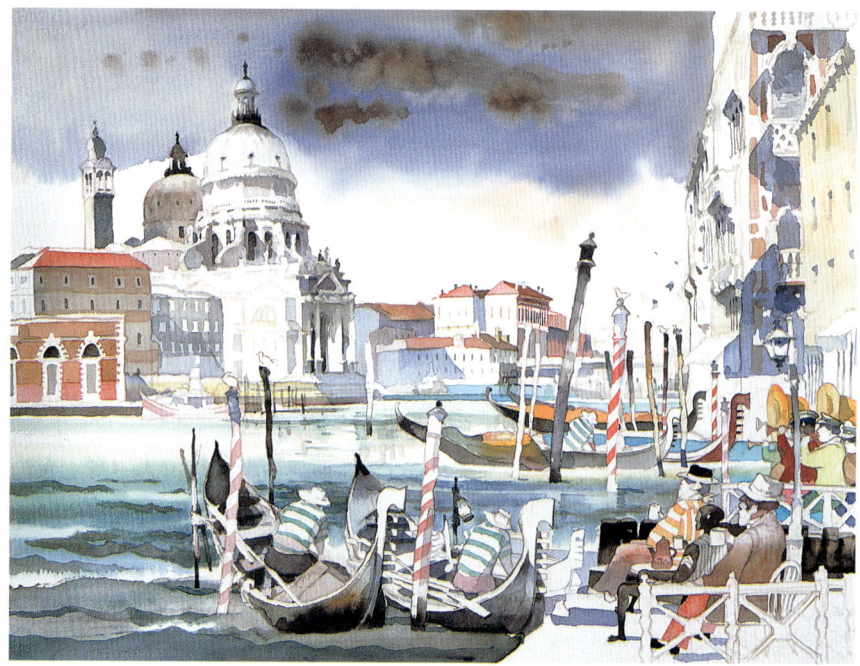

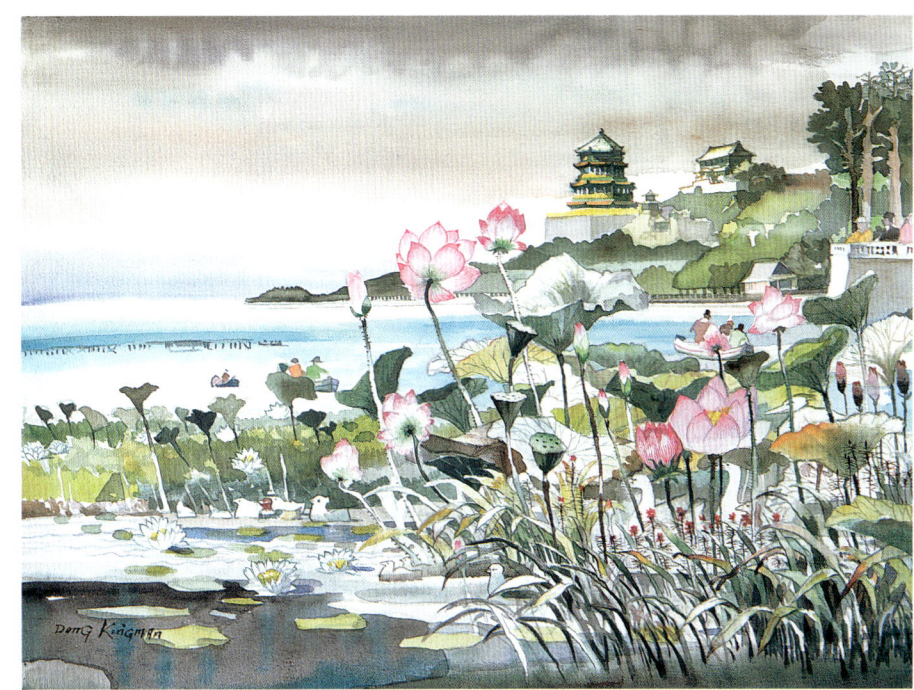

Lotus Pond in Summer Palace in Beijing, collection of Mr. Ed Singer

Oslo, collection of Mr. & Mrs. Chen Yang-Chuan

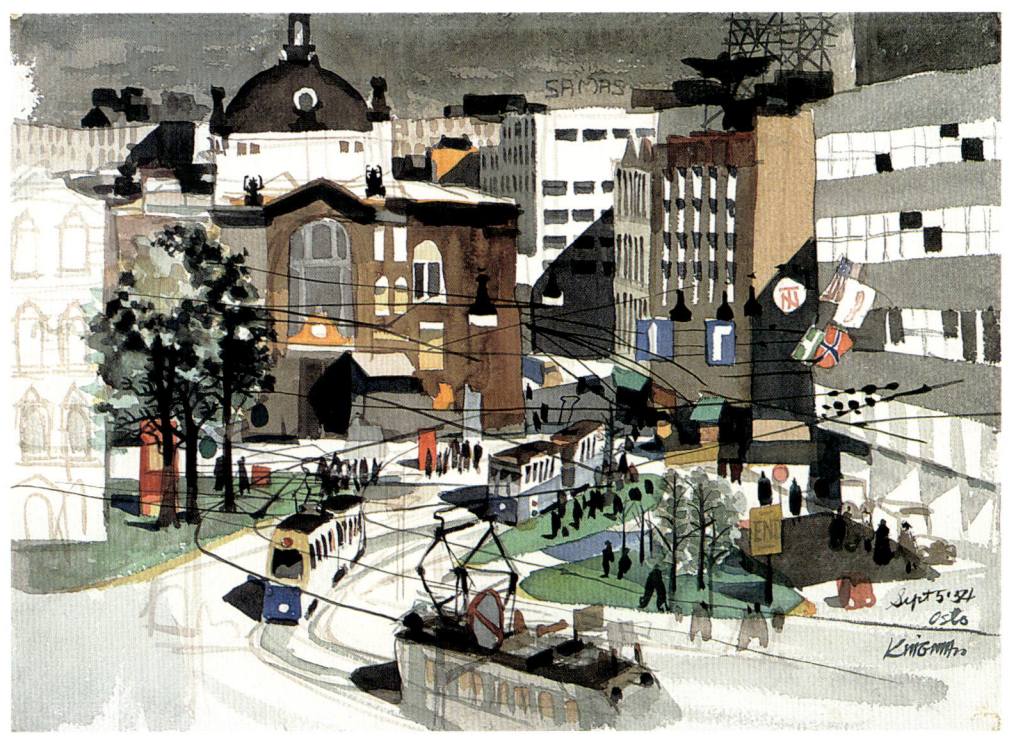

PICTURES

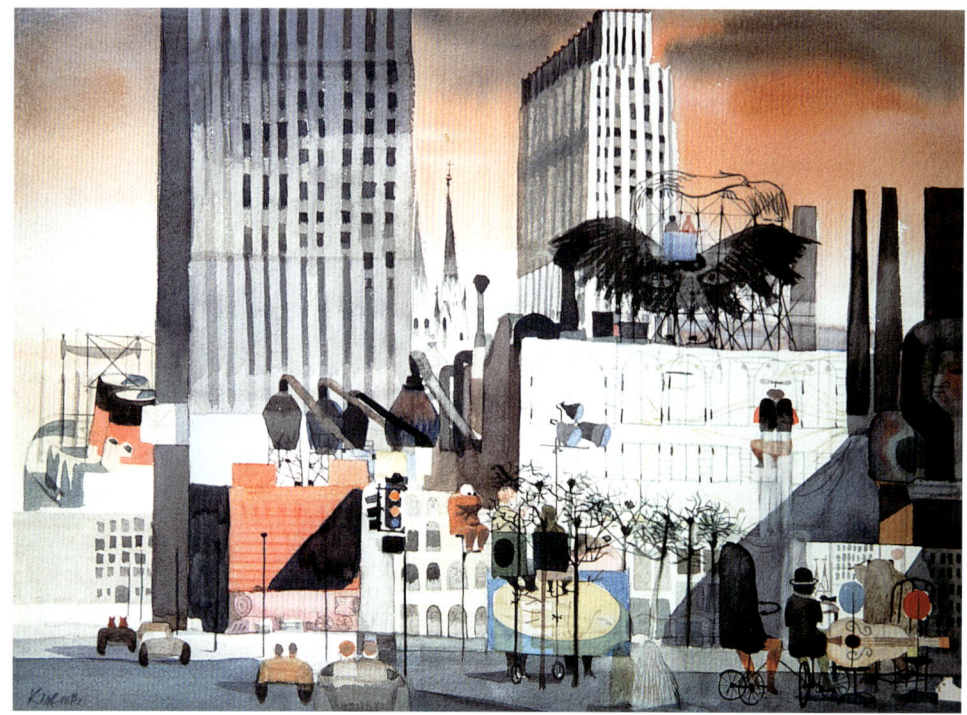

Self Portrait, collection of Mr. & Mrs. Twig Gallemore

Lion Dance, collection of Mr. Eddie Kingman

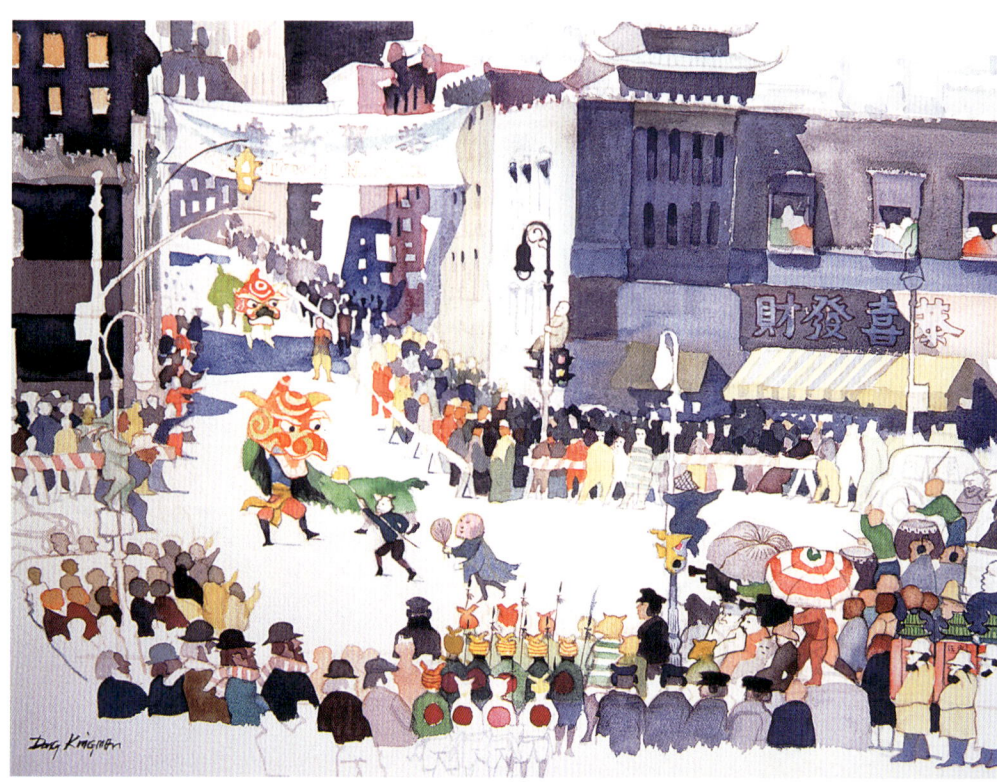

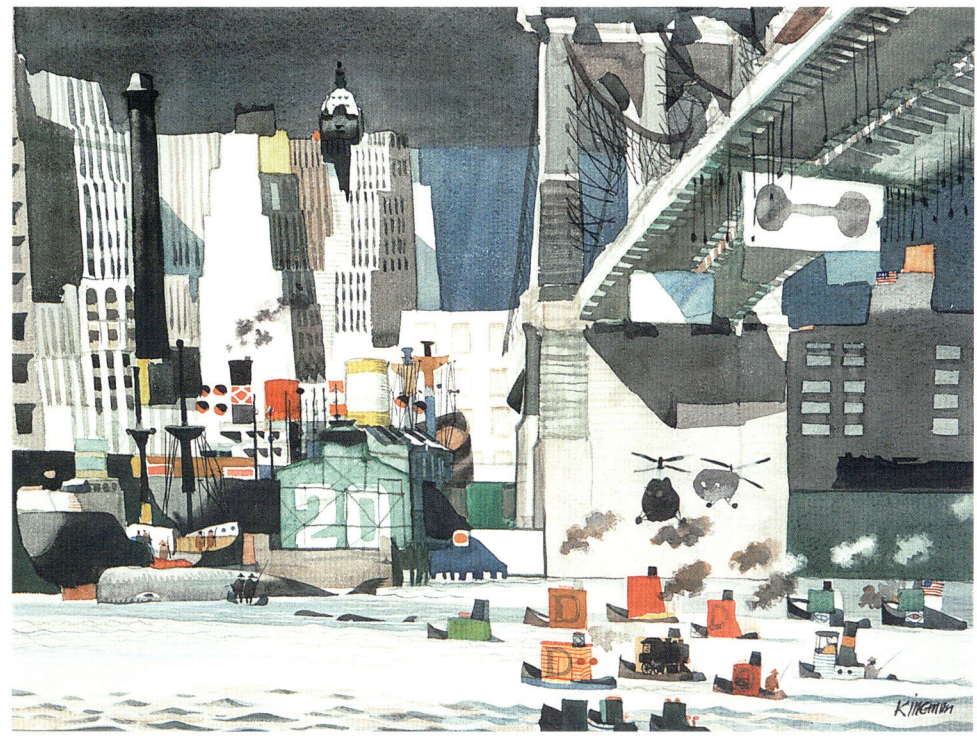

Brooklyn Bridge, collection of Bill Cullen

Grand Central

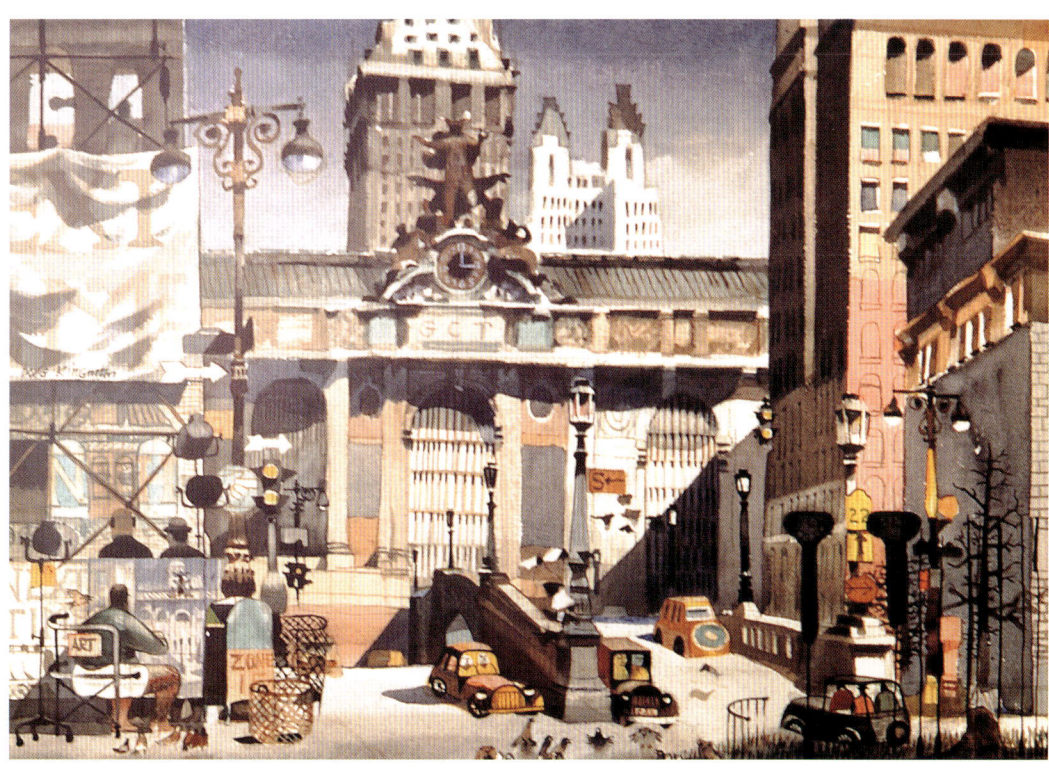

57

Pictures

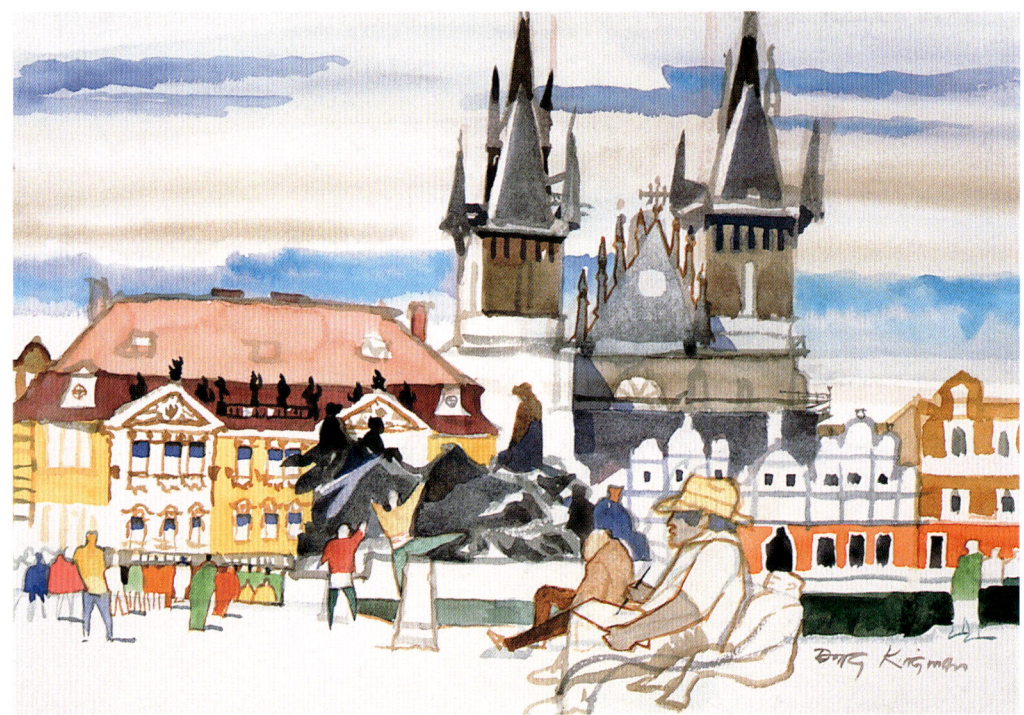

Prague, ollection of Mr. & Mrs. C.C. Lee

Locomotive to Great Wall

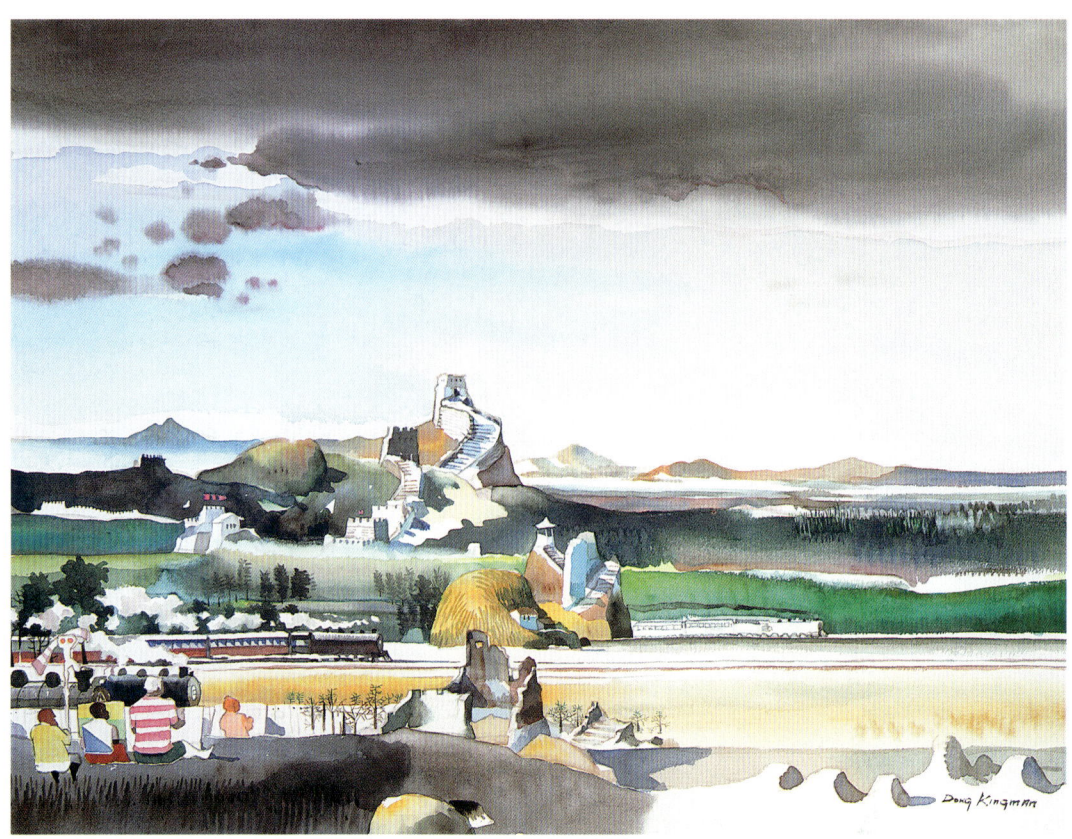

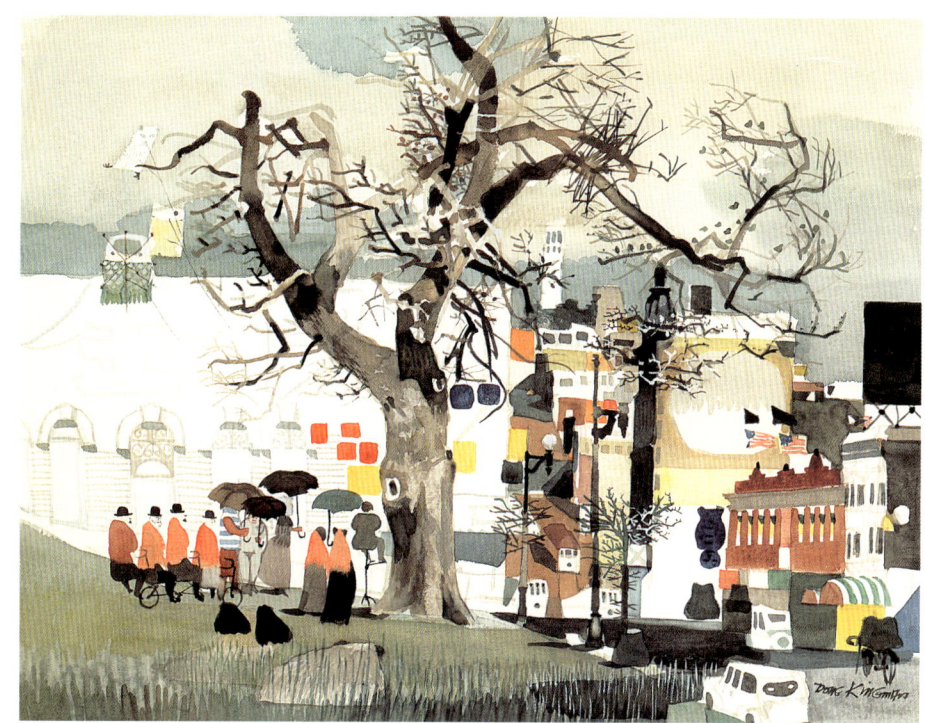

Kearny Street, San Francisco, collection of Mr. and Mrs. John Bower

Cow Looking North, collection of Mr. and Mrs. Norman Kirk

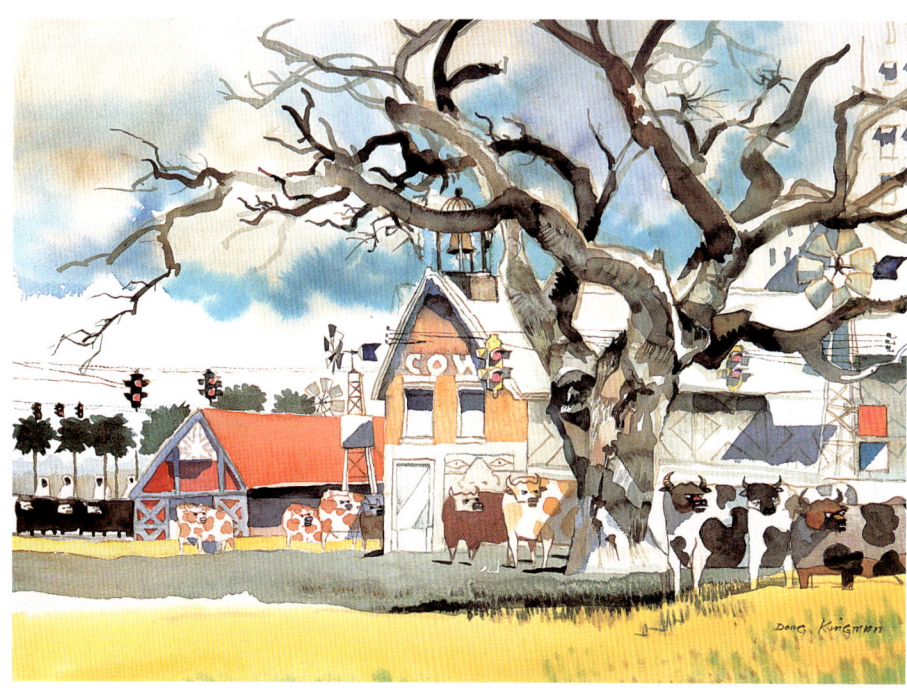

PICTURES

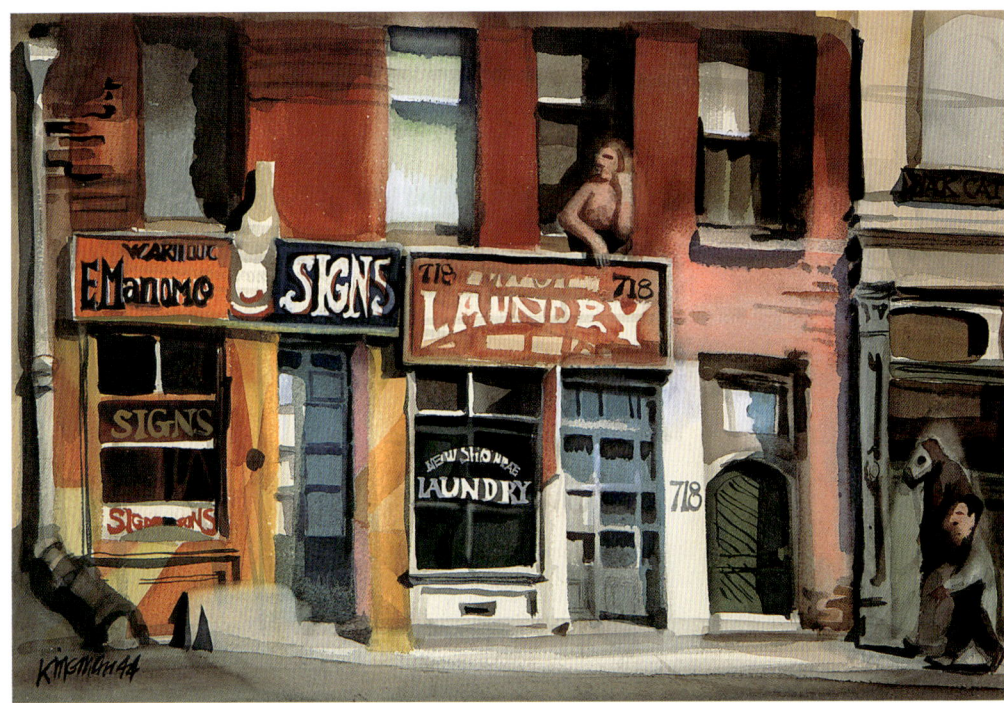

Chinese Laundry

Kyoto

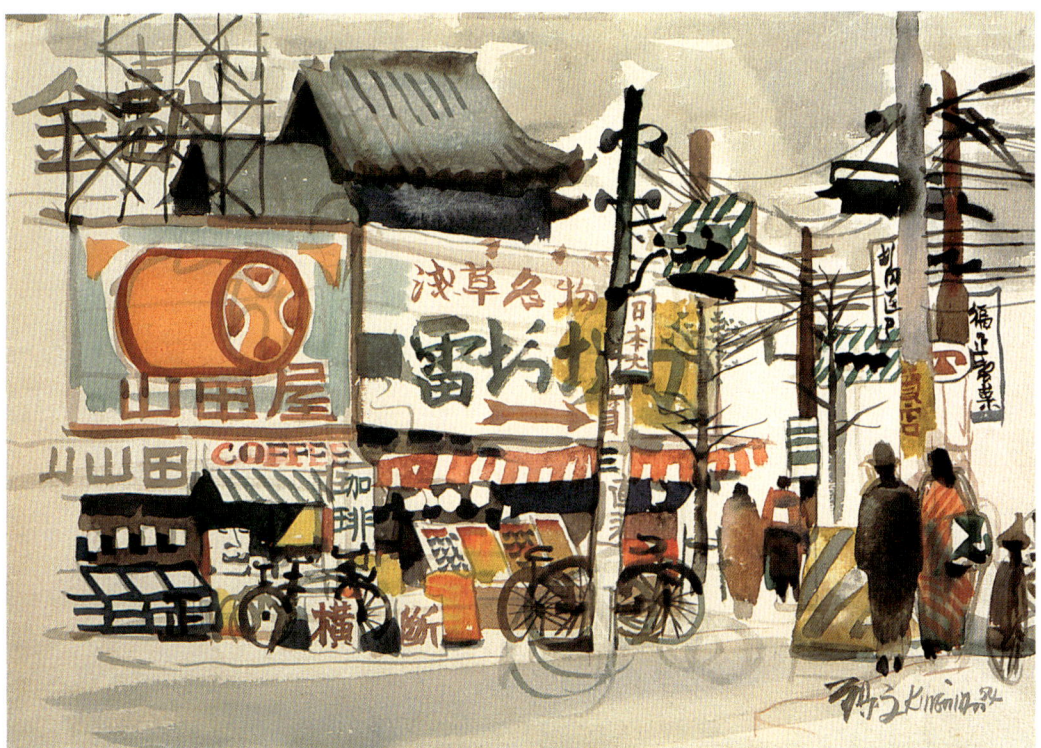

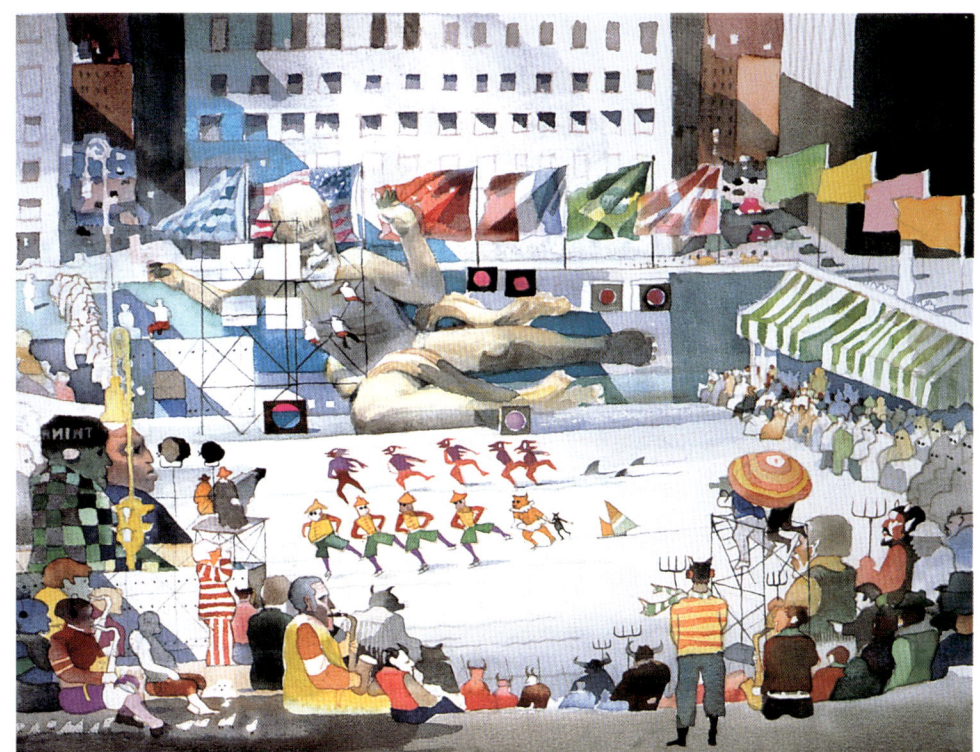

Rockefeller Center

Mount Rushmore, American Watercolour Society Mary Pleisner Award 1991, collection of Mr. and Mrs. Putra Massagung

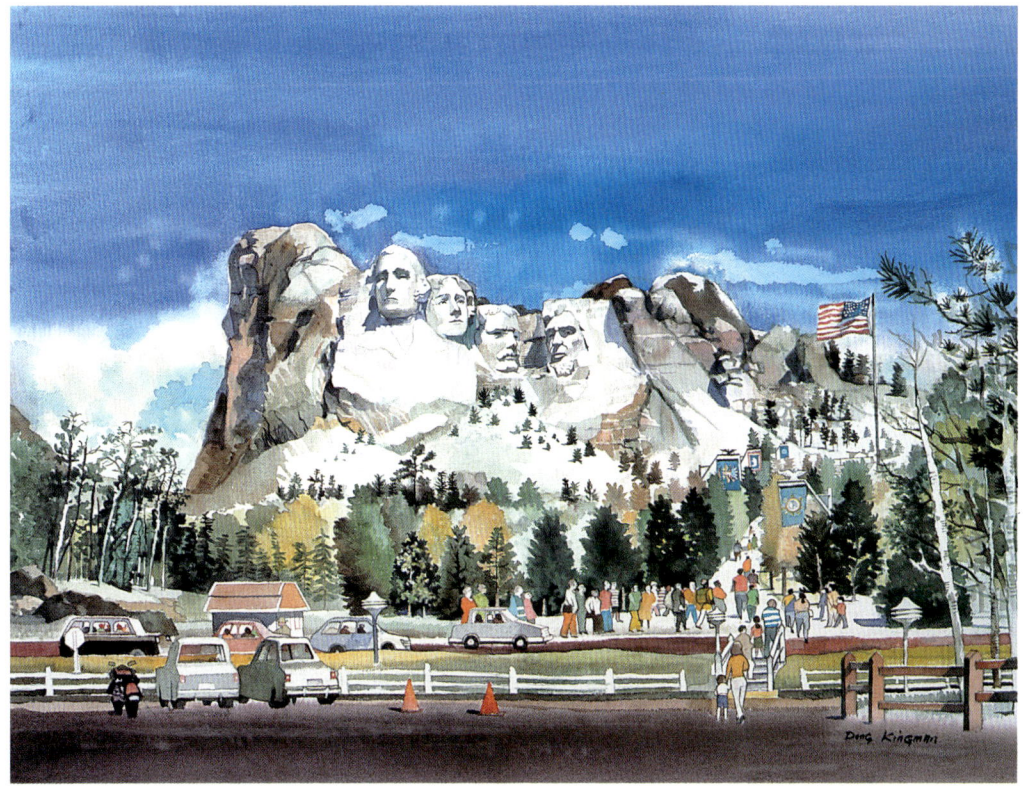

PICTURES

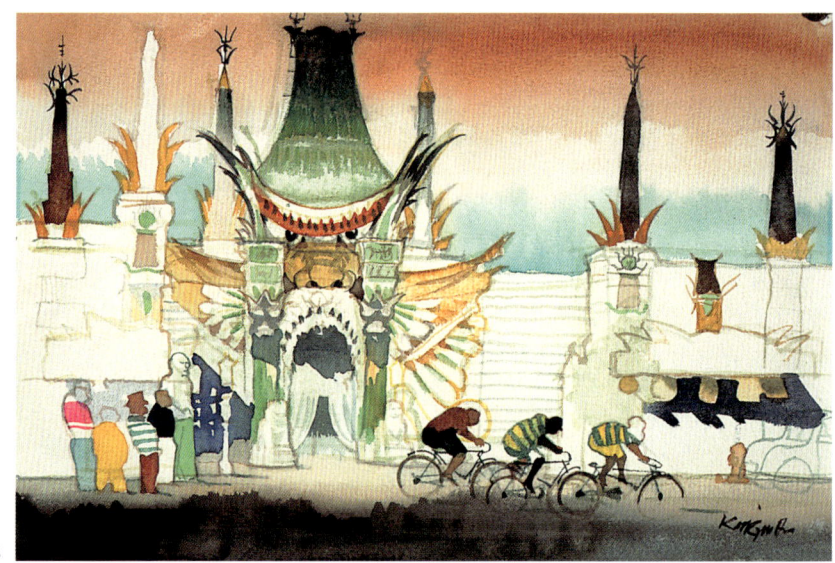

Chinese Theatre, Los Angeles

Vatican, collection of American Tourister International

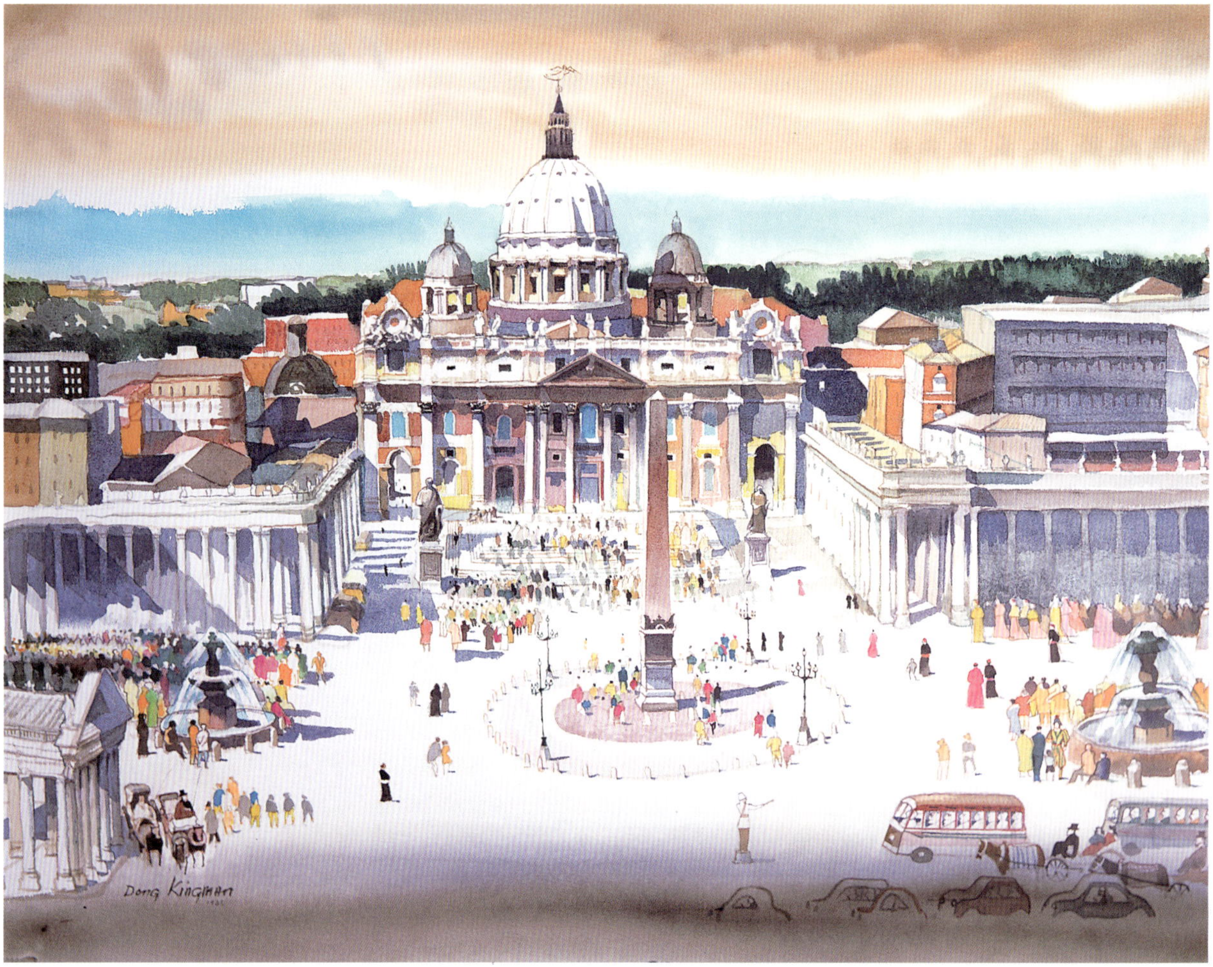

62

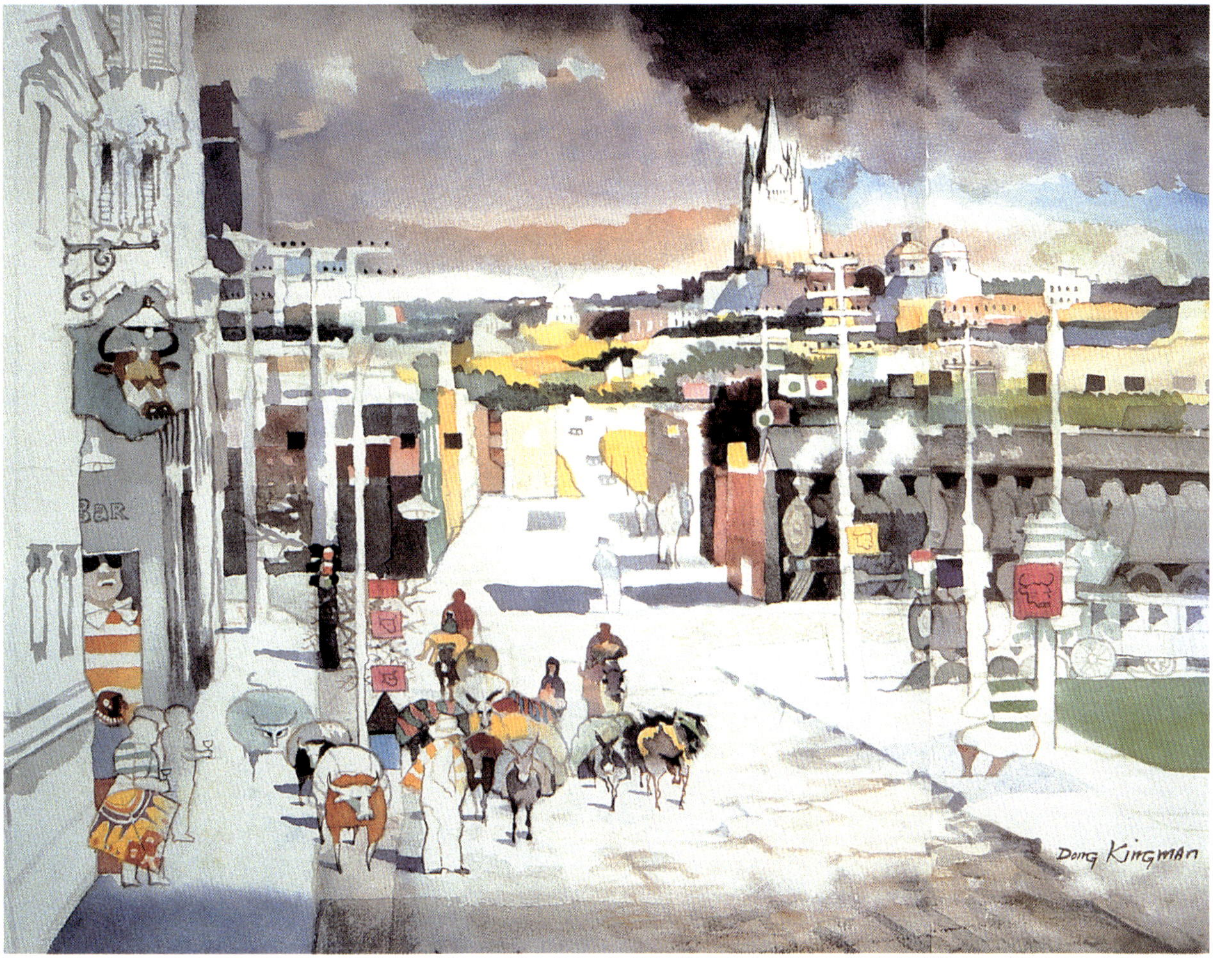

Ox Head Bar, collection of Mr. Heri T. Kato

When I was giving a one-man exhibition in Fresno early 1996, I also found time to go sketching outdoors. This building sitting amidst large trees fascinated me.

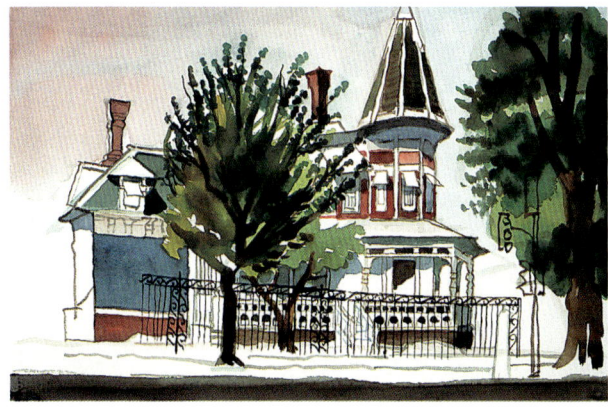

Meux Home.

PICTURES

Park Ave

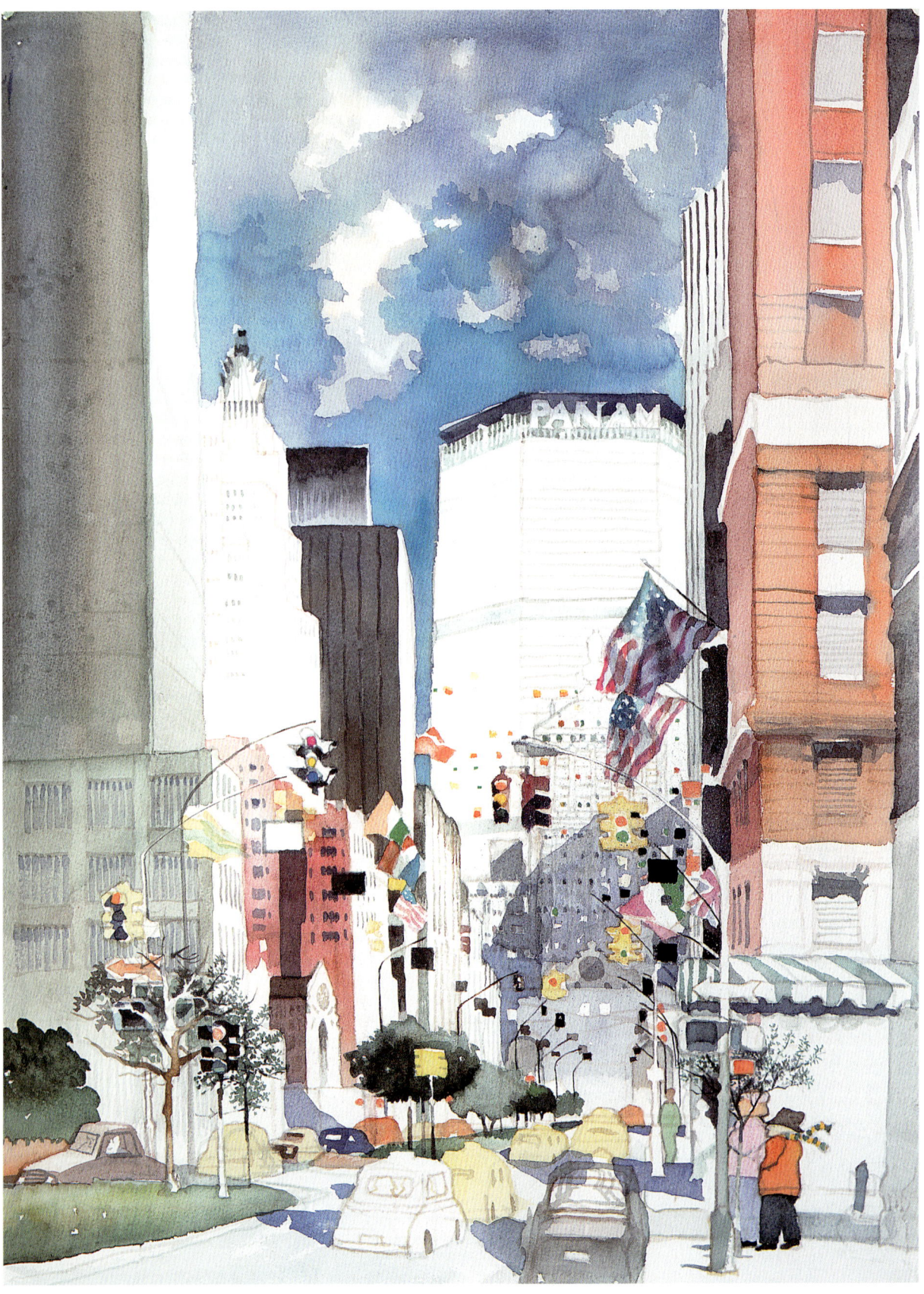

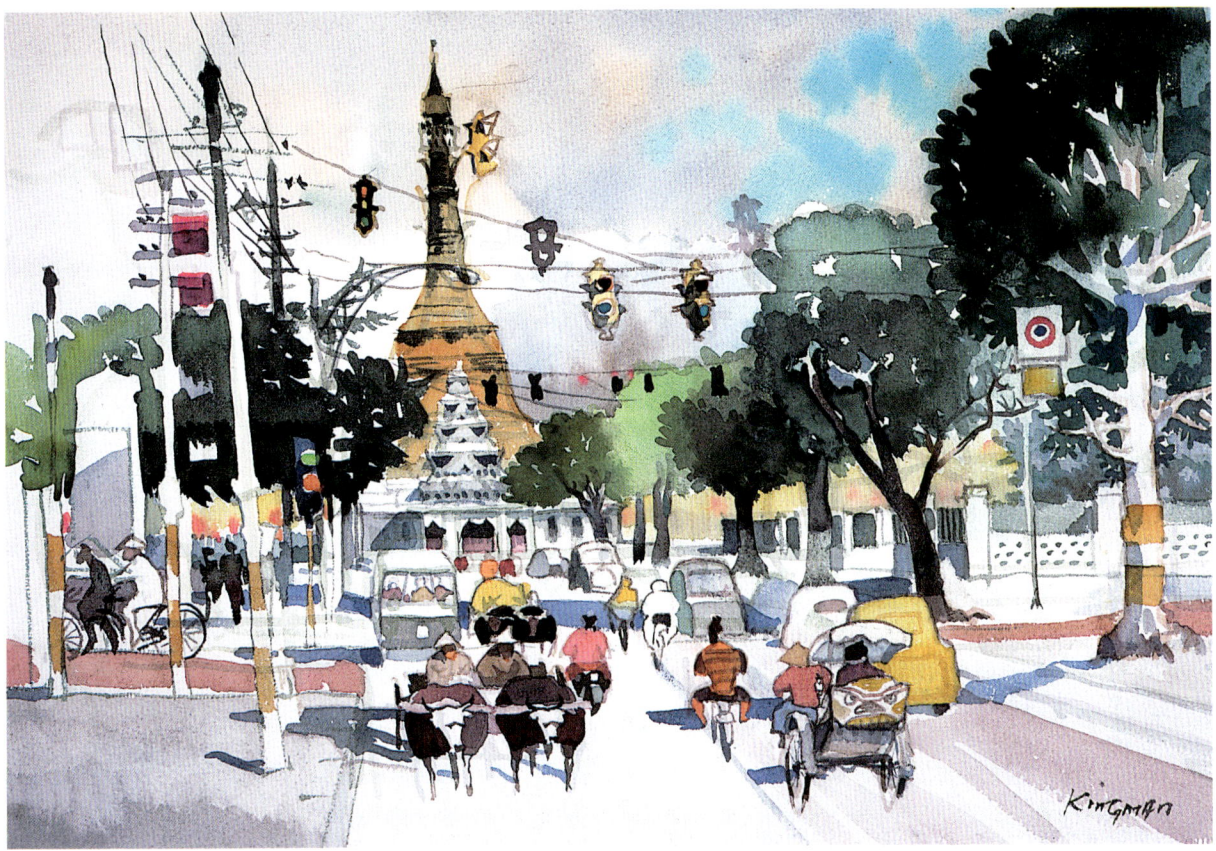

Rangoon

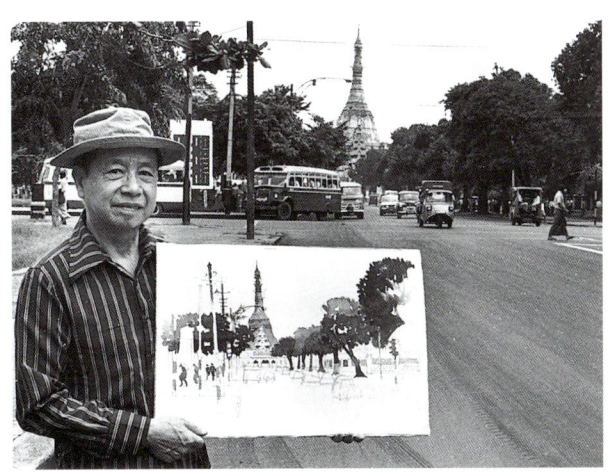

Cable Cars

Big cable car, little cable car.....going up and down like a Charlie car, from Powell Street up to North Beach to Fisherman's Wharf, from Market Street to Chinatown, to Nob Hill and Van Ness Avenue... Dong... Dong...You are in Hong Kong.

Cable car, cute little cable car, with cable attached to its bottom, it can go very near or very far...When the cable car goes downhill, the conductor would yell, *"Hang on Gai Ding..."* If you had said the same thing to a Chinese waiter in a Chinese restaurant, he would have brought you a dish of Almond Chicken, and a Fortune Cookie...

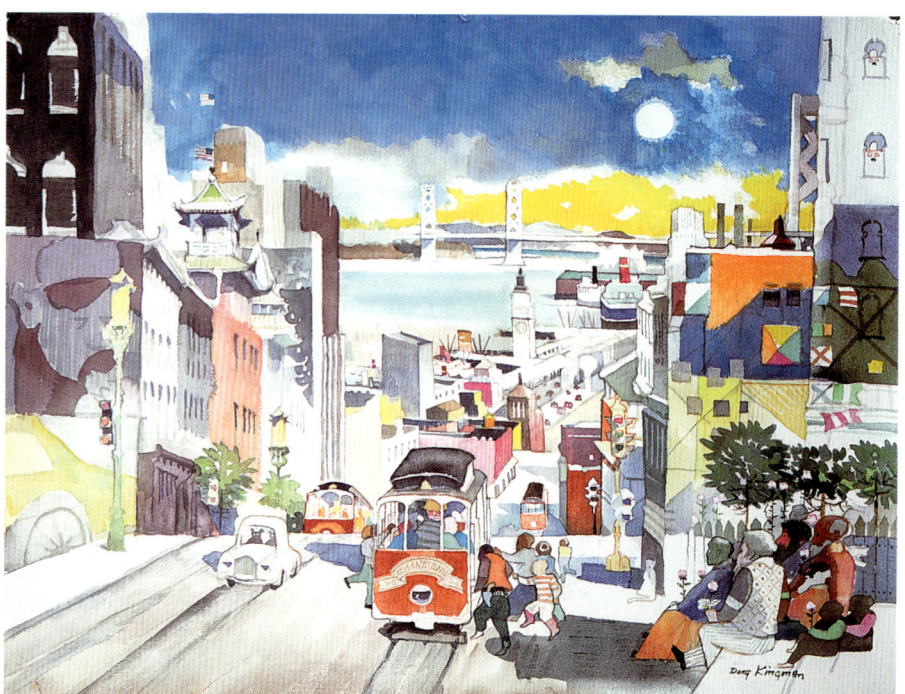

Nob Hill

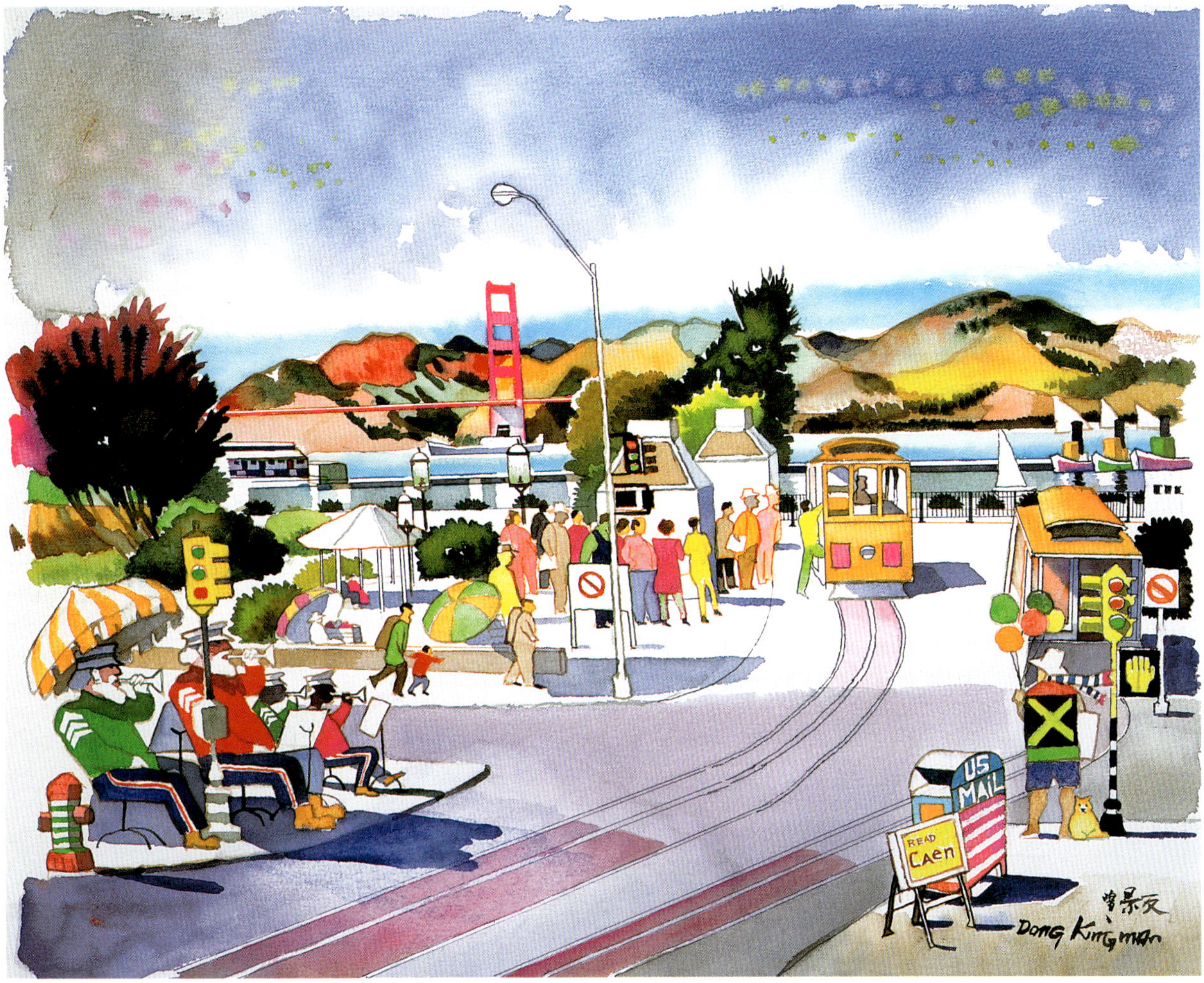

From the Beginning

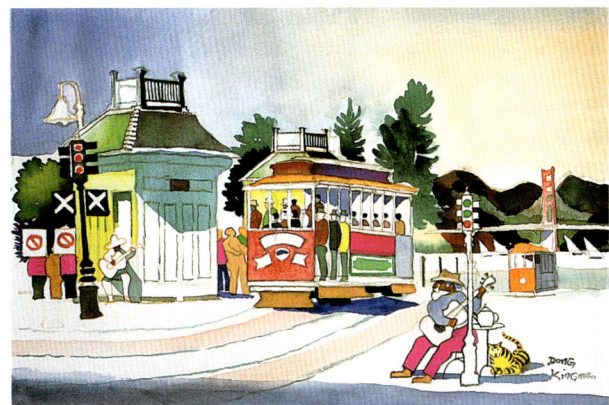

Cable Car

67

Cable Cars

Chinatown Festival

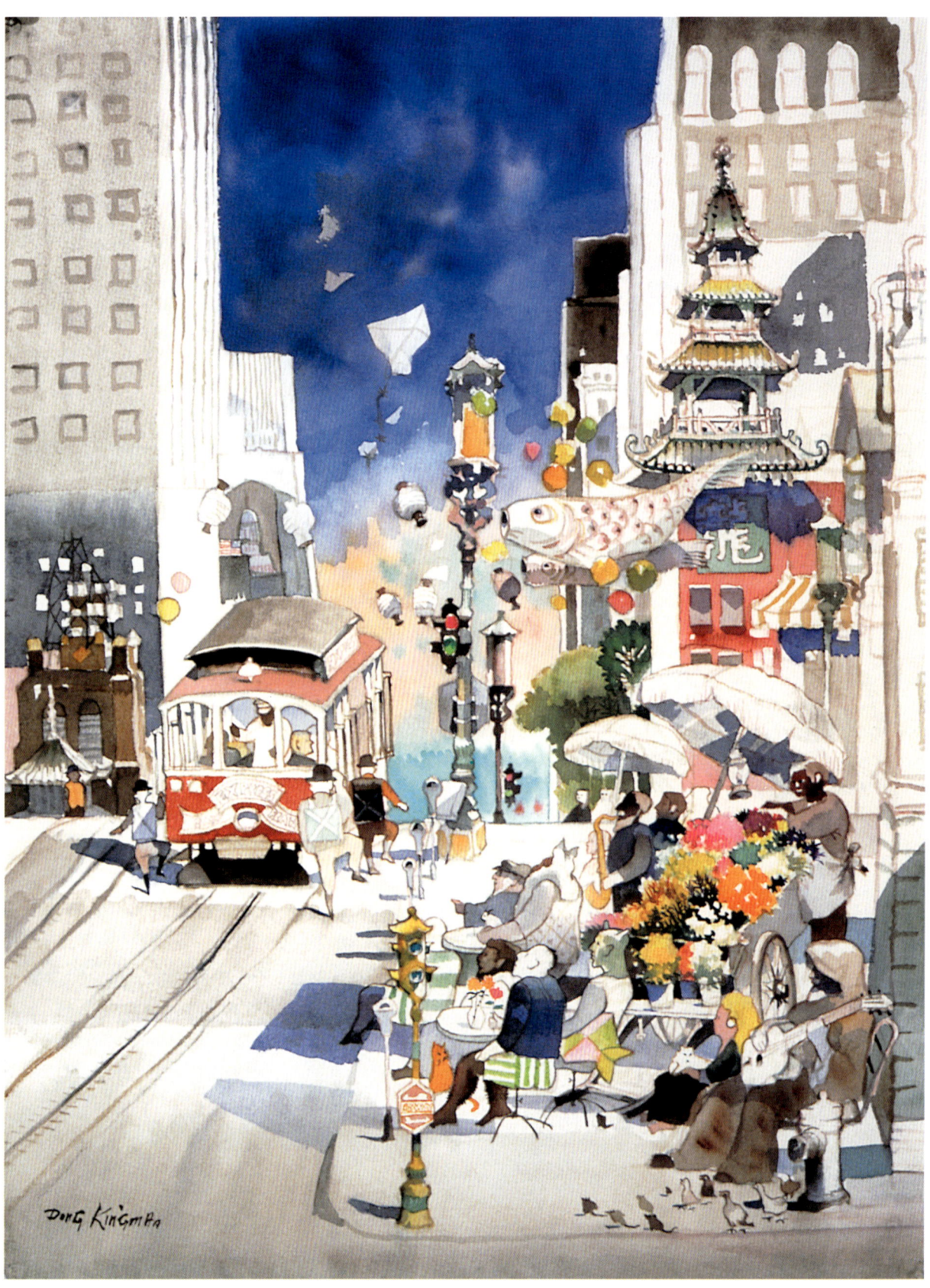

Powell Street, collection of Herb & Pat Little

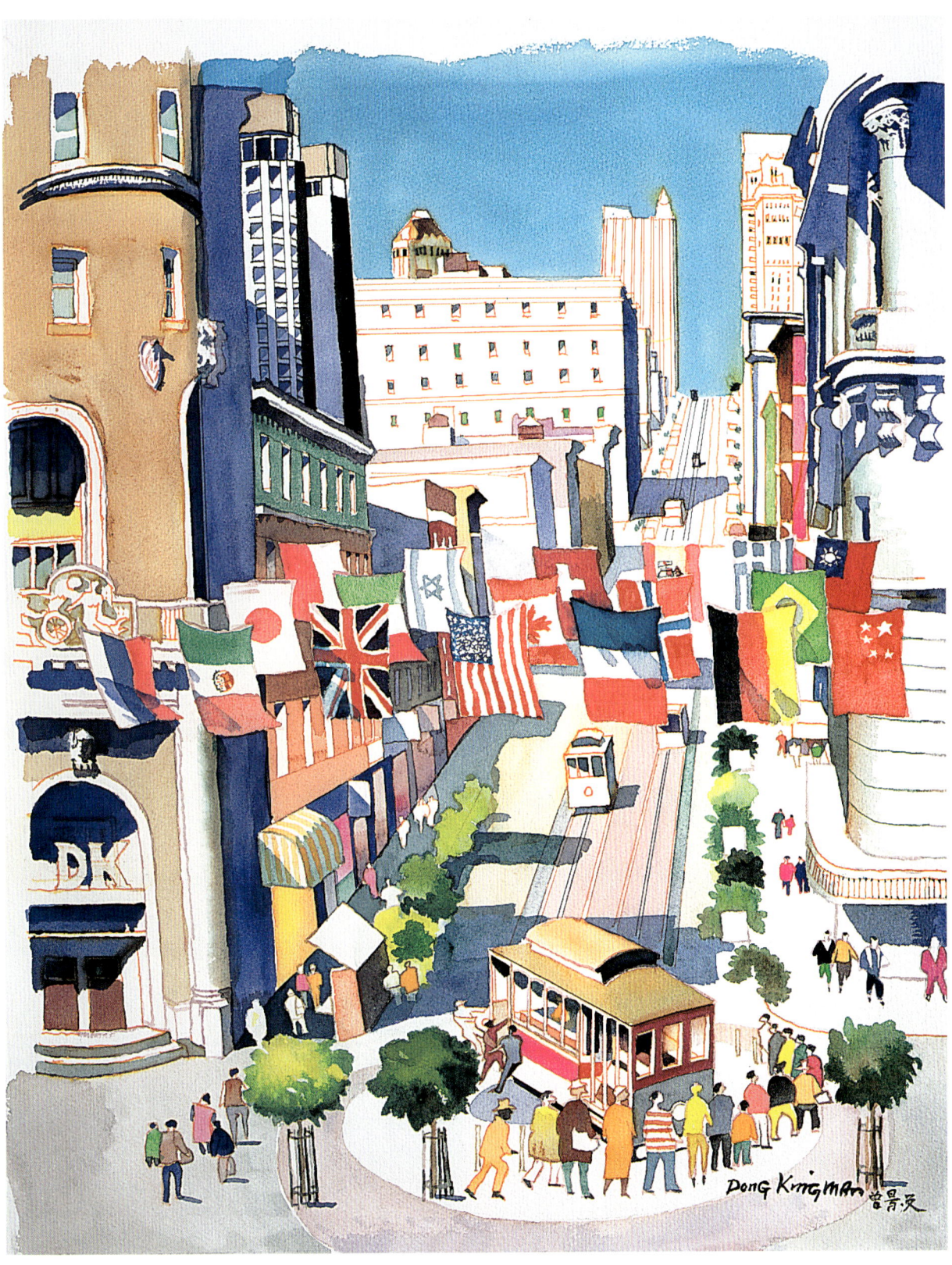

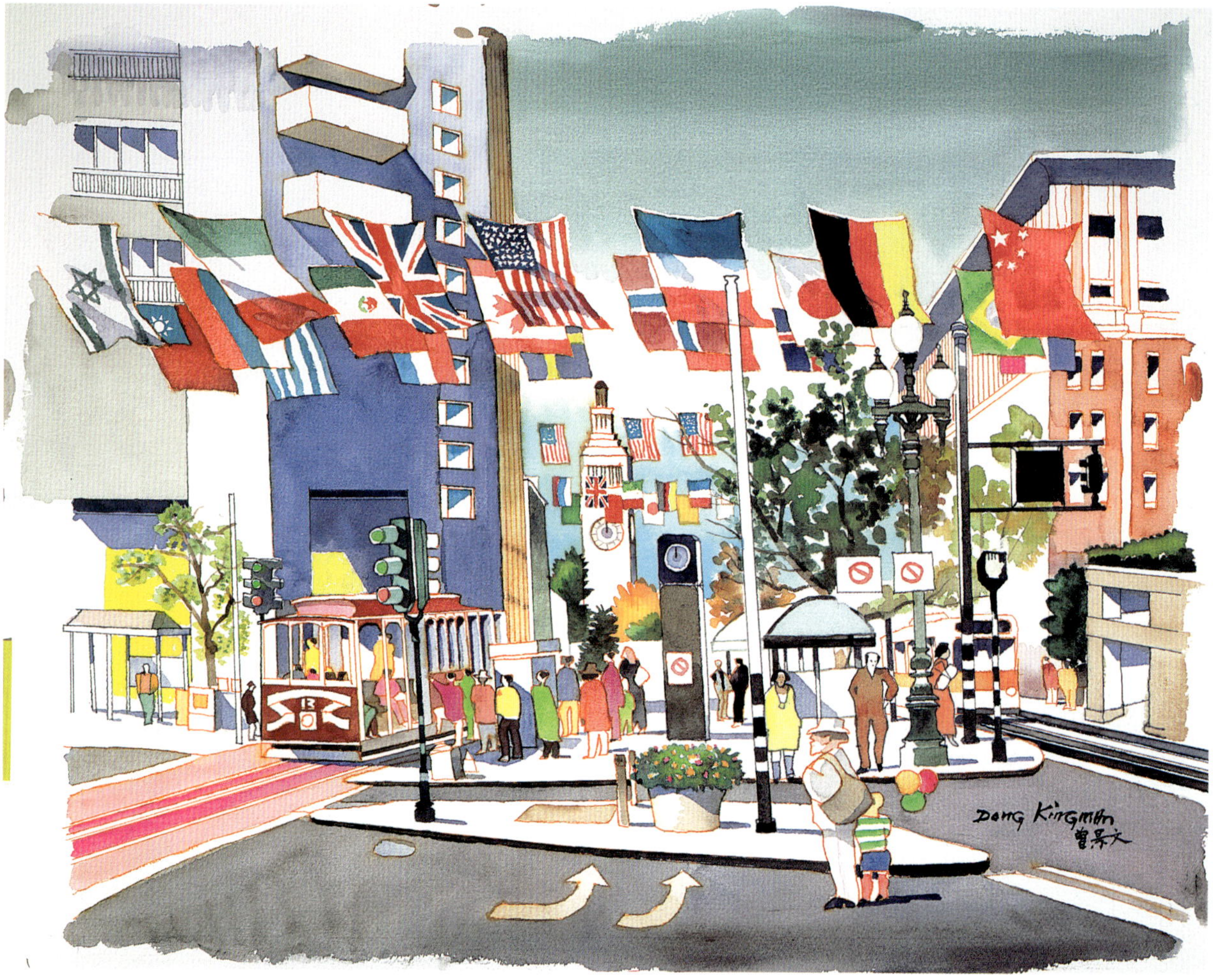

Cable Cars

Ferry Building

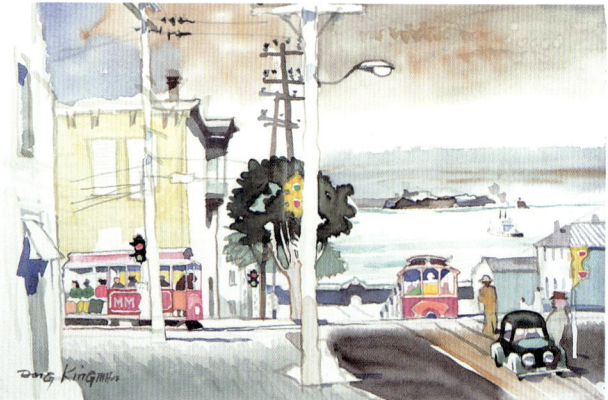

Two Cable Cars

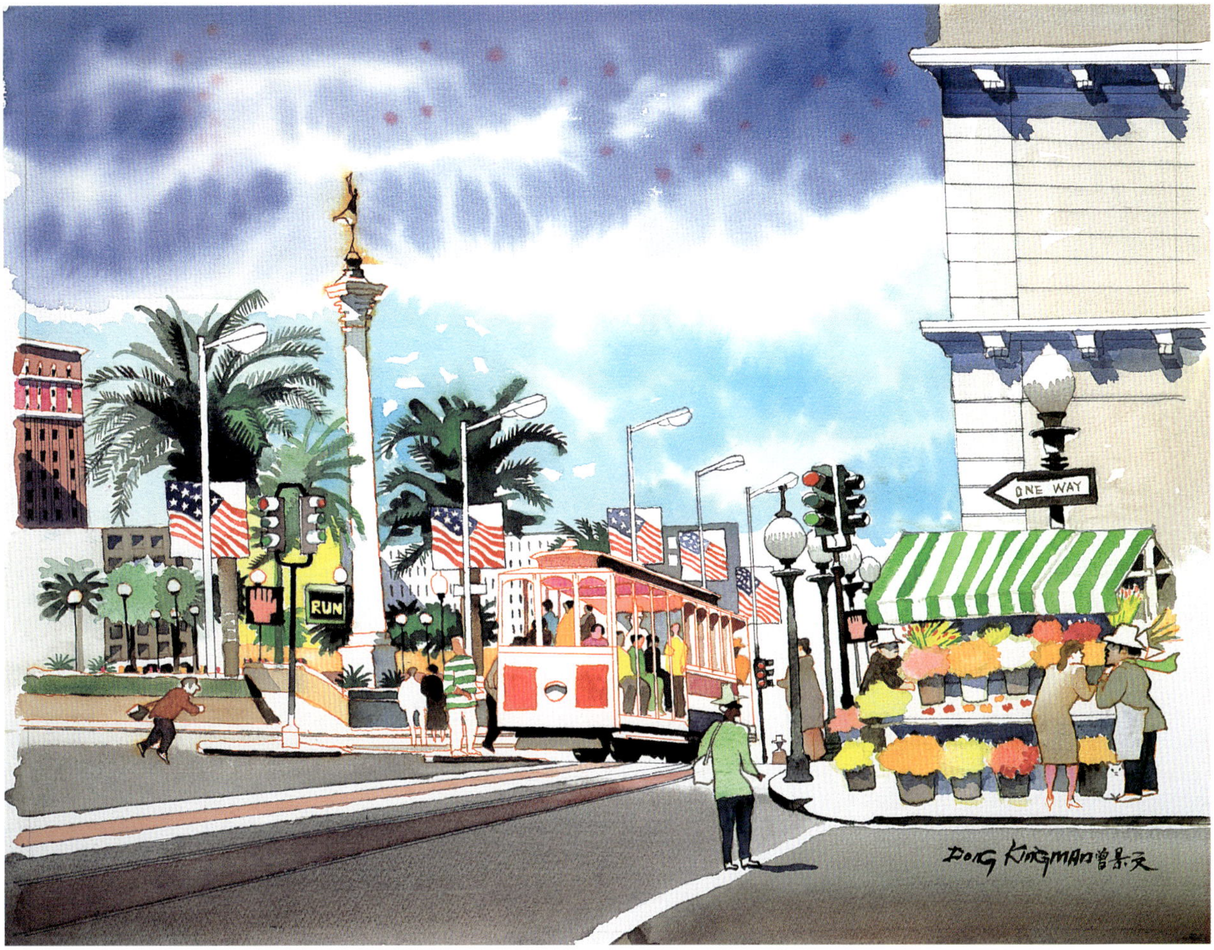

Union Square

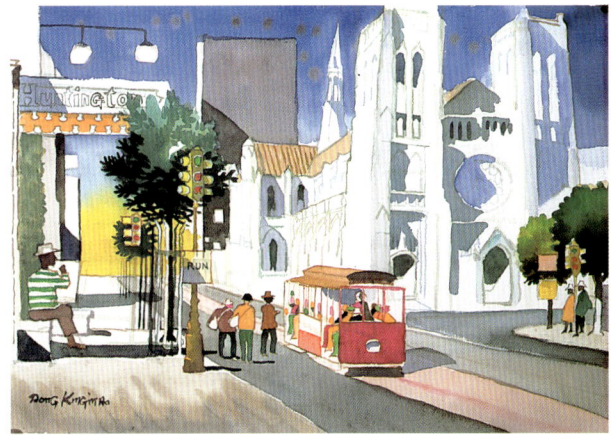
Gray Church

71

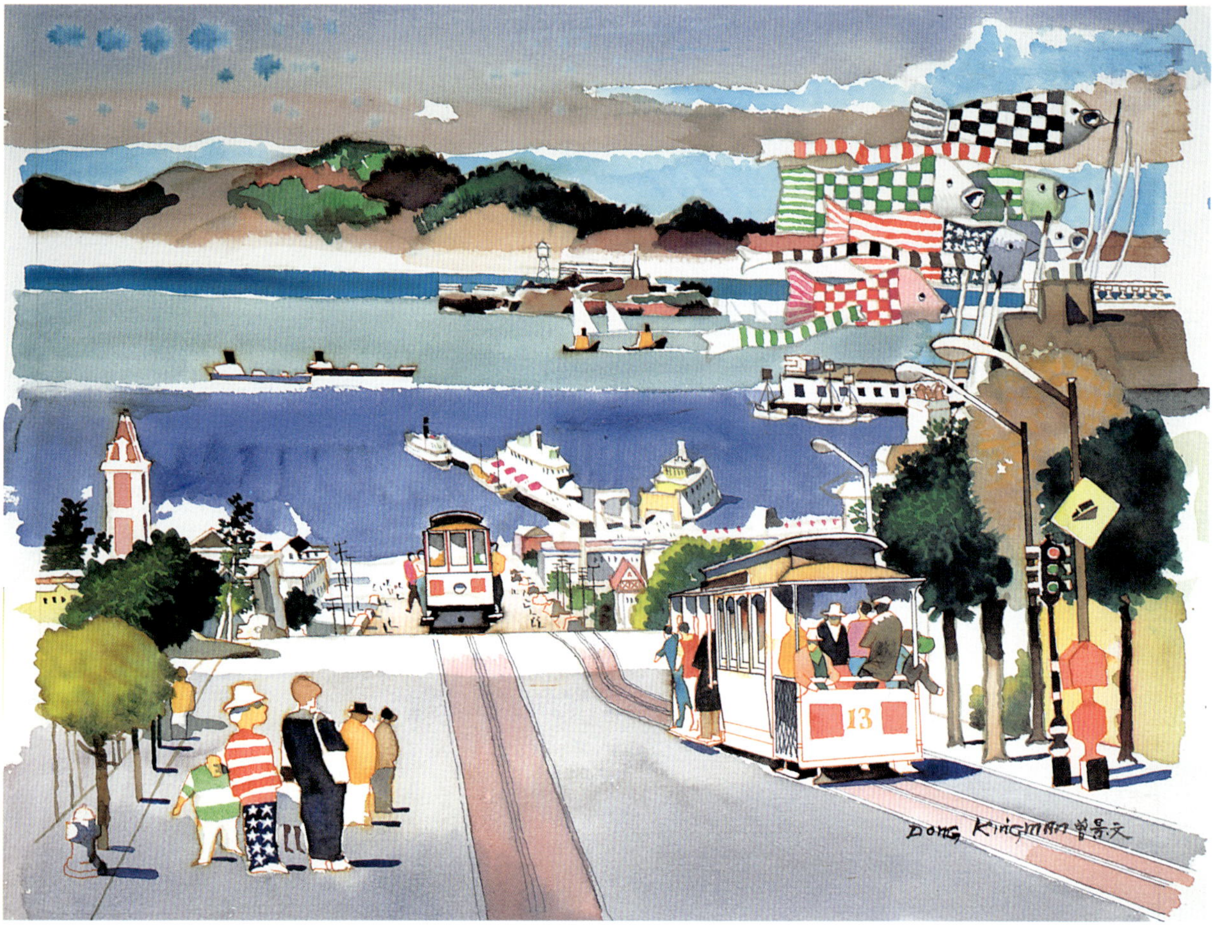

CABLE CARS

Up Hill Hyde Street, collection of Gerald Blum

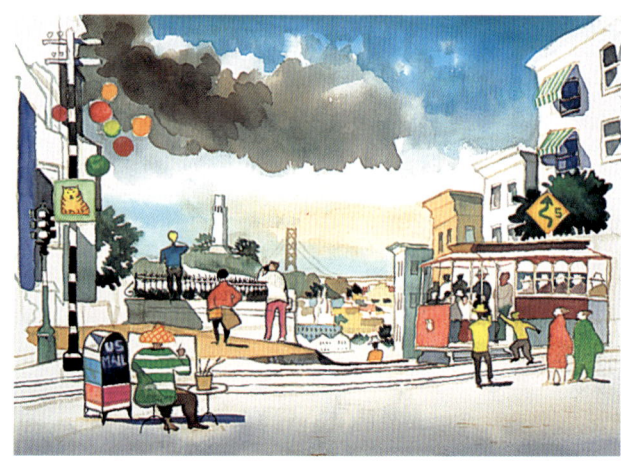

Telegraph Hill, collection of Ms. Tucky Ramsey

California Street

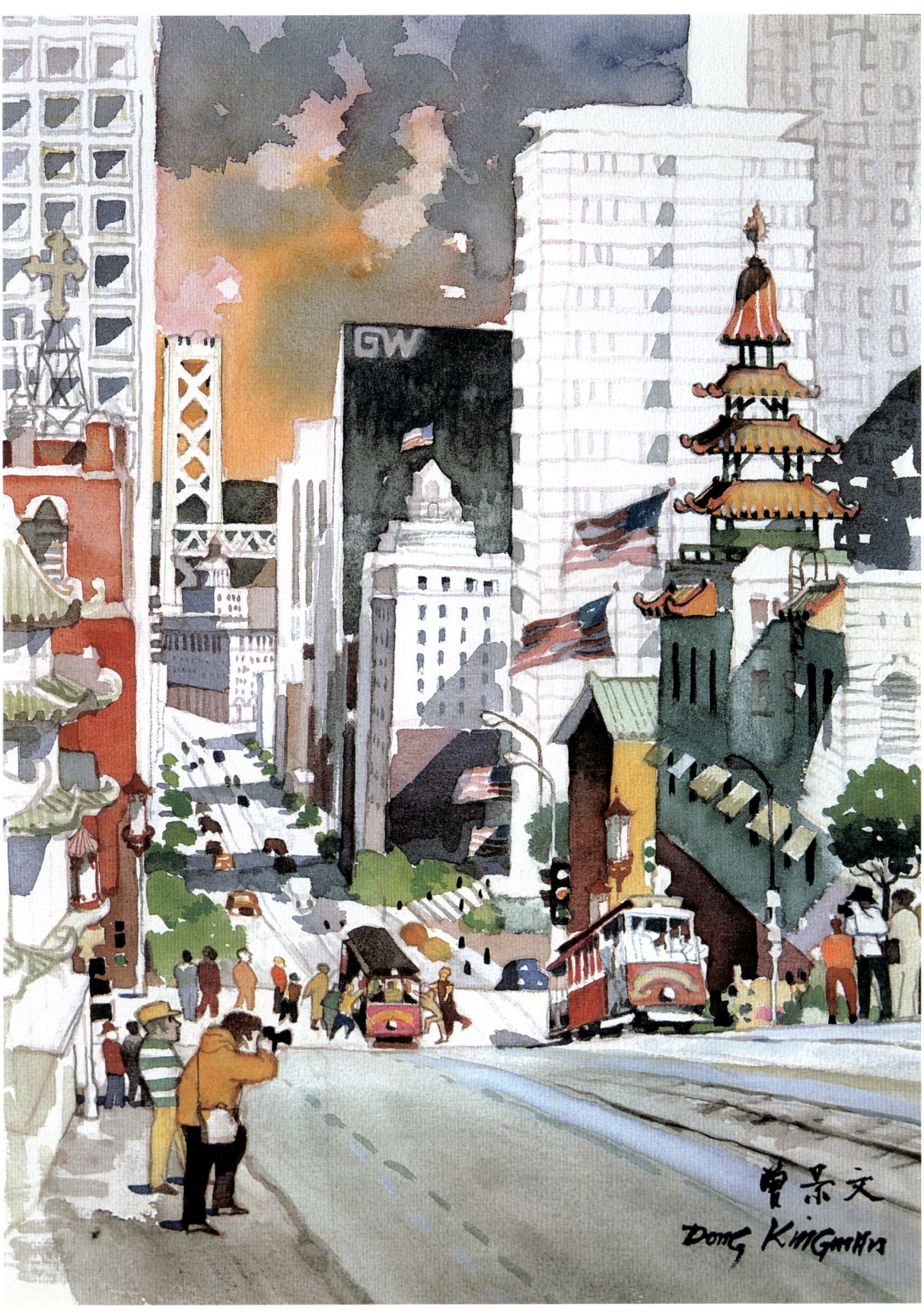

PORTRAITS OF CITIES

I am a painter of portraits, not of human faces, but of the human spirit which arises from the contours of citites and landscapes around the world.

It takes only one painting to do the portrait of a person. But it takes many drawings and sketches in a painting to do the portrait of a city, specially when you come to do portraits of cities like San Francisco, Hong Kong, New York City, and the like, so many beautiful and yet so complicated.

My interest in painting portraits of cities started in 1954, when the U.S. Department of State invited me to do a lecture /exhibition goodwill tour around the world, with special emphasis in the Far East and East Asia including Korea, Japan, Taiwan, HongKong, the Philipines, Singapore, Thailand, and Malaysia. For the next 40 years, because of my continuous assignments for the former Pan-American World Airways, IBM, and other commercial concerns, giving exhibition and lecture tours, being on the Judge Panel for Miss Universe almost 20 years, and conducting classes for the annual travelling Hewitt Painting Workshops, I have been to some of the world's most famous and interesting out of the way places like London, Paris, Rome, Iceland, the Scandinavian countries, Russia, Hungary, Poland, Czechoslovakia, from the Swiss Alps to the Swiss Lakes on the Italian border, North, Central, and South Americas, and to exotic places like Pago Pago, Fiji, Tahiti, Bali, Guilin, Penang and Kuala Lumpur, to mention just a few.

If you happen to see a painting of mine with elephants and lions with Mount Kilimanjaro of Africa in the background, I was there. If you see a picture of the luxury Palace Hotel in St. Moritz in the rain in Switzerland, I was there too getting soaking wet painting the scene.

And of course, the Golden Gate Bridge in my hometown San Francisco, Mount Rushmore with huge heads of our Presidents known as the Shrine of Democracy, I was there too, and many other cities in the United States.

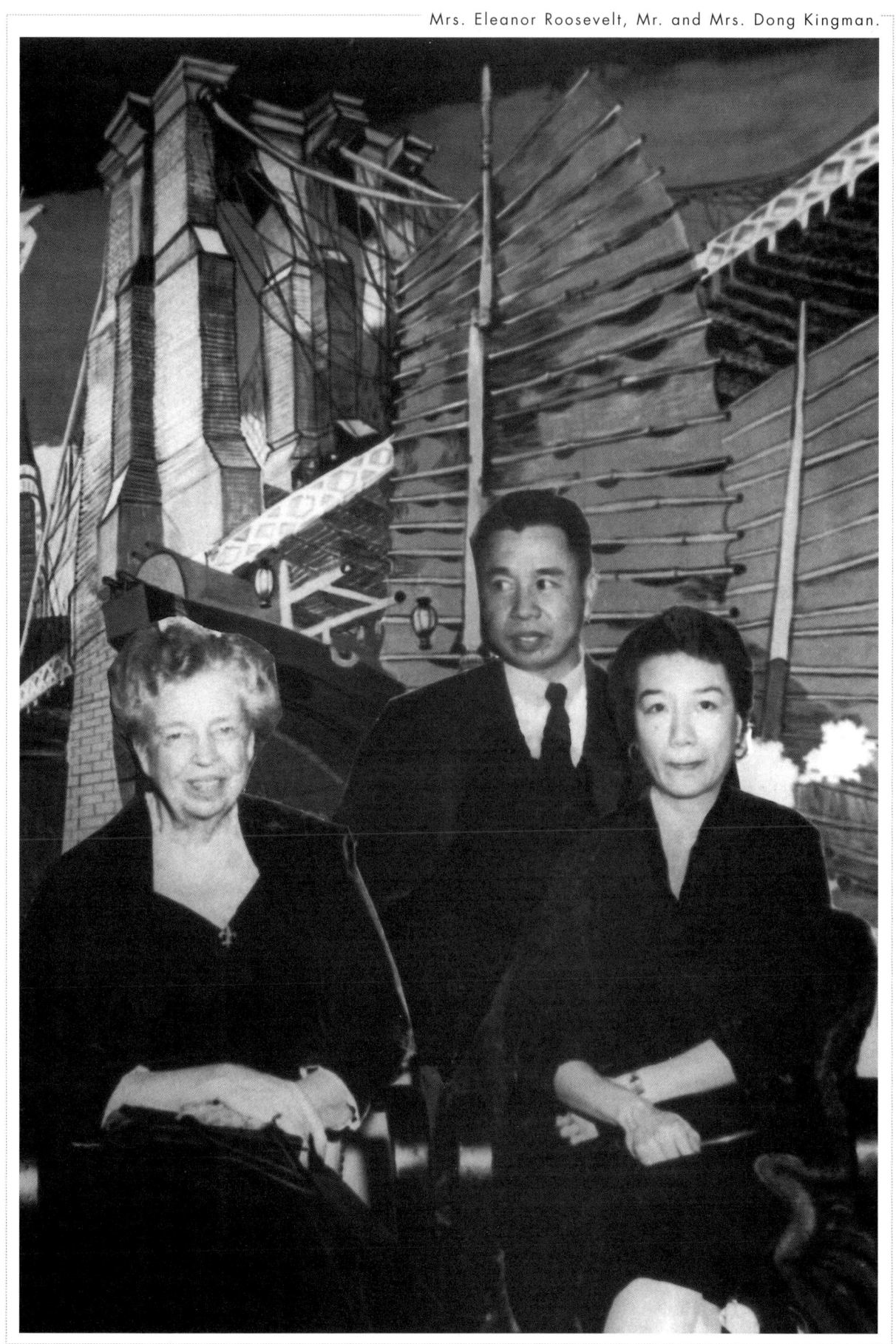

Mrs. Eleanor Roosevelt, Mr. and Mrs. Dong Kingman.

Life Magazine

14th May, 1951

Dong Kingman's U.S.A.

Artist gives American scenes a lively oriental flavour

To Artist Dong Kingman the world of Chinese junks is as familiar as that of Brooklyn Bridge, and both worlds come together in cheerful tumult in his paintings. Although he was born midway between East and West, in the Chinese section of Oakland, Calif., Kingman was introduced to the land of his ancestors at the age of 5, when his Chinese-American father closed up his dry-goods store and took his family back to Hong Kong.

There Kingman practiced drawing with chalk on the sidewalks until he was old enough to attend school, where he learned to handle a brush in an adept Oriental fashion. But at the age of 18 he sailed back to San Francisco and, in between jobs as factory worker, cook and houseboy, began to turn out his lively impressions of America: Trolley cars, signposts, pigeons and skyscrapers tumbled into his paintings in bright profusion, and humdrum city streets were transformed into colorful scenes as festive as firecracker celebrations on Chinese New Year's. In 1946 he moved to New York where, along with teaching five art classes a week, he puts in a 15-hour day at his work. Today, at 40, Dong Kingman is one of the country's foremost watercolorists. Already represented in more than a dozen major museum collections, this month he is being honored with a large retrospective exhibition of his paintings in New York's Midtown Gallery.

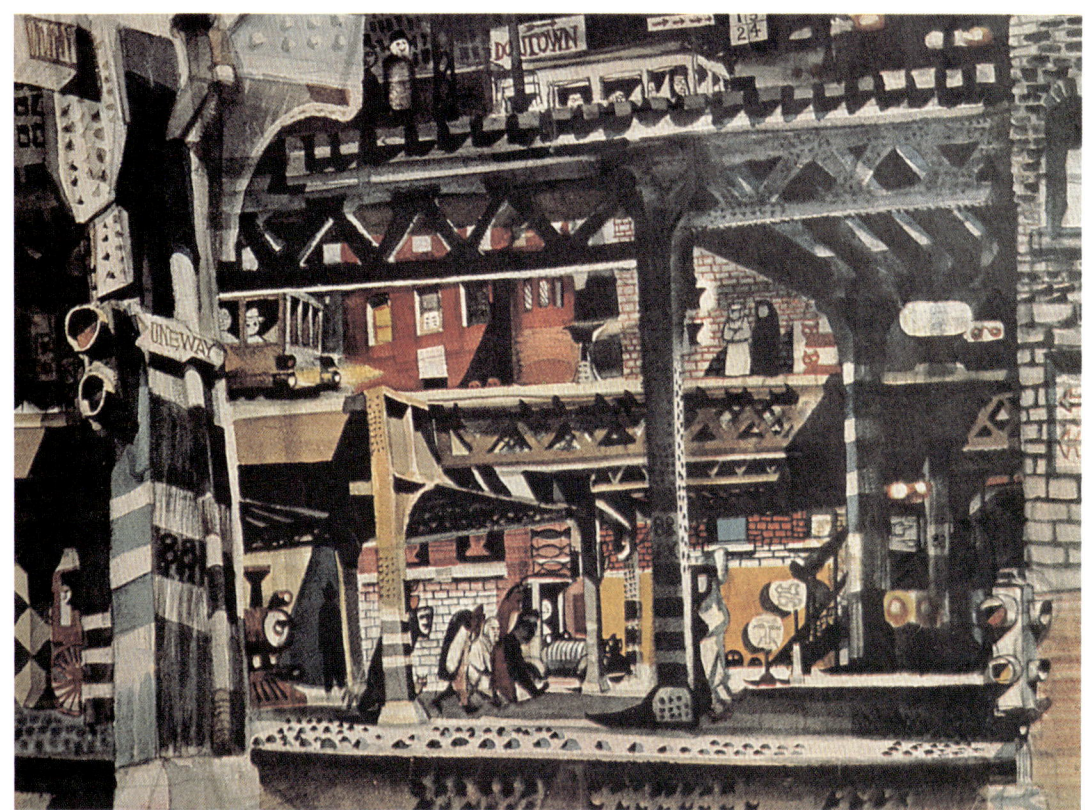

Trestles and Traffic angle through New York's Chinatown, which Kingman often paints. He added locomotive because it is his favourite shape

Blue Moon, Boston Museum of Fine Arts collection

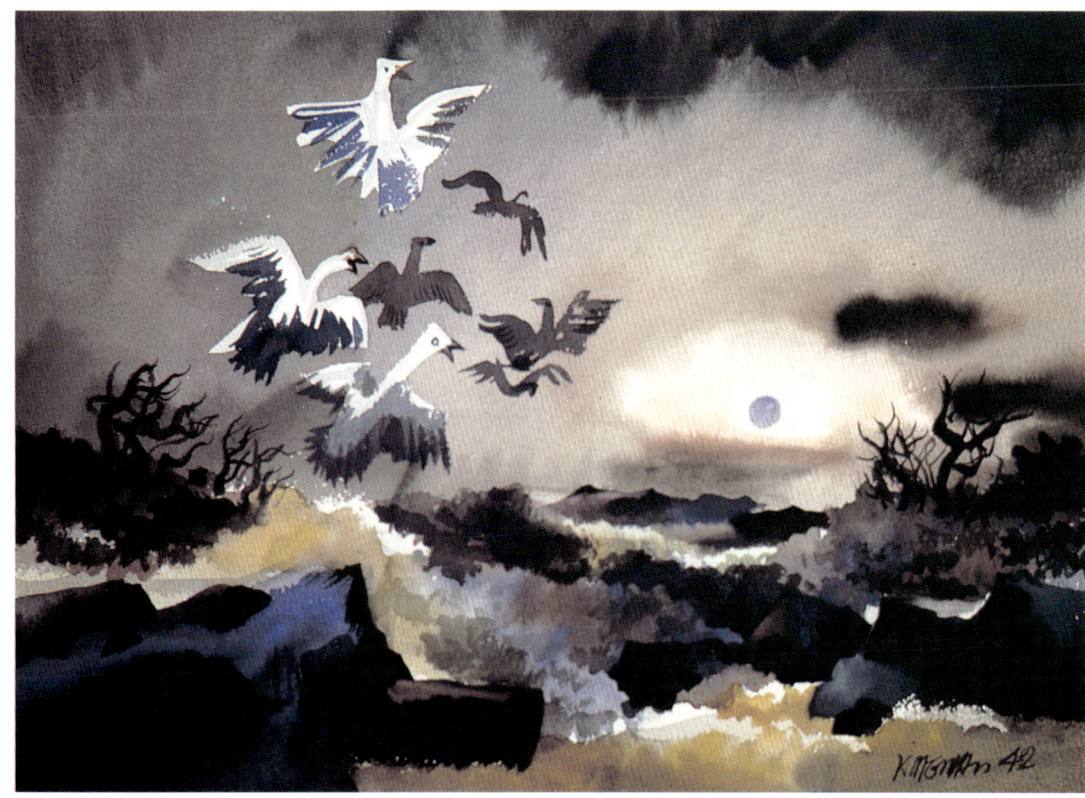

Turrets and widow walk on a Victorian mansion caught Kingman's eye when he was vacationing in Provincetown, Mass. The house had been turned into a staid museum, but Kingman livened up scene by putting optician's charts in the windows and railroad tracks and wires out in front.

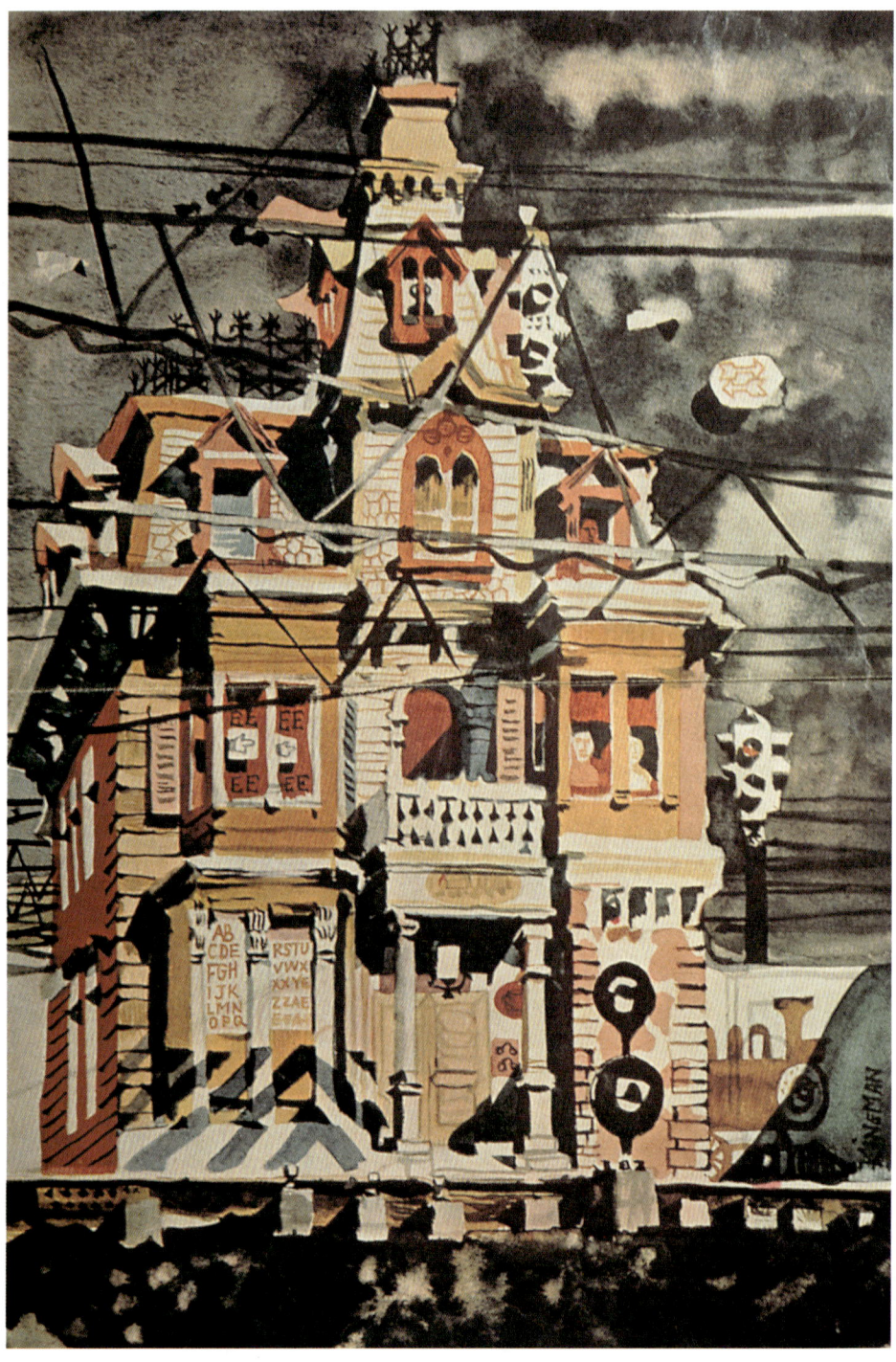

Life Magazine February 14, 1955

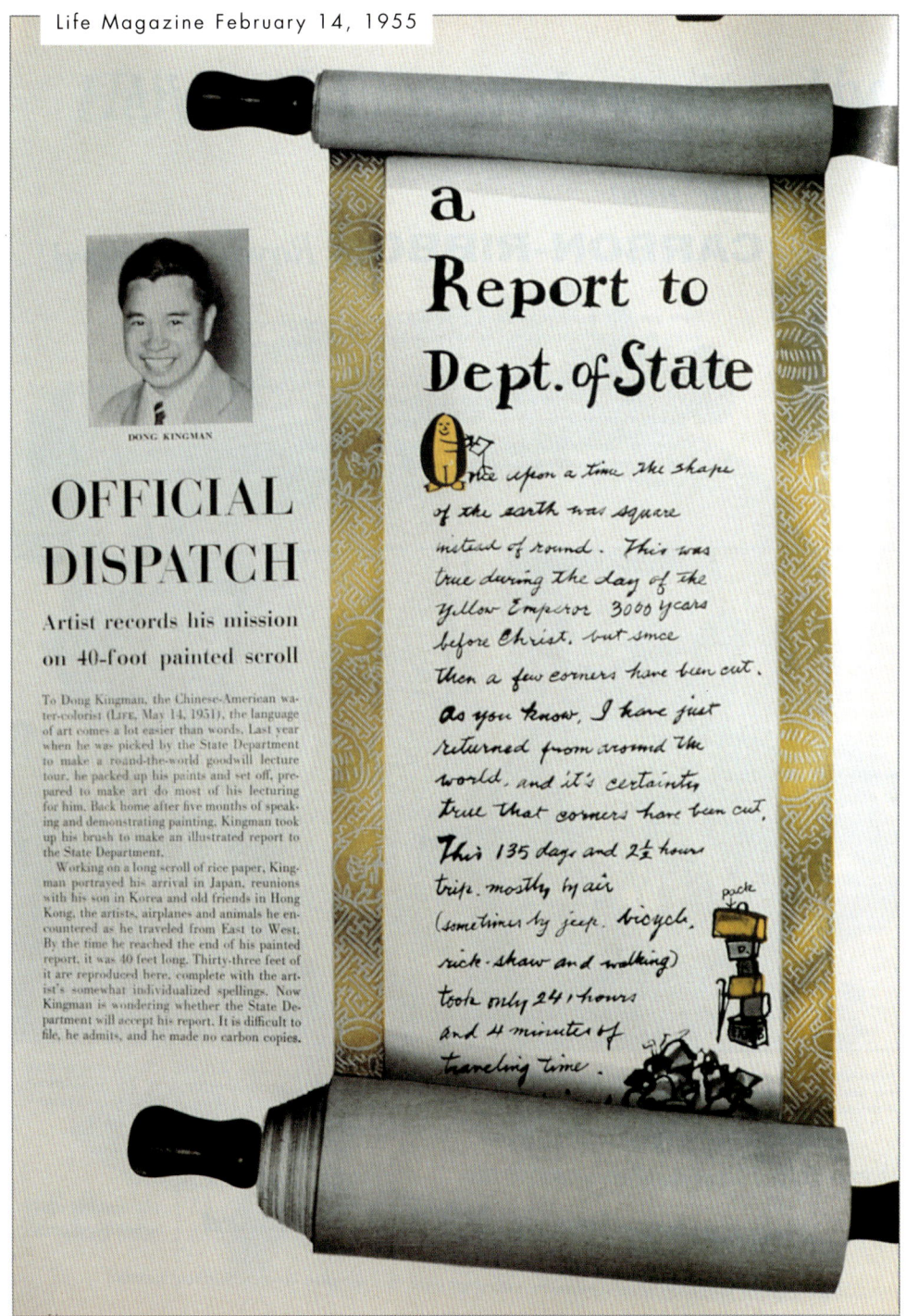

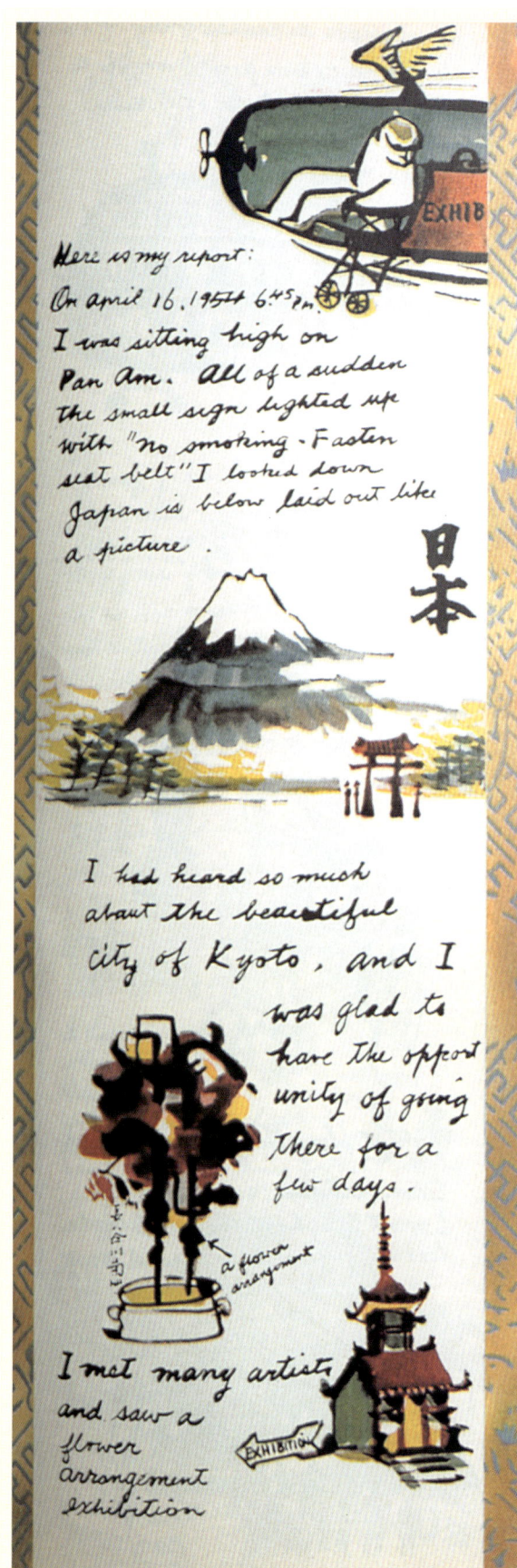
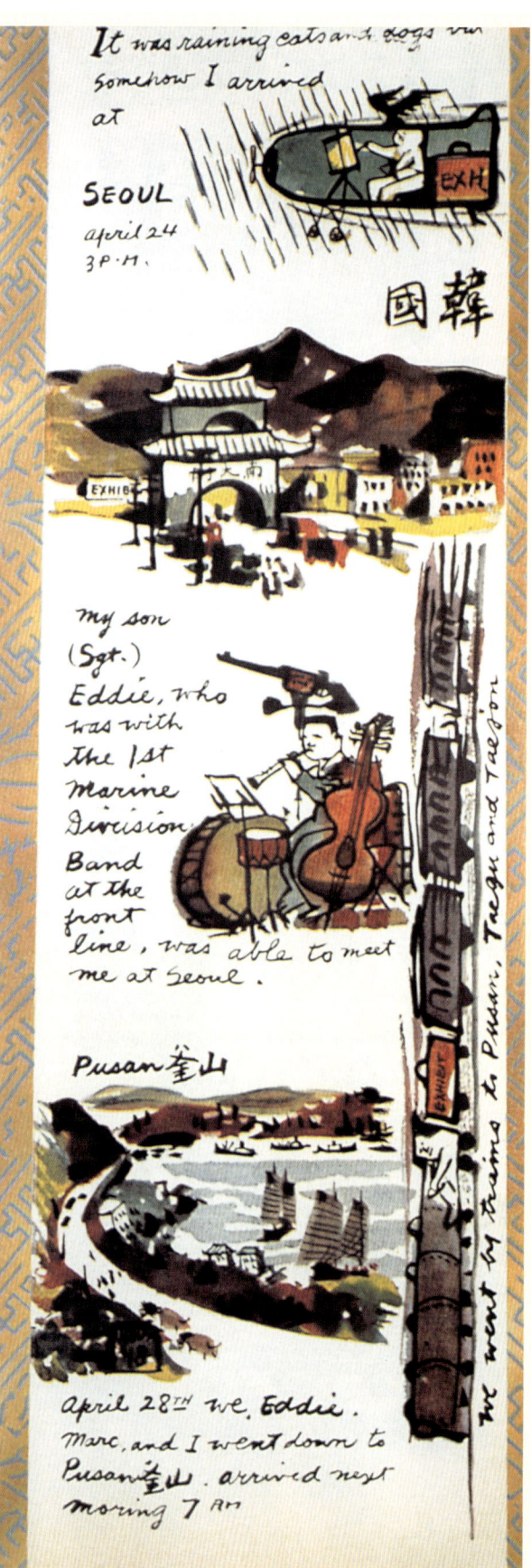

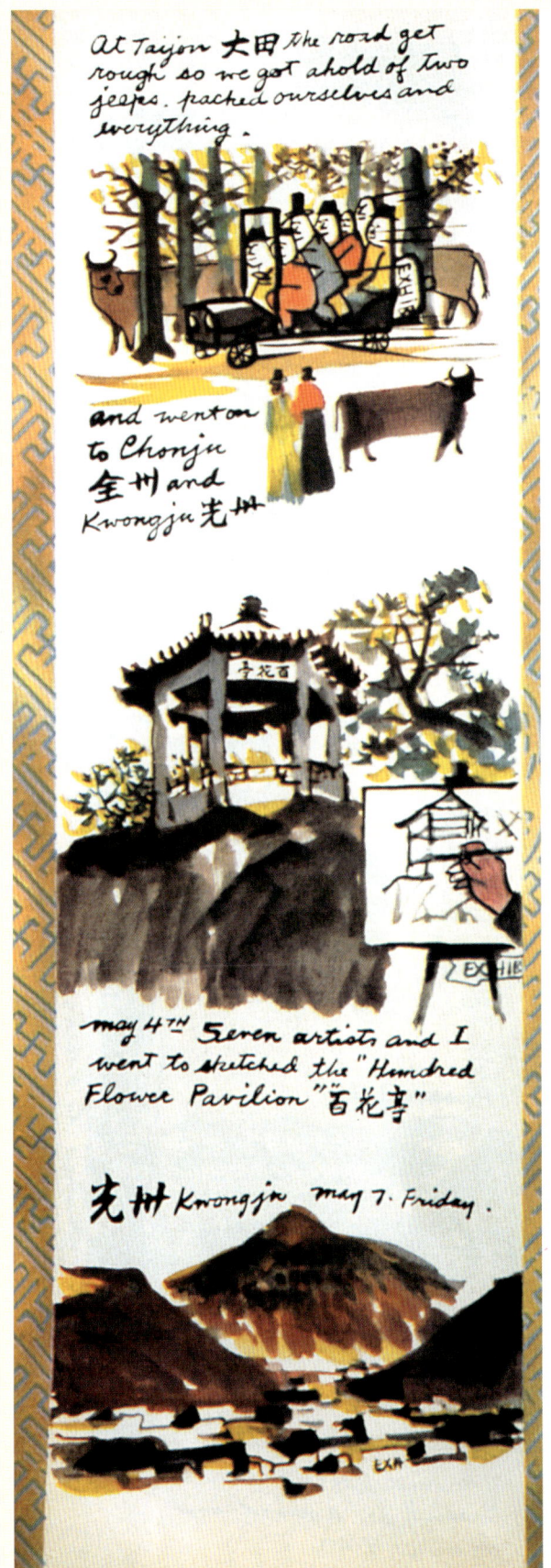
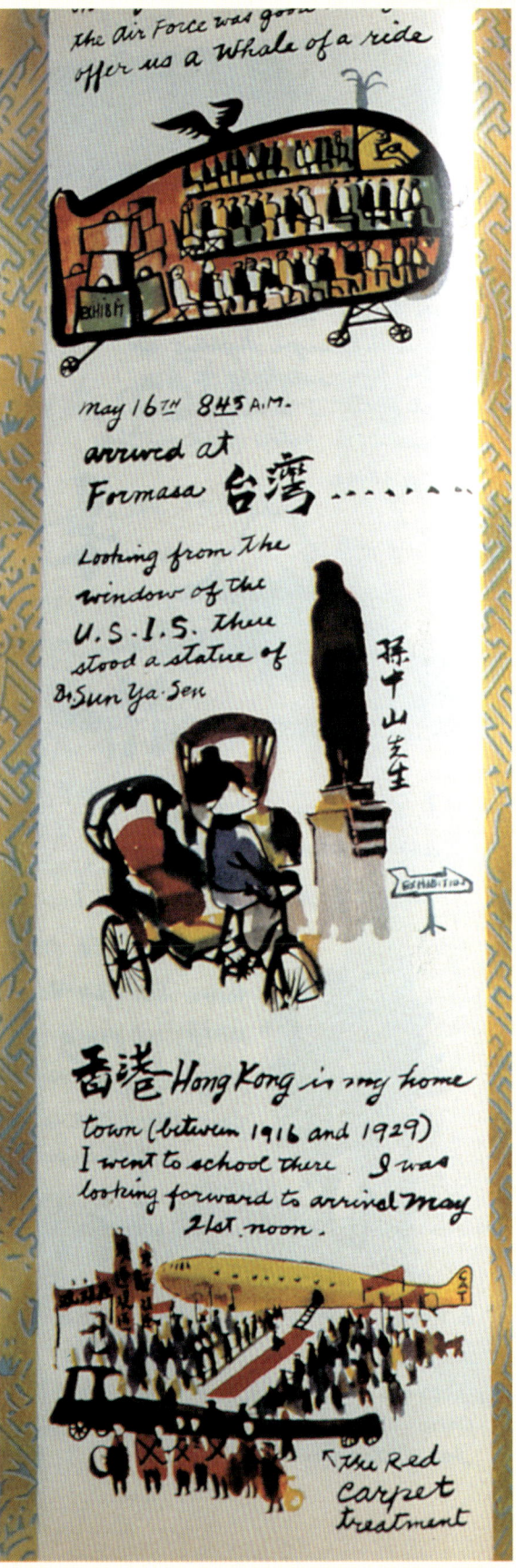

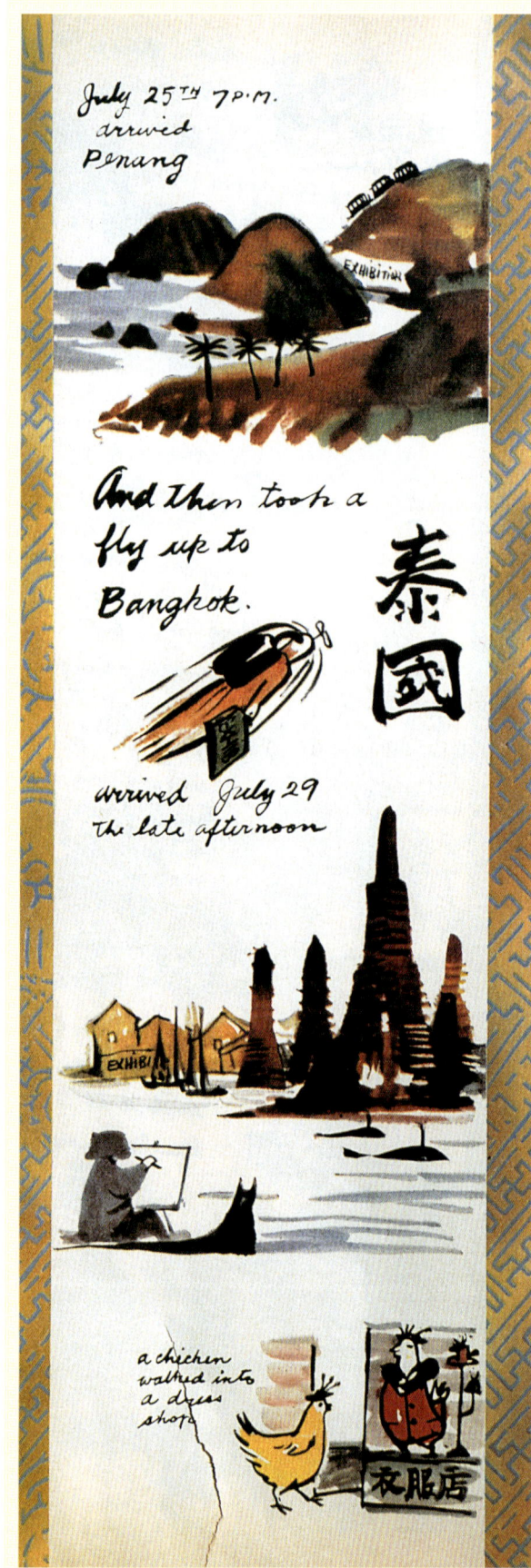
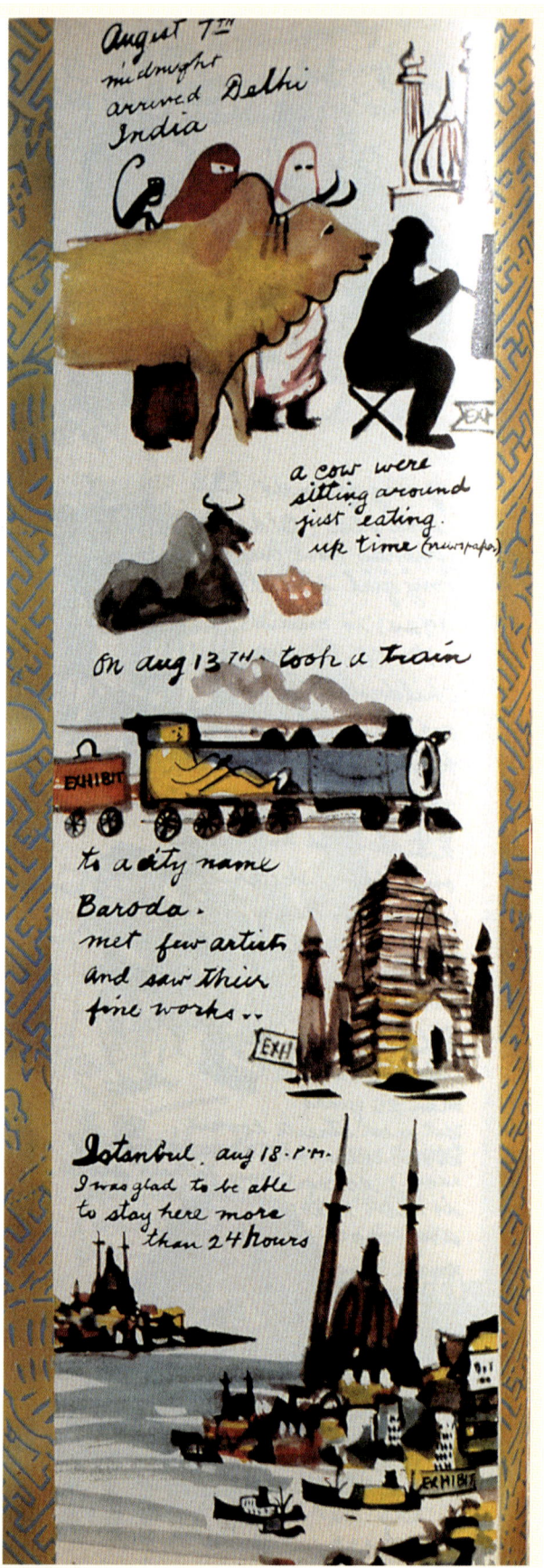

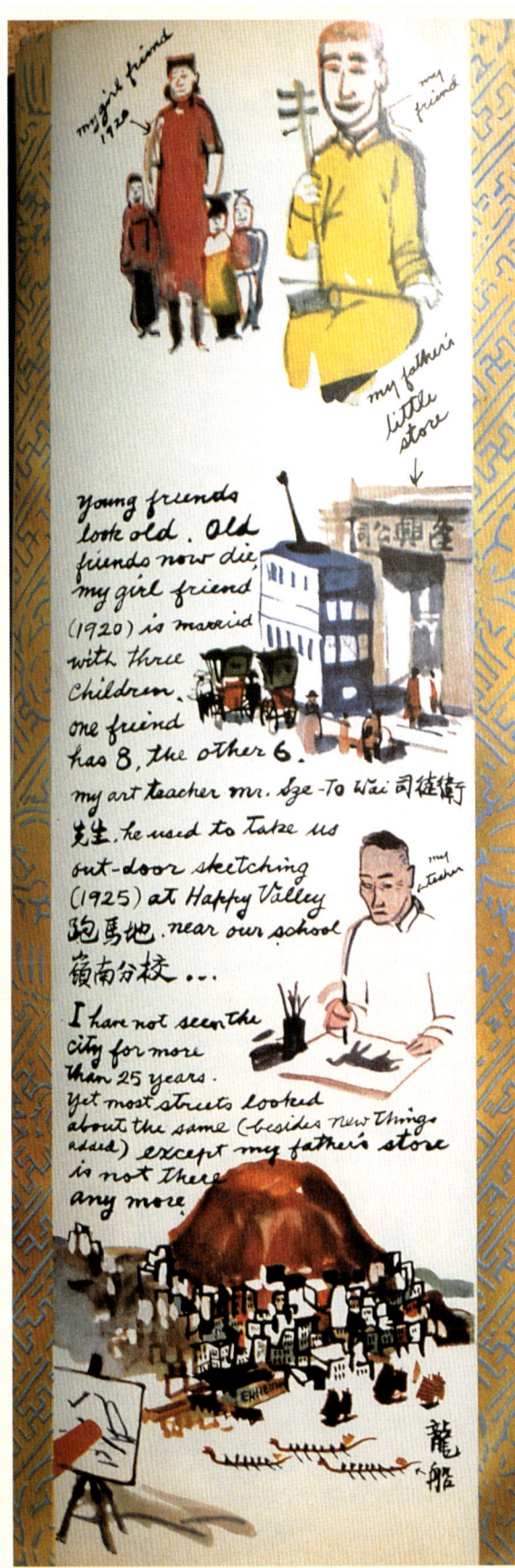
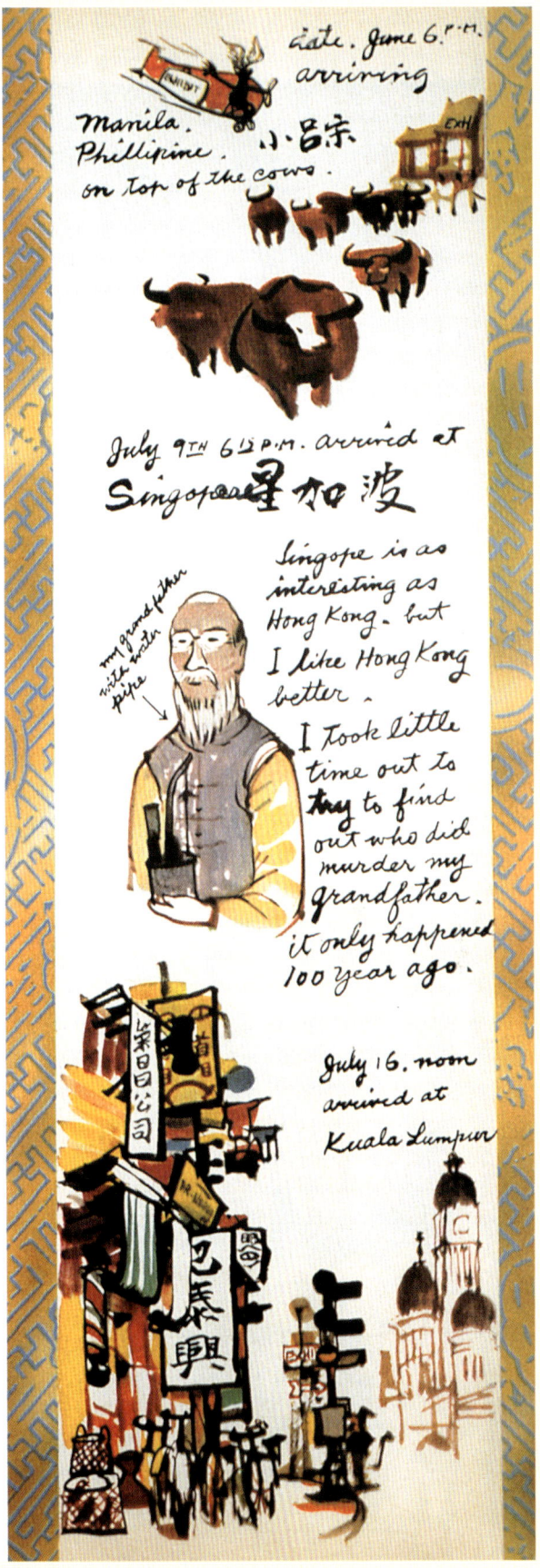

The Eye & Hand of Dong Kingman

by William Saroyan

He looks at New York as no one else does—as no other painter, writer, composer, photographer looks at it, and of course New York is the world. That's where he is. That's where his looking at the world is steadiest. That's where he goes to sleep, and where he wakes up.

He really looks at the place, and he really sees it. Everybody whose business it is to look and see looks at New York and sees something different, perhaps new, perhaps important, perhaps special.

But I don't know anybody who sees what Dong Kingman sees, and I'll try to talk about it in just a moment. I've got to be very careful about it because in a thing like this it's easy to go off.

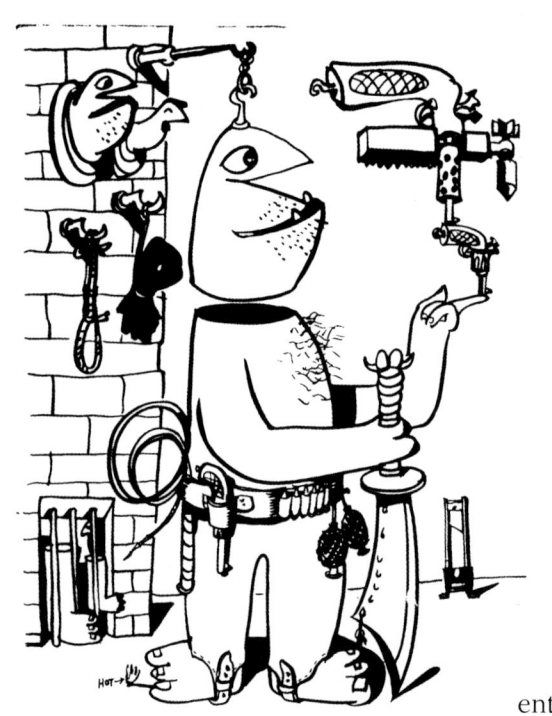

This is it, I think: he sees the world this instant, and in his glance, in the instantaneous and miraculous reality of matter and color, of living vision, of memory captured in the painter's great skill, he sees the world gone—forever. Not smitten to smithereens by silly explosives, not worn away by time and wind and decay, but gone forever in the very instant of its immediate reality—mixed, colorful, plain, heavy, but lighter than a man's soul, right there now and gone forever.

This quality in his city paintings is deeply moving, both delightful and sorrowing. We are not looking at a human face—eyes, nose, mouth. We are looking at the configuration and color—the mass of a place, a part of a city, a part of the world, that's all. Nothing of the human being himself is in the frame, and yet the picture in its entirety evokes The Human—gladly, and simultaneously with a stab of loneliness, longing, love, loss—irreparable loss—ache. The locomotive—what part of the soul, the heart, the hope, the memory of The Human is the locomotive? No one can answer that with accuracy, but the locomotive just naturally is some part of man. It is not a locomotive as a locomotive is a locomotive on a railroad, in the heart of a city, on the waterfront, or out in the plains. And this has nothing at all to do with such literal relationships as lights being the equivalent of eyes, or anything like that. That sort of thing is trickery, and nonsense. Nothing in Dong Kingman's painting looks like something else, something it isn't. It looks like what it is. It's the way he paints that makes the thing painted—a traffic-signal arm, for instance—evoke a spiritual condition out of common experience.

You see, I have both got to guard against inaccuracy, and at the same time try to say as clearly as may be what Kingman does and has in his paintings.

Now, it has always been inevitable for the skilled painter of landscapes to achieve a quality of man's soul, in one or another of its dimensions, in the far-off turnings of streams upon the land, or the lonely grandeur of grasses and trees, human paths, roads, places, dwellings, and so on. The skilled landscaper of nature evokes in his paintings as a rule a lyric, or almost religious, quietude—nature's own far-off aloofness, serenity, anonymity, universality, and perhaps even indifference. Good landscapes are always good to look at. They do the eye and the heart, and possibly the mind, a lot of good. I won't ever be willing to knock a "View of Toledo," for instance. The clouds, the castle, the road, the wind, and the Greek's great skill are forever irresistible.

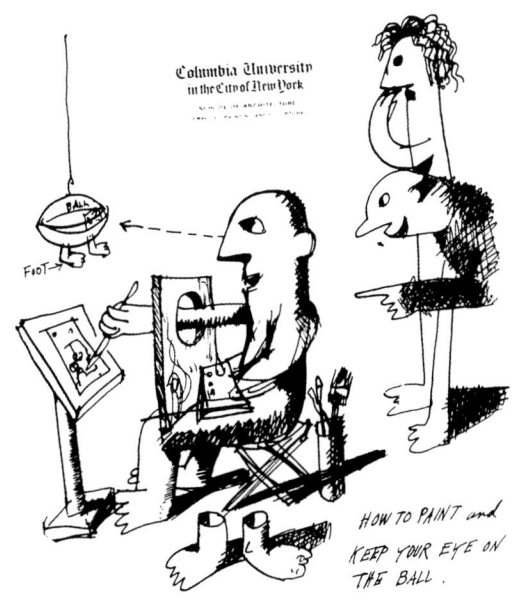

Well, here's Dong Kingman holding an eye on the jungle and clutter of a city—an eye that's both microscopic and far-seeing—here he is holding that eye on a small patch of a vast city, an infinitely var-

The Eye & Hand of Dong Kingman

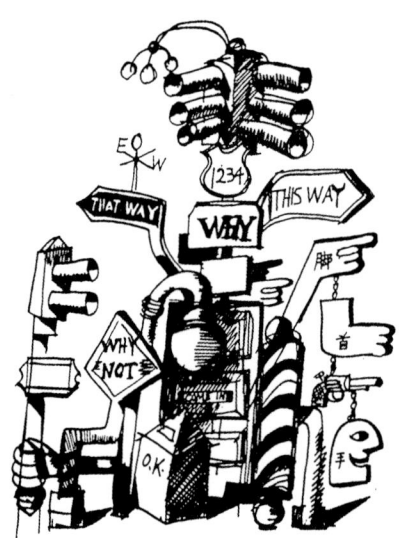

ied world, and by the miracle of his great skill, here he is making asphalt and steel, stone and glass, brick and board and iron and tin, streets and buildings, automobiles and trains, junk of all kinds—here he is making all of these things into an entity that is instantly real, forever gone, and somehow immortal, as if in his junk is man's monument, the image of his lost and indestructible soul. And this juxtaposition of rubbish and grandeur is just naturally beautiful. You look and you see, and you don't know why, but you're awfully glad about the whole business—man's proud futility, his brilliant failure, his heroic loneliness, his awareness of his end and his refusal to care about it. His refusal to stop in his tracks and let it all go. If he can't make a miracle, he can make locomotives. If he can't go to heaven, he can go to Hoboken.

He's an American, out of China, out of San Francisco. He's a wit. He tells some of the funniest stories anybody has ever told. His eyes twinkle with laughter and affection—for all things. All people. But never for an instant is he far from profound and steadfast earnestness. Perhaps even sorrow.

The foot of time, unpainted, without image, seems to be in each of his pictures. It is an enormous foot, vaster than the earth. It seems either to have just stepped upon everything, or about to do so. This foot of time seems to stamp the world as a side of beef is stamped by a government inspector, but there's no telling what the message is. Sometimes it seems to be the end, and then suddenly it's forever, and then now, and then the beginning, and back and forth and all together, so that the sum of the feeling evoked is a mixture of new, old, ended, started, gone, indestructible. Beautiful, and tragic. And yet nothing he paints may be considered beautiful in any conventional sense. It's something, an assortment of things, made by man, seen every day, unnoticed every day, ignored, forgotten, much too familiar to be truly beautiful. But Kingman makes these things terribly beautiful. How does he do it? I doubt if he can say, and I know I can't.

The better part of any real work of art is essentially unaccountable. Still, it would be absurd not to understand that he does it by skill, by technical skill, by the skill of a painter. That is to say, he does a good part of it by skill—by eye and hand, paint and brush. The rest—the mystery—belongs to art, to human experience, to Kingman, to me, and to all of us. We don't know how he does it, but he does it, and that's what we care about.

He makes his paintings in a studio, on paper with paints and brushes. That's a fact, but there is another fact that can't be measured, weighed, or identified—the fact of how. How does he really do it? All great art appears to come from all men through one man. In one man it comes in one way, in another it comes in another. In still another it comes entirely from paint and brush, and you always know it, however cleverly the images and colors are arranged. There is a lot of good technical painting. There isn't a lot of painting that is good both technically and as true art.

Anything at all that is looked at carefully is worth seeing. Looking carefully makes it—whatever it is—a thing of fresh reality. The careful looking is the thing that does it. The act of careful looking, the event of seeing, is in itself the creation of beauty, and possibly truth, or at any rate meaning. But to look and to see, and then to be able to achieve the miraculous, the unaccountable, that is the true thing, the rare thing, the deeply moving thing, and that's exactly what Dong Kingman does in his paintings.

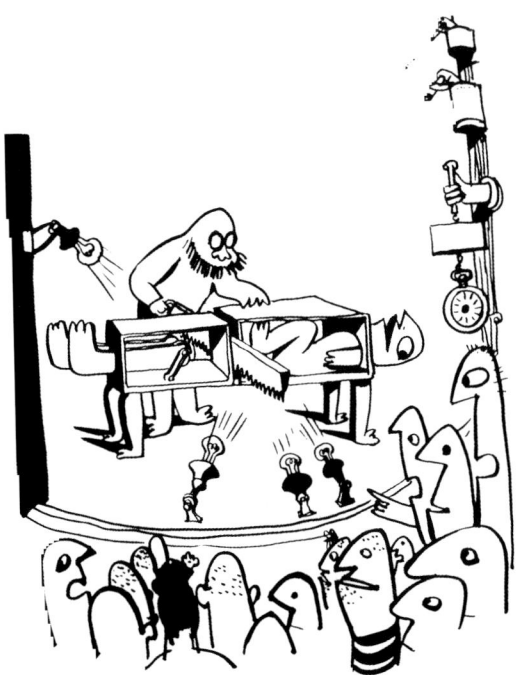

I believe I am a wiser man for having looked at a few of his paintings. I'm sure I'm a better writer for it, for the achievements of one art impel fresh achievements in another. This is my warm thanks to Dong Kingman.

Reprinted from Dong Kingman and How the Artist Works

My Art In Films

By Dong Kingman

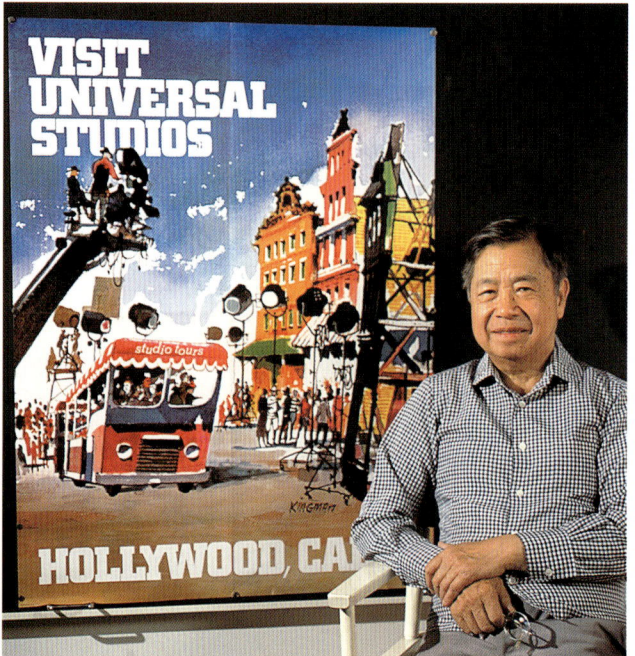

Something amazing happened to me as a child in Hong Kong when my art teacher and mentor Mr. Ssetu Wei took the whole class to see a movie. It set forth the direction of destiny for the rest of my life.

The movie was *The Thief of Bagdad* starring Douglas Fairbanks. The story was so fantastically incredible, yet so vividly appearing before my eyes that the swashbuckling adventures of the undaunted hero stirred at the very core of my admiration and inspiration lasting till this day.

I had always wanted to be an artist since I was five. But now, after seeing this movie, I was more determined than ever to work myself into one of the seven arts in the movies when I grew up.

I established myself as a fine artist after I returned to the United States.

My first chance came in the 1960s when Paramount Pictures invited me to make promotional sketches for the film The World of Suzie Wong starring William Holden and Nancy Kwan in Hong Kong. Next came my assignment

My Art In Films

for main title background paintings for Universal's *Flower Drum Song* in Hollywood, and for Paramount Pictures' *55 Days in Peking* starring Charlton Heston in Madrid.

In the 1970s, Columbia Pictures sent me to cover the film *The Virgin Soldier* starring Tom Courtney and Lynn Redgrave in Singapore, and again for Paramount Pictures' *Desperados* starring Jack Palance in Madrid, and *King Rat* by James Clavell in Hollywood. I also worked for the movie *Circus World* starring John Wayne in Barcelona, and the musical version of The *Lost Horizon* in Hollywood, etc

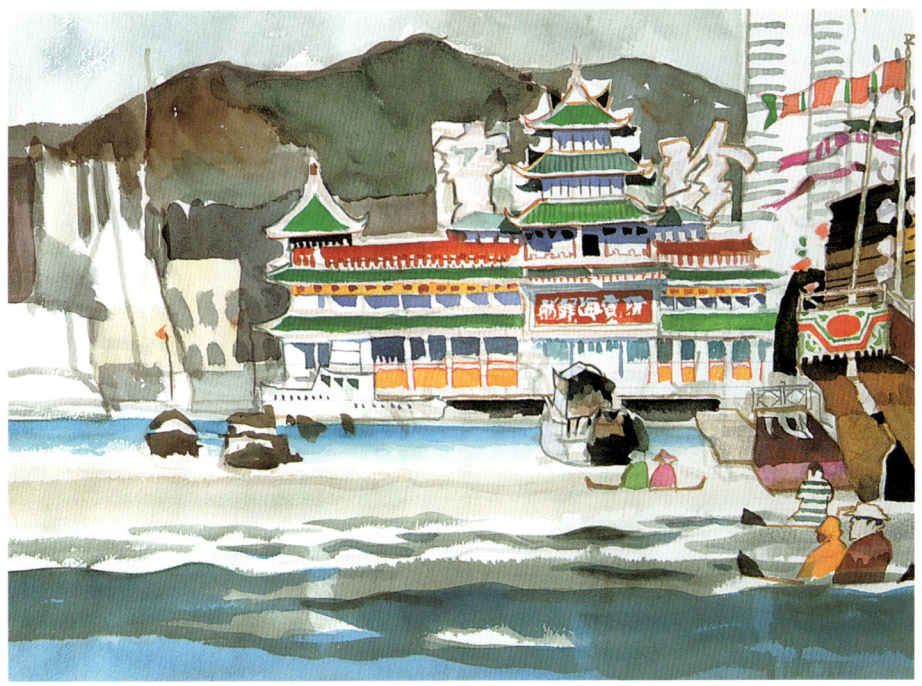

FILMING IN HONGKONG

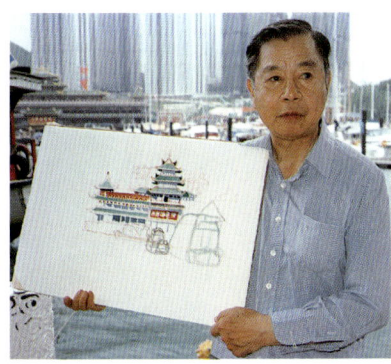
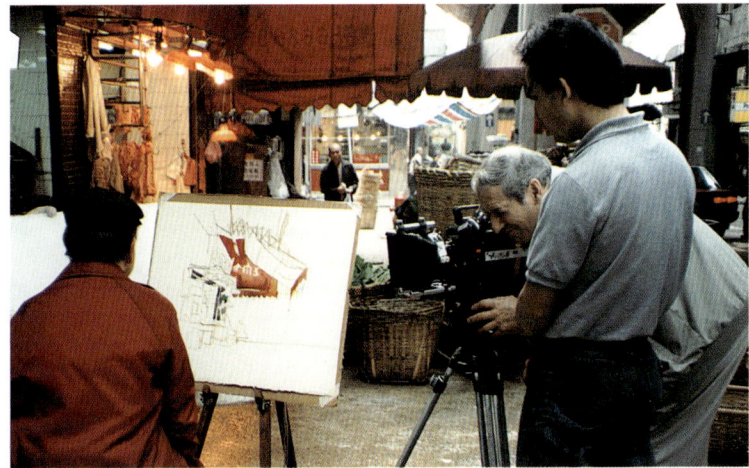

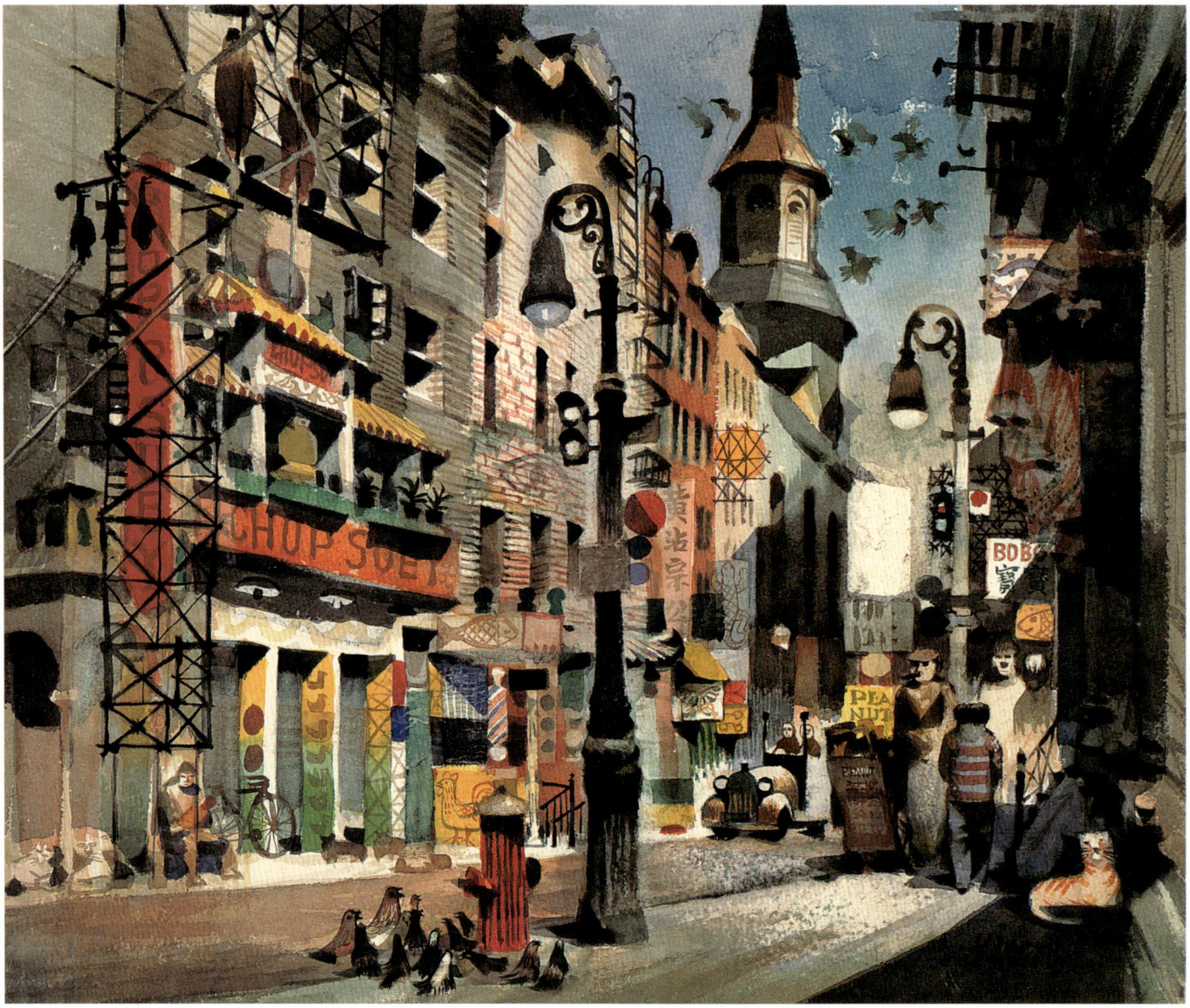

Mott Street, 1953, collection of Mr. Philip H. Greene

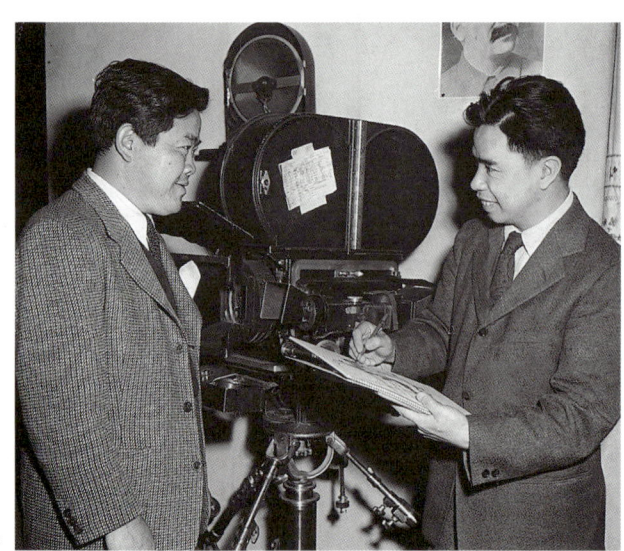

James Wong Howe

My Art In Films

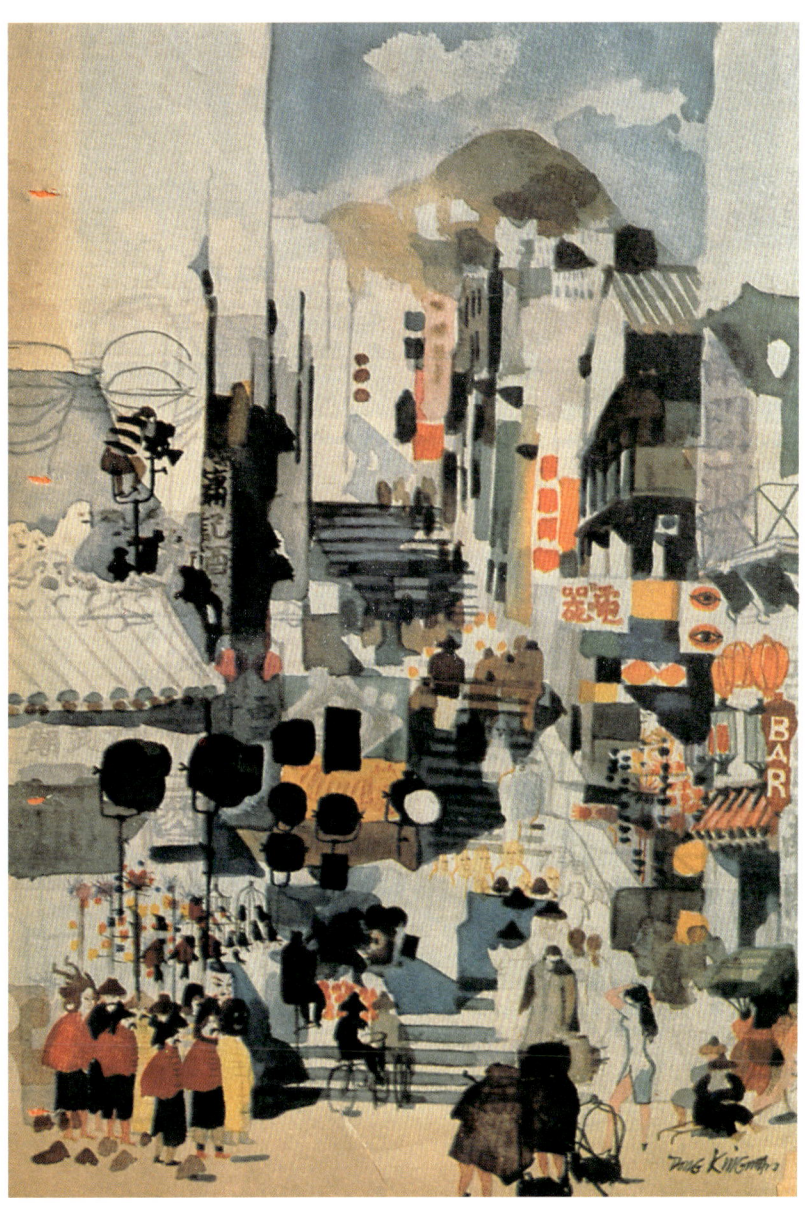

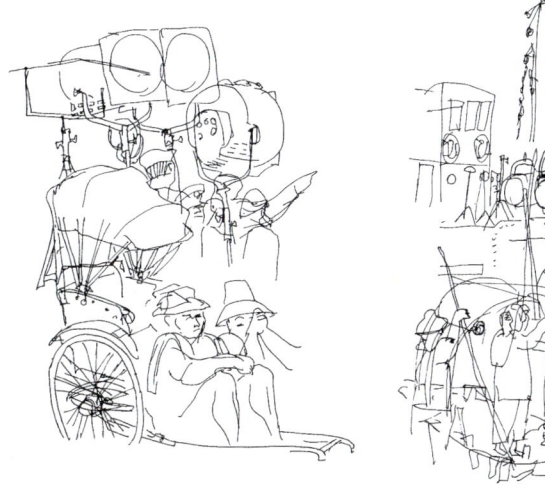

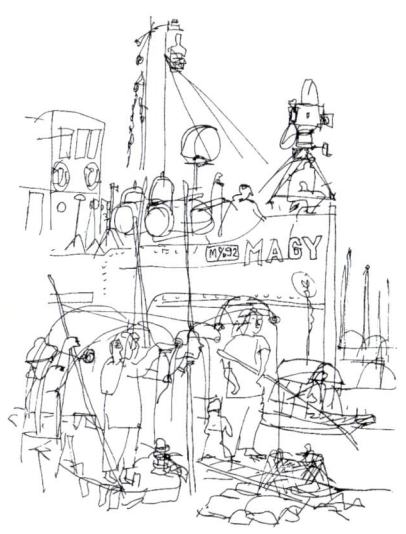

WORLD OF SUZIE WONG
This picture was created specially for the movie from Paramount Moving Picture Co. Studying where is S. Wong's place is with stairway going up hill.

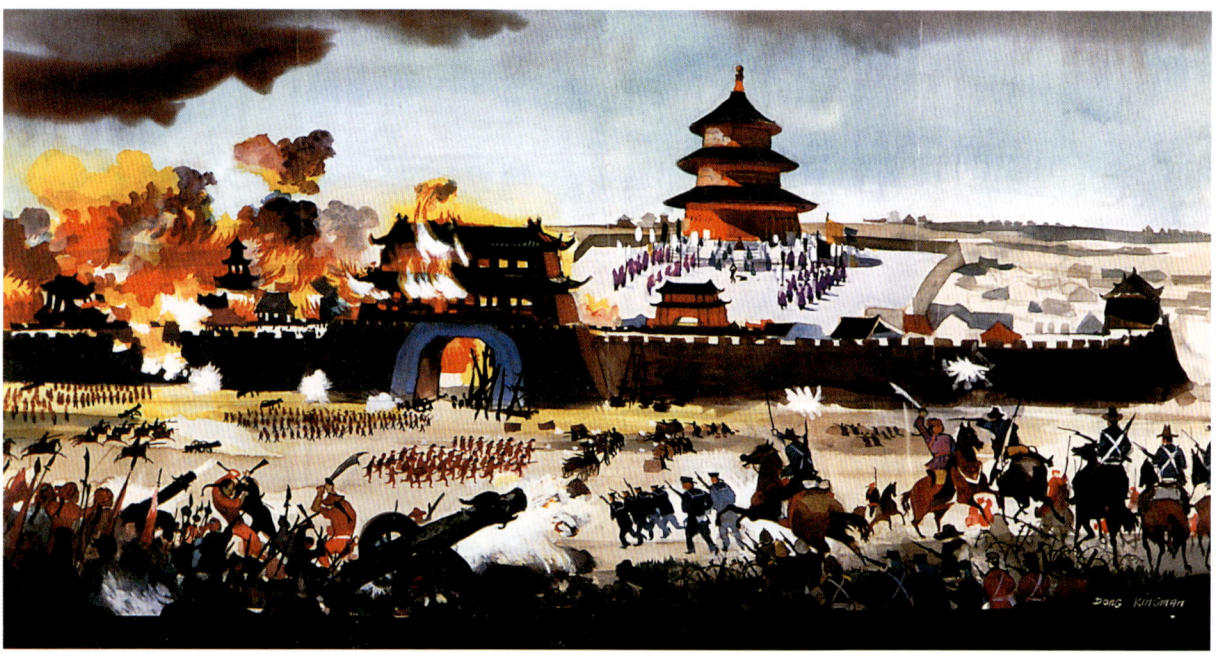

55 Days in Peking

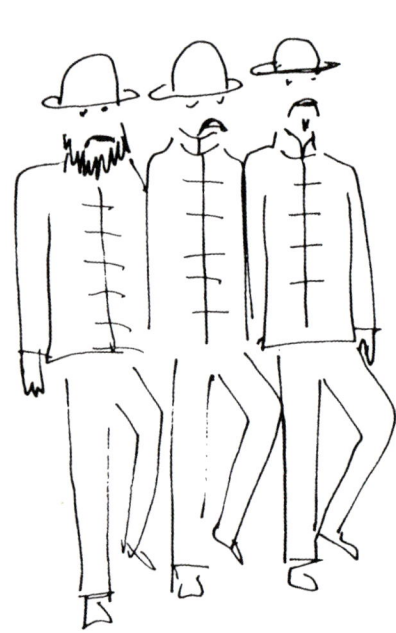

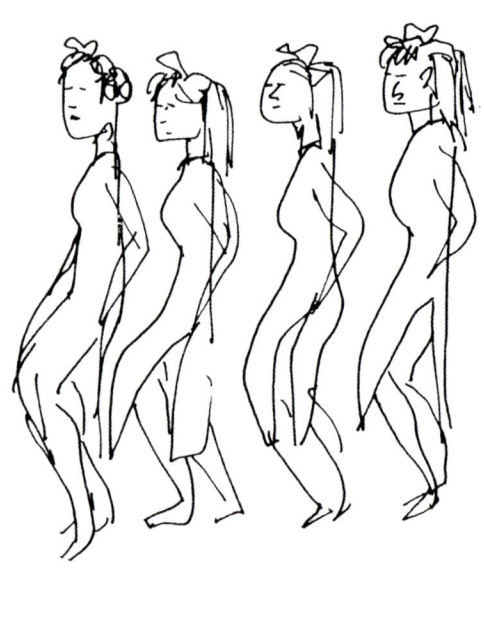

Flower Drum Song

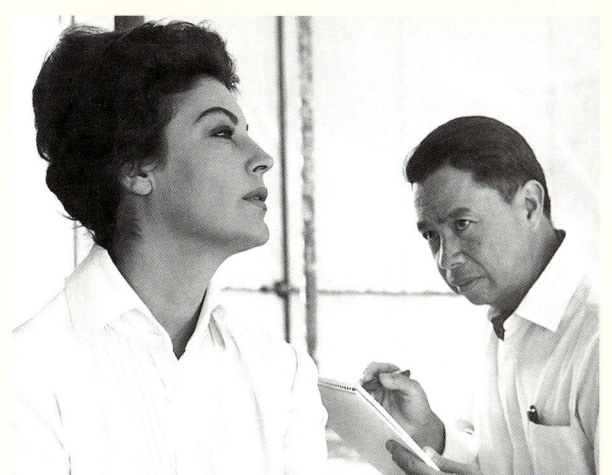

Ava Gardner poses for Dong Kingman

Dong Kingman Paints Peking in Spain

55 *Days at Peking*, a film about the Chinese Boxer uprising of 1900 against the foreign legations in Peking is a handsomely produced action filled, colorful movie that will delight every artist. For us at AMERICAN ARTIST held special interest. The film had its American premiere in Palace Theater on Broadway in the building which our offices have been located since last January. Secondly, Dong Kingman played an important part in the interpretation.

The producer, Samuel Bronston, commissioned Kingman to do a series of background paintings on location. He was flown to the movie set in Madrid, where he painted about fifty watercolors of the filming. Prior to the premiere, this collection of brilliant paintings was exhibited at the Knoedler Galleries in New York. They revealed both the natural kinship between the artist's background and the subject of the film, plus his interest in the theater, an inclination cultivated by his father during Kingman's childhood in China.

The first image flashed on the screen for 55 *Days At Peking* is a long panoramic watercolor which sets the mood for the play. Seconds later, the title is superimposed. Successively, other Kingman watercolors fill the wide screen, and again, each picture frame is held briefly to singular the view before all of the usual film credits appear. Then at the end of the film—like a demitasse to a fine meal—the screen lights up with another Kingman watercolor and it gradually fades.

55 *Days At Peking* stars Charlton Heston, Ava Gardner, David Niven and was directed by Nicholas Ray from the original screenplay by Philip Yordan and Bernard Gordon, with music by Dimitri Tiomkin. While the important role of artists in the movies—costume and set designers, art directors; illustrators, and photographers—is known and appreciated within the theatrical profession, the public is primarily concerned with the identity of stars. However, readers of AMERICAN ARTIST, like subscribers to other technical journals, are also interested in the purposes for which art is being employed in business and entertainment, and we commend Samuel Bronston for his tasteful use of Dong Kingman's work. Though few painters are as natively equipped by background and talent to interpret the illustrative flavor of the average movie, we hope that producers will provide similar opportunities for other artists.

Execution at the Temple of Heaven on the set of 55 Days At Peking.

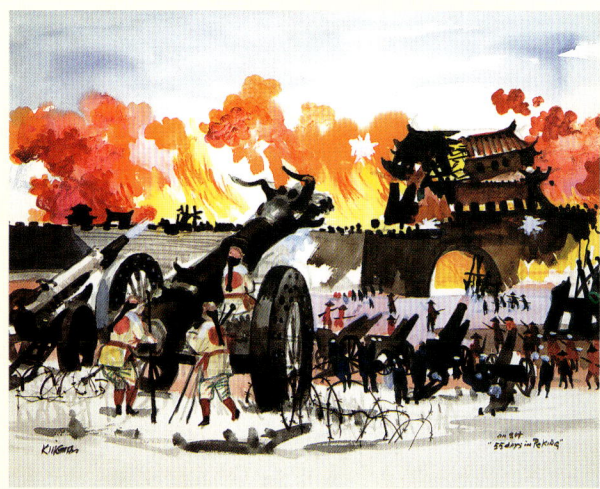

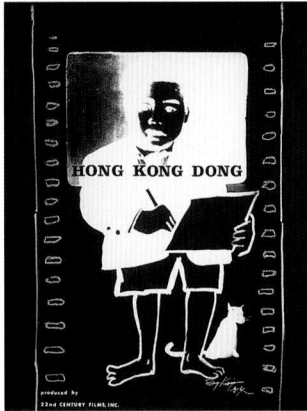

PAINT THE YELLOW TIGER -
a documentary film by Dong Kingman:

Following are some of the highlights of the above new film.

I produced, wrote, and painted the animations of a short subject film about my childhood life in Hong Kong in 1970 called Hong Kong Dong. This film has been shown in International Film Festivals and theaters in the US. and abroad.

In 1990, CBS-TV Sunday Morning show did a feature on me painting under the Brooklyn Bridge.

In Hong Kong for the past 20 years, whether I was there on painting assignments or painting workshops, my good friend Charles Wang, Chief Executive of Salon Films Ltd. worldwide, often sent a crew and equipment to photograph me giving painting demonstrations in Aberdeen to my group of American students, or on assignments painting market in a street in Causeway Bay, on sidewalk of my father's old store, in front of the Star Ferry, and he sent crew and equipment to film me all the way to my ancestral home in Toysan inside China, and on other occasions.

In this film, there will also be clips from short subject film *The World of Dong Kingman*, produced and filmed by the late James Wong Howe, a Hollywood Oscar-winning cinematographer. For this film, my friend Charlton Heston had done the narration for me.

Right now, my nephew Richard Chuang, V.P. of Pacific Data Images, is putting the above packages together into an hour-long film, hopefully will be ready for release sometime next year.

Again, the title of this new film is *Paint the Yellow Tiger*.

American Artist

Since the late Mr. Ernest W. Watson, Editor of American Artist Magazine, wrote a cover story about me in 1943, the magazine has been consistently writing about me through the years.

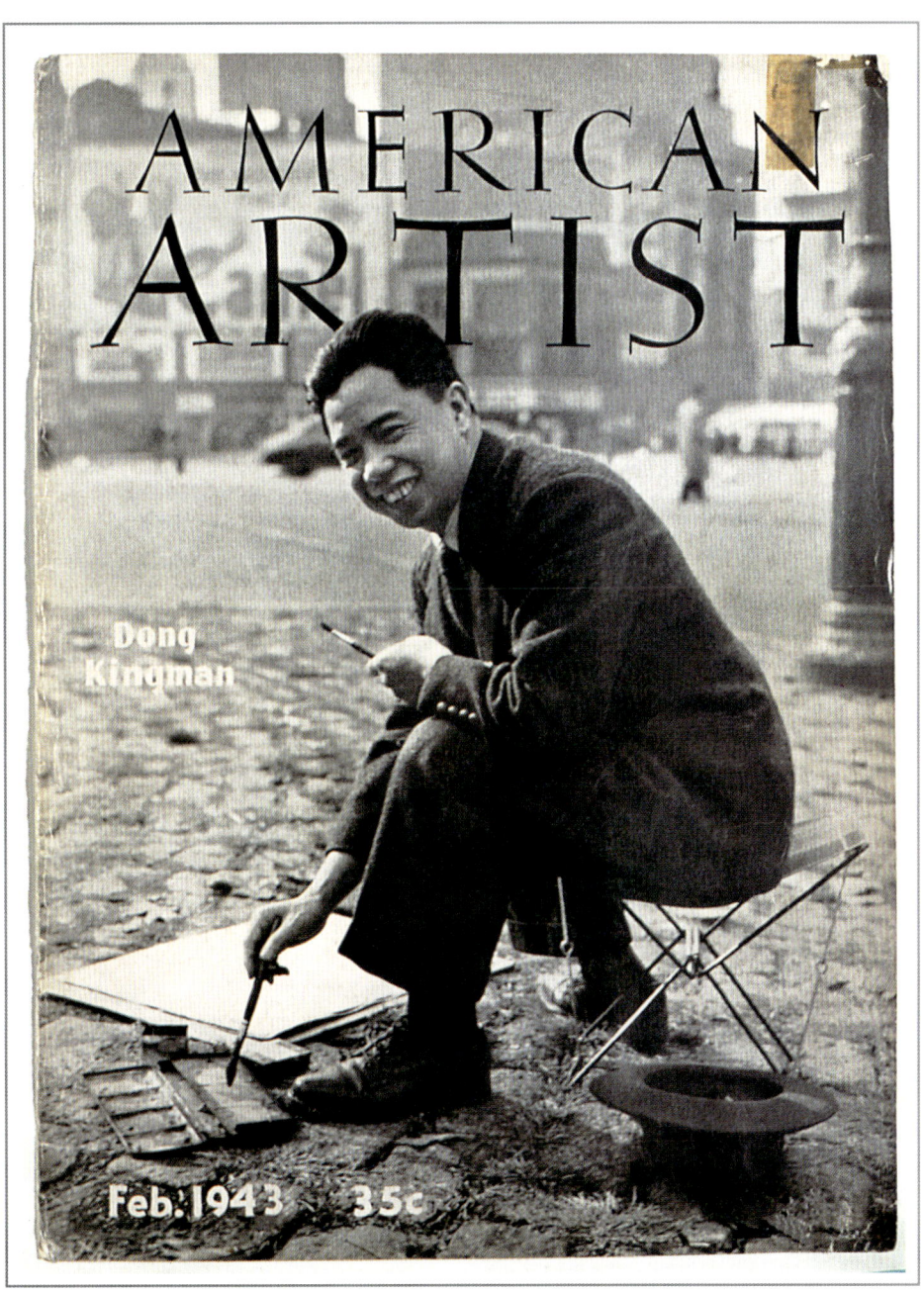

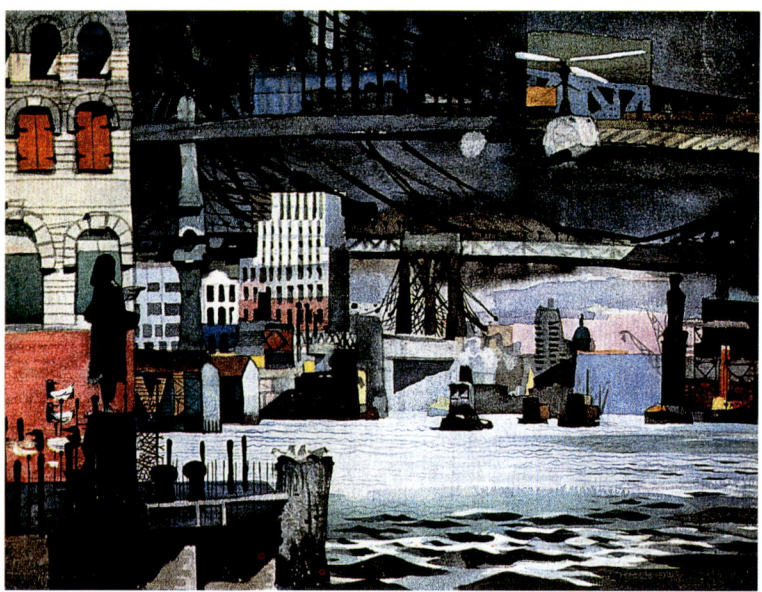

Helicopter, collection of Atlanta University

Dong Kingman
ON AN INDIVIDUAL APPROACH TO WATERCOLOR

DONG KINGMAN IS THE SUBJECT OF A FINE NEW BOOK: The Water Colors of Dong Kingman (and How the Artist Works) authored by Alan D. Gruskin, the artist's Midtown Galleries dealer, and recently published by Studio-Crowell, New York and London.
From a technical chapter entitled "The Making of a Watercolor," contributed by the artist to this book, we have been given permission to extract the following notes and observations, along with the reprinting of the color plate opposite. Kingman writes:
"I personally use three or four good, round sable watercolor brushes, small, medium, and large. Sometimes a Chinese brush is helpful too. I select about nine tubes of the best-made watercolors—I prefer the tube, as the paint remains fresher in it. My palette of colors is composed of the following: cadmium yellow, cadmium orange, cadmium red, alizarin crimson, thalo blue, French ultramarine blue, halo green, burnt sienna, and ivory black. With these basic pigments I can mix almost any color or shade I desire. I keep the brush and tubes in a tin watercolor box. I carry a folding chair and a small water container, which are both kept in a knapsack. I ordinarily paint in one of two sizes, 15"x22"/ 22"x30", using either a good thick watercolor paper or watercolor board, for they are both easy to handle.
"It is a common belief that the watercolor medium is a quick, spontaneous method of painting, and that no revisions can be made without ruining the paper and losing the freshness characteristic of the medium. I have found through years of experience, and with the exercise of considerable care and patience, that watercolor can be kept fresh and sparkling, and the paper kept in good condition despite constant changes and revisions. I compose on the paper, wiping out and changing various areas of the picture as I progress, often working months on a watercolor—sometimes years. Wiping off can be done with a clean rag or soft paper handkerchief."
"One late afternoon in the summer not so long ago, I was walking in downtown Manhattan all by myself. Suddenly the storm clouds gathered and the sky hung low. I looked around for a shelter, there standing

before my eyes was a full view of three giant bridges: the Manhattan, Brooklyn, and the Williamsburg."

"'What a wonderful subject this is for a painting,' " I said to myself, "and the weather!" The power, the vitality, and the intricate pattern of the city architecture all woven together. I could not wait to get my collapsible stool and painting equipment to put all this down on paper.

Early next morning, when the city was still half asleep and there was practically no traffic, I dashed back to the scene — Pier 6 on the East River. From there, the magnificent view of the three bridges interwoven with Manhattan's skyscrapers on the left and the Navy Yard in Brooklyn on the right unfolded before my eyes. Here and there on the rippling surface of the water were tugboats and steamers trolling lazily by. I knew then that I had found the spot. The picture I painted is shown in color on the next page.

"How I began my painting. Locating the subject is, of course, an important step in beginning a picture. My next step is to sit myself down as comfortably as possible on the collapsible stool and lay out my watercolor equipment. I was ready for action."

"A painter's eyes must see what another person does not see. They must be able to absorb what is good for a picture and what is not." With brush in hand and a 22x-29 inch piece of 300 pound watercolor paper in front, I was ready to put down a few brief lines to indicate the center of interest for the picture.

" I wetted my brush and worked with the colors — learning what to put in and what to leave out as I went along. It generally takes two to three hours, or a good part of the morning, for me to put down the essential parts of the scenery in a picture, the surrounding areas to be finished later in the studio."

"I also believe in sketching and painting the actual subjects on the spot, as this is the way, the only way, to feel the atmosphere around and to capture the mood right there on location."

"The Composition. Every artist has his own method of working. My method of course, is what I have developed for myself. My picture is generally 25% to 40% finished on location."

"For me, it is always better to have the semifinished picture hanging around the studio for a while. This gives me an opportunity to study and plan more carefully before completion."

"Looking at the unfinished picture on the easel, I may make preliminary sketches, with as many different ideas, to experiment with the colors and tonal values."

"One lesson I have learned in my years of painting is that it would be distracting to have a direct line, or lines, cut across the top of a picture, or for that matter, across any part of a picture. To stop the line of the bridge from cutting across the picture, I placed a perpendicular building on the left-hand side in front of the bridge."

"You may notice the square area at the top of the bridge on the upper right-hand corner. I had put it there on purpose. I was thinking, at first, of hanging a sheet of cloth, or a towel, over the bridge. But when I studied more of the composition of the painting, I came to the conclusion that I should put a helicopter there instead—the top part of the picture very dark, expressing the threatening storm, and the lower part in light colors for the churning sea."

"If you ask why I put a statue instead of a tugboat on the lower right-hand corner, my answer is that I like to give the feeling of being in an open park in the picture. And who doesn't enjoy being in an open park?"

"And why the wooden ducks in the foreground? Well, they are for the fisherman when they go fishing. This is a picture of the waterfront, remember?

"A Closing Thought. One must learn all he can about handling brush, the choice of colors, the tonal values, the use of techniques, all the necessary tools and knowledge to become an artist. But that is only the beginning. An artist must continue to search — for himself, and for something which is always there but may not be there."

"One may continue to search, on and on. But be does not have to straddle heavily and clumsily along the way. He can enjoy the task of painting, because painting is fun."

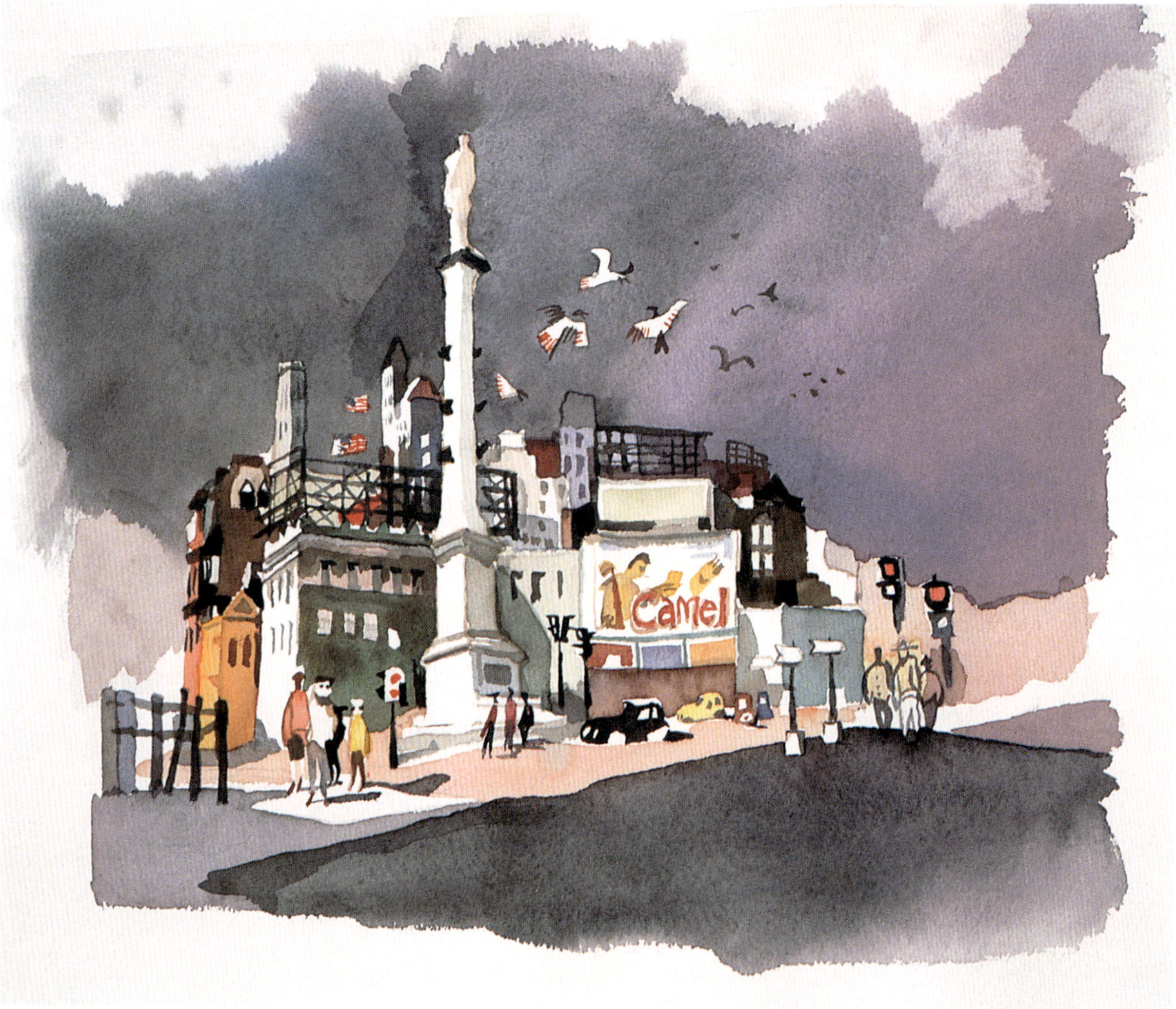

Columbus Circle, New York

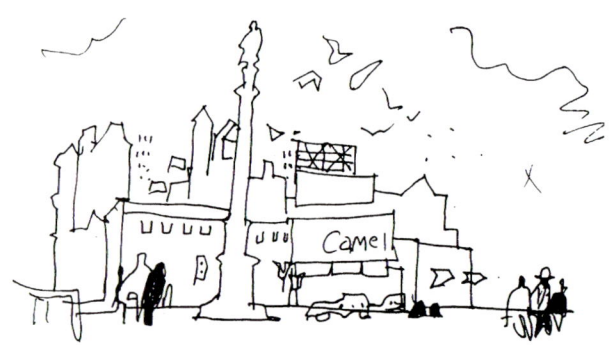

Dong Kingman

An Interview

by Ernest W. Watson

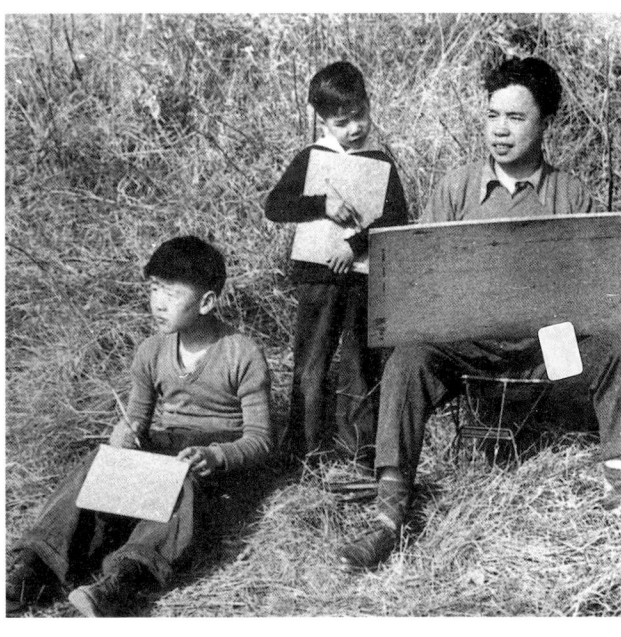

Dong kingman, noted Chinese-American artist and his two sons, Eddie, 12 and Dong Kingman, Jr., 6.

It is not often that pictures are printed upside-down through intention, but Dong Kingman's watercolors should first be viewed in that manner.. That is because Dong goes the world walking on his hands—figuratively, of course—and stands on his head—again figuratively—while he studies his subjects, then paints them. This is merely another way of saying that he is inspired, principally, by color, pattern, movement and tonal qualities — abstractions which can, if they are sufficiently charged with vitamins, make any picture exciting regardless of subject content.

Any chance reader who is more interested in just what Columbus Circle looks like should, of course give his attention to the photograph taken from the spot where the artist painted. Such person will be terribly disappointed with the watercolor because Dong wasn't at all concerned with architectural verisimilitude and, it will be seen, he departed radically from the literal aspects of the scene before him.

What did catch his eye were the startling accents of sunlit planes contrasting with darkening clouds, splashes of brilliant color intermingled with tonal grays, stabs of dark accents, the sweep of the whole colorful mass against a windy sky; these are the things that excited Dong that brilliant October morning when he first walked into Columbus Circle, the things that will, I believe, do something to the reader's insides if studies the watercolor upside-down without asking to give him a guide book impression of this famous New York landmark.

Dong has told a deliberate lie, factually, about that hodge-podge mass of brick and stone and advertising clamor which owes much of what charm it may possess to just those startling beauties which have been revealed to him and I hope to readers.

Forget for a moment that this Columbus Circle study is a picture; think of it as a color symphony and enjoy, for example, such handsome passages as the sequence of yellow, orange, red, brown and gray at the extreme right (viewed upside-down). Just to concentrate upon that choice bit, cover all of the picture except an inch and a half vertical strip at this side. If that isn't as palatable a color morsel as you're likely to find in any painting, I'm just plain color blind. Try the same experiment with other details. Cut a 2 or 2.5'square opening in a piece of white paper and slide it over the picture. If color were the only phase of Dong's work worth mentioning his pictures would be noteworthy. But there are many facets to his genius. One is his keen awareness of the activity of all things in this swift moving world. Even in Blue Moon, as quiet a subject as one could select, we are made conscious that this is but a transient effect of a restless nature in which things are always on the move. His startled birds accentuate this mood as do the reaching fingers of leafless trees.

Yes, those birds are a bit amusing, from an ornithological point of view.

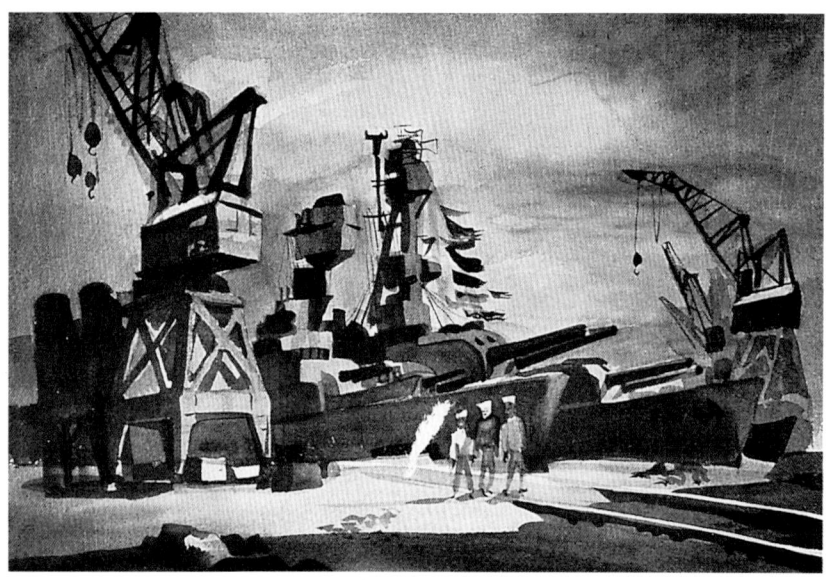

Pacific Coast Navy Yard, **Midtown Gallery**

COMPARING THIS COMBINATION WITH "PASSSING LOCOMOTIVE" WE NOTE A SIMILARITY OF ACTION; PROWS OF SHIPS, GUNS, FLYING FLAGS AND RAILS HAVE A POWERFUL HORIZONTAL THRUST TO THE RIGHT. THIS MOVEMENT IS TURNED BACK BY THE SHADOW SWEEPING ACROSS LOWER RIGHT CORNER, THE GREAT CRANES, AND SWEEP OF DARK CLOUD IN UPPER RIGHT.

One Way Bridge, **Midtown Gallery**

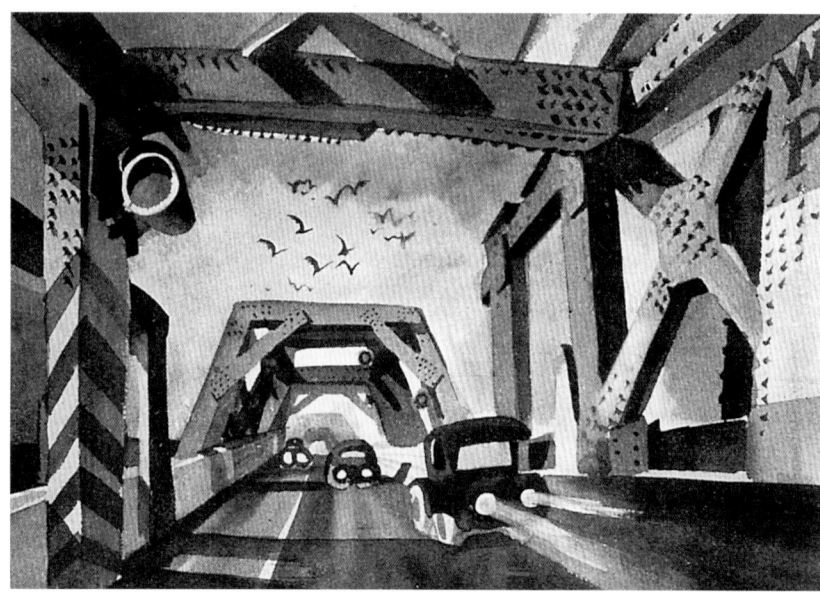

But Dong, when painting, isn't any more interested in ornithology than in architecture, as such. He can, I happen to know, draw a bird with the utmost anatomical perfection, as (did the Chinese masters whom he once emulated), but a bird in flight really has no anatomy whatsoever.

In Passing Locomotive the artist revels in the rush of modern life. Here he becomes ecstatic in the emotion of lines and colors sweeping across his picture. But note how he prevents the eye from hurtling right off the paper. The diagrammatic notes show how vertical elements and shadows falling across horizontal lines prevent them from flying off into space, how they succeed in sweeping the eye back into the vortex of the picture.

Kingman, it will be seen, is somewhat partial to a diamond-shaped foundation for his composition. Note how he uses it in Blue Moon and in Columbus Circle. He never relies upon a frame to confine his composition; he insists that the nucleus of the picture's interest be enfolded within encircling lines or masses of tone and color. Well, you see I like Dong

Kingman's watercolors. So do others. Boston Museum of Art has just purchased Blue Moon. The Museum of Modern Art owns a Kingman, as do the Metropolitan, the Brooklyn Museum and the San Francisco Museum of Art. He has won several important watercolor prizes. His latest one-man show was held at Midtown Galleries in New York. During the past year he was the recipient of a Guggenheim Fellowship, has taken him about the country on a painting tour.

And Dong is just at the beginning of his career. He was born of Chinese parents in 1911 in Oakland, California. At the age of five his parents returned to China where Dong spent the next thirteen years. His education and art training are thus of Chinese origin. He studied painting under traditional Chinese masters and from Sze-To Wei—a Chinese painter, returned from Paris, having acquired the philosophy and methods of the modern French painting. Against this contrasting background of the old and the new, of orient and occident, Dong has developed his own original expression in which the sources of influence, however, are clearly observed. "In the old tradition of China," explains Dong, "Chinese artists often painted their pictures from memory. First they would go on a trip to a mountain or, as their fancy chose, go down near a river for a sketch trip. They took along only a small sketch pad, one or two brushes and black ink. With this scanty equipment they repaired to the place of their choosing to study and enjoy the landscape, perhaps etched in silhouette against a full moon.

"These trips were generally made for observation only, rarely did the artist paint directly from the scene. Back in the studio he developed his picture, his memory aided by the scanty scribbles he may have brought back in his sketchbook. All of this, to my understanding, produced some very satisfactory results and I very often follow the same procedure."

"Something Missing Here" ~here and there, some of the buildings, and the background, I then proceeded to lay in the sky, after which I worked, in detail, the rest of the picture. I had not yet put the shadow in, when a few drops of rain came, causing me to go back to my studio, which was just as we because many of my pictures are completed indoors anyhow."

Contrary to the somewhat general practice, Kingman usually leaves the painting of the sky until almost the last. He feels that in so doing he can better adjust this vital factor in the all-over effect of the picture. His color is strong, varied and clean, a result it is hard to believe can come out of that tiny paint box seen lying on the pavement at his feet. All the water he requires is carried in the rectangular receptacle standing at one end of the palette. It holds barely a half pint. We see no paint cloth for the cleaning of those two brushes which do all his work. How he manages, under these conditions, to produce colors of such purity is something to wonder at. Dong Kingman is very much of an artist. Every new place or thing seen is at once analyzed as potential picture material.

As he and I sat down together at a luncheon table, from which lower New York and the Harbor could be seen, he at once whipped out his pencil and began sketching on the back of his menu. For several minutes he was oblivious of all but the glory of what was, to him, a new and exciting scene. I wouldn't be surprised if these scanty lines plus an extraordinary memory of what he saw during that hour atop the McGraw-Hill building sufficed to produce a watercolor of Manhattan's famous skyline.

At that luncheon, by the way, I had more than a hint of Dong Kingman's ardent Americanism in his refusal of a cup of coffee for patriotic reasons.

Dong Kingman is an extremely personable young man, as may be surmised from the cover picture. That smile was not produced by a photographer's request; it is wholly characteristic and heartwarming. It's a real treat to meet this Chinese-American artist from whom, I predict, we shall continue to hear in the coming years.

The Intimate World of Dong Kingman

By Eugene M. Ettenberg

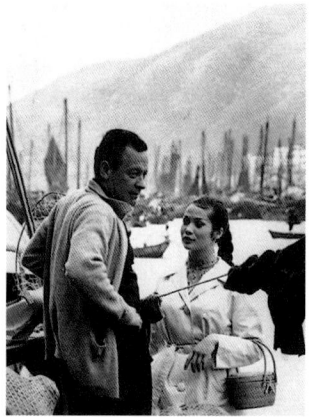

Actors Nancy Kwan and William Holden flank Dong Kingman on location in Hong Kong

Dong pays tribute to his teacher, Mr. Sze-Tu Wai, in his portrait

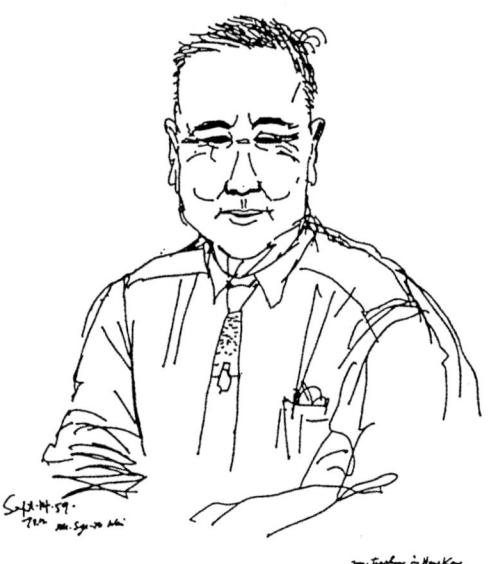

IT WAS ORIGINALLY OUR INTENTION to report on the more recent work of Dong Kingman to celebrate his reaching his mid-century in years. What dissuaded us was the fact that so much has already been written about him in magazines (Life alone has done five illustrated stories), newspaper features, and a book. And three film demonstrations of his paintings, two by the Harmon Foundation and another by Hollywood's world-famed cameraman, James Wong Howe, have been made. This magazine, too, has done its share; in 1941, Editor Emeritus Ernest Watson saw Kingman's first New York exhibition and featured his work in an interview article. Then too, a story on his latest successes, such as the recent sellout of all his paintings before the opening of his last exhibition of watercolors of Hong Kong—pleasant as it is to tell of such things—seemed inadequate and surface reporting. We felt a more meaningful story could be told by inquiring into the roots of his skills and penetrating, if we could, the surface of his art.

Poring through Kingman's sketchbooks as a proper beginning, it occurred to us that we need go no further, for these were our answer. There in a closet in his West 58th Street studio, stacked from floor to ceiling, were literally hundreds of these books. They go back sixteen years— eight by ten, and eleven by fourteen sketchbooks, some spiral bound, some sewed, some with paper covers and others in black leather. Dong Kingman calls these his diaries—records of his day-to-day doings. He has accustomed himself to taking a sketchbook with him wherever he goes—to his luncheon dates, the theater, television studios, circuses, on trains and planes, and even when he visits his barber. Self portraits with a barber's sheet tucked around his neck crop up in these diaries, as well as sketches of the barber snipping away and resigned males seated in the back leafing through tattered Esquires as they await their turn. Then there are sketches of his friends in the entertainment world, lolling in easy chairs, talking animatedly in a night-club or restaurant, sweating out a part in rehearsal. Leafing through, we see laughing Carol Channing, Charlton Heston, bewhiskered Peter Ustinov, Charles Laughton holding forth, Shirley MacLaine while the movie, "The Apartment," was being filmed, Danny Kaye in a Chinatown restaurant, or a sketch succinctly labeled "Eddie Albert's Dressing Room, 11:30 P.M."

It is remarkable how much of Kingman and his world peers out from these pages, and how much more they reveal the artist than a written diary. Each sketch is done quickly; he has trained his eye to be selective and his hand to draw with an economy of effort. His is a very special sort of eye. It selects the essence of the bustle of a crowd; the faces are little more than circles or child-like masks, but the bent back here and the stretched neck there bespeak nameless pushing people en masse better than any detailed photograph or most written descriptions. Like Saul Steinberg, he is titillated by the over-ornate, the garish and tawdry. Rococo ceilings in plush nightclubs, Broadway signs, fire escapes, street lights, telephone booths and traffic signs fill many pages.

His friend, William Saroyan, has to say about the very particular way Dong sees: "He really looks at the place and he really sees it." Everybody whose business is to look and see looks at New York and sees something different, perhaps new, perhaps important, perhaps special. But I don't know anyone who sees what Dong Kingman sees. . . This is it, I think . . . he sees the world this instant and in a glance, in his glance, in the instantaneous and miraculous reality of matter and color, of living vision, of memory captured in the painters of great skill, he sees the world gone—forever."

If we are to try to understand the Dong Kingman eye, what it selects for recording as well as what it omits as not material to the moment, we must review some of his life experiences. As we do, his gentle satire, a satire with no sting, will become understandable. His wide-eyed enjoyment of man-made vehicles, machines, and structures will show its origin, as will his return to the Oriental semi-stylization of water, sky, flying geese, and feathery-leafed trees.

As Dong grew up in teeming Hong Kong he worked at all sorts of jobs, from a pattern factory hand to a newspaper vendor. When he turned eighteen, his father sent him back to California where he worked for two years in his brother's overalls factory; later he bought a restaurant for seventy-five dollars and promptly lost it; then became a houseboy for the Drews, a San Francisco insurance executive's family. He worked there afternoons and evenings, and in his spare moments painted in their basement. Mornings he cycled to school. At this time he had his first exhibition of twenty watercolors in San Francisco's Art Center and was promptly hailed a find by the city's art reviewers. He was off, and not even the Depression of the 1930's could stop him. The ninety dollars a month he got from the W.P.A. for five years, as well as the friendship of such art patrons as Albert Bender, enabled him to keep busy sketching and painting. A $5000 two-year Guggenheim Fellowship permitted him to travel through the country, recording the Rockies, the cornfields of Illinois, and Chicago's Loop. Then museums started to acquire Kingmans—the Metropolitan, Brooklyn, Boston, Whitney and DeYoung, the Art Gallery of San Diego, Art Institute of Chicago, and Butler Art Institute. With the outbreak of World War II he was sent to Camp Beal in California and then to Washington, D.C., making charts and graphs for the Office of Strategic Services. It was while in Washington that he began filling sketchbooks, his first ones peppered with the feverish activities of the war-

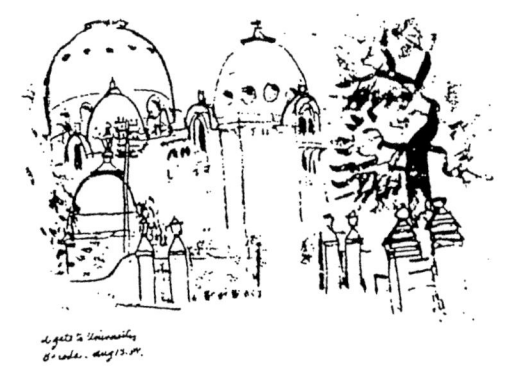

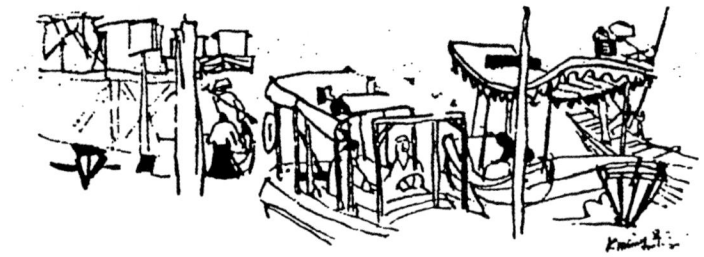

time capital.

Next to Hong Kong, Kingman perhaps felt most drawn to New York, and as soon as he could he bought a house overlooking the New York harbor in Brooklyn Heights where he set up his studio. Soon thereafter Hunter College appointed him a full-time instructor in painting, and in 1951 he was elected to full rank in the National Academy. Then in 1954 the U. S. State Department, as part of its educational and exchange program, invited him to go on a world tour to "sell" democracy. This he did and covered himself with distinction. (The department called him "the five-foot all American.") The forty-foot scroll report he made to the State Department may be recalled by readers of Life magazine where it was reproduced. On his return, in the intervals between his one-man shows, he made covers for Fortune Magazine and Holiday, painted murals, illustrated two books on China, played chess and bridge, taught watercolor painting Saturdays at Columbia University, became a member of the Famous Artists Schools faculty and married Helena Kuo, a Shanghai journalist and author.

Since 1935 he has painted about fifty pictures a year, finding a ready market for each and every one. At this moment he does not own a single finished watercolor of his own, and only about a dozen in various stages of completion.

Inevitably Hollywood beckoned, sending him back to Hong Kong as a technical adviser during the shooting of "The World of Suzie Wong." As this is being written he is off to act in a similar capacity for the filming of "The Flower Drum Song." Many artists carry sketchbooks, having in mind that they may serve for studio compositions later. How many of Kingman's sketches find their way into his watercolors is hard to determine. They seem to be without purpose and about as simple and unmeaningful as the fun one might have at a good party or watching a dog chase his tail. However, we get a clue to how these sketches affect his painting in a comment Kingman made regarding his harborside watercolor, Two Bridges. "The mood of the sea and sky remind me of the time I was in China . . . the bridges I saw and sketched many times in San Francisco . . . the buildings we see every day here in New York. Thus the paper was painted with all my thoughts together—Hong Kong and San Francisco in the back of my memory and New York in front of me."

Robert Fawcett, in his book On The Art of Drawing, has a good deal to say about the accurate eye and the trained and obedient hand. "What holds imagination back more than anything else is sloppy seeing. We must first see, then we may safely imagine more. Vagueness and blurred seeing are not the same as an inspired transformation of reality."

The accuracy of putting down and transfixing the passing moment did not come to Kingman overnight. Along with such formal training as was given him by Sze-Tu' Wai, he had six months in an architectural drafting office (though the office and he agreed at the end of that time to call it quits). This was followed by a short period with a motion picture company, for he dreamed then of becoming a movie director, or at least doing something with the theater.

Love of the theater was bred in him by his father, who took him as a schoolboy to see the Cantonese opera every night for months, getting home at two or three in the morning. No wonder his school teachers the next day found it hard to compete for

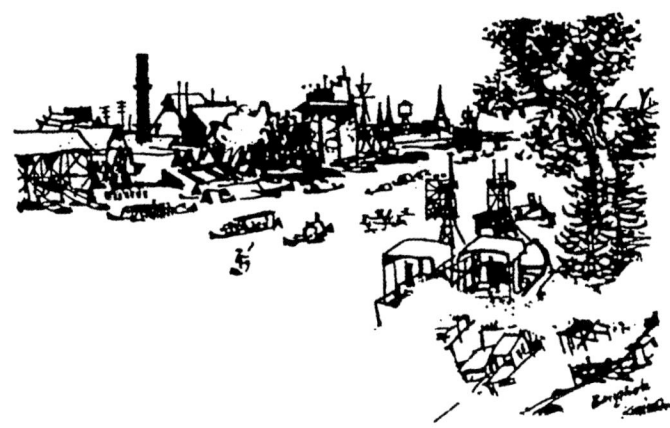

his attention. He was sleepy-eyed, half in the make-believe world of Chinese epics filled with dragons, flashing swords, and beautiful, sorrowful heroines who died at his feet to the sound of tinkling bells.

Many of his friends ask him why he is forever sketching and are amused by his reply —that he does it to learn how to draw. But he assured me soberly that he means it, and what's more, he feels he is slowly improving! The pen he uses is an imported model that holds ink and has fine, hard bristles for a point. It produces a fat, even line, slightly less than the width of match stick. The paper he prefers is a satin-smooth texture. About other sketching tools, such as crayons or pencils, he said that he felt anything other than a solid black line tempts one into suggesting something with blurred and fading edges rather than drawing the object or person precisely. Dong holds his pen straight up and down at right angles to the paper in oriental fashion, drawing swiftly without pause to catch the fleeting expression or shifting light. In the darkened theater he draws on his lap, not seeing what he has done until lights up during the intermission or after the performance. Quite a neat trick that, and only to be appreciated by those who have tried drawing in the dark! Remember those parlor games when you ordered to draw a cow, your teacher, or your best friend in pitch darkness? The results often brought many a laugh—and derision, if you were considered to have talent.

Kingman has achieved the artist's ultimate goal of using mind, eye and hand as one. His pen line at the end of the process responds, like the antenna of an insect, how he feels. Often the result is sly and puckish, or appears with eyes a-twinkle. Almost always it reveals Kingman's good humor and affection for all about him. Noise, dirt and smells are somehow suggested in these sketches as clashing lines weave in and out like a tapestry.

Howard DeVree, art critic for The New York Times, noted the selective detail in Kingman's paintings, "vitalizing the commonplace through observation and rearrangement to suit the needs of his pictorial design." This is also apparent in his sketchbooks. His sketches are impressionistic, but they also contain much of camera kind of realism, as if at times he sees everything about him, and at others peers intently at some detail that strikes his fancy. The conventions of perspective to convey distance, the thinned and thickened line to suggest rounded forms or shadowed areas are second nature to him. A telephone booth on Broadway, an antiquated automobile or railway signal are put down with minute detail as surely as though he might want to construct it later in wood or metal.

Accustoming himself to draw from any angle of perspective, he describes one harbor scene he had done as seen through a fish eye. Other paintings, such as rooftop views of Pusan's harbor or a mountain in the Grand Tetons looking down through the mist into the valley, appear equally effortless. As evidenced by these sketchbooks, it is this ability to draw, the fountainhead of the artist's craft, that gives him his self-confident line. Unchained from academic, realistic shapes, he now soars, putting together combinations of happy memories—of popping fire-crackers, people, bridges, locomotives, sampans and cats—collages of what excites him and thinks amusing—that make up the world of Dong Kingman.

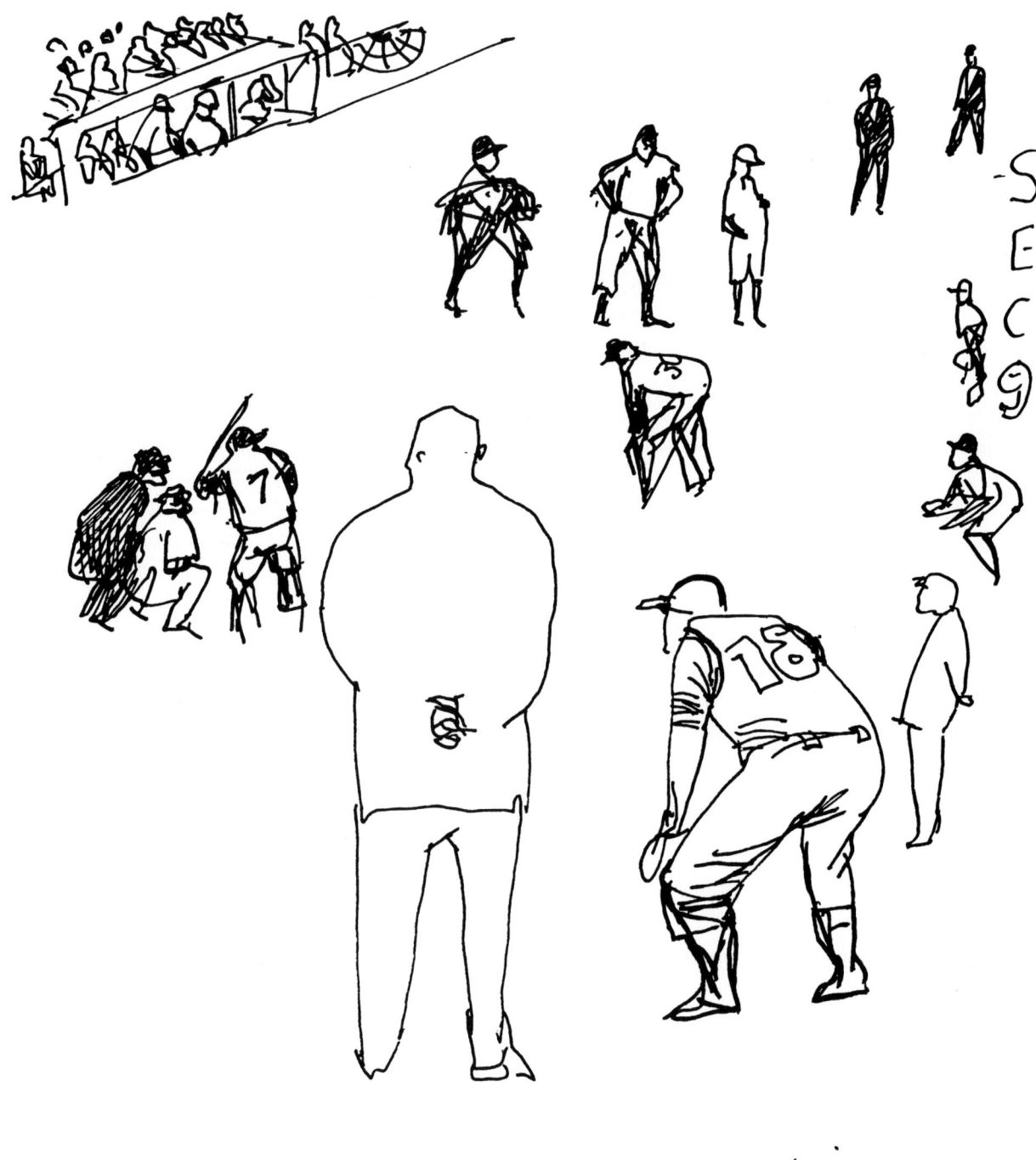

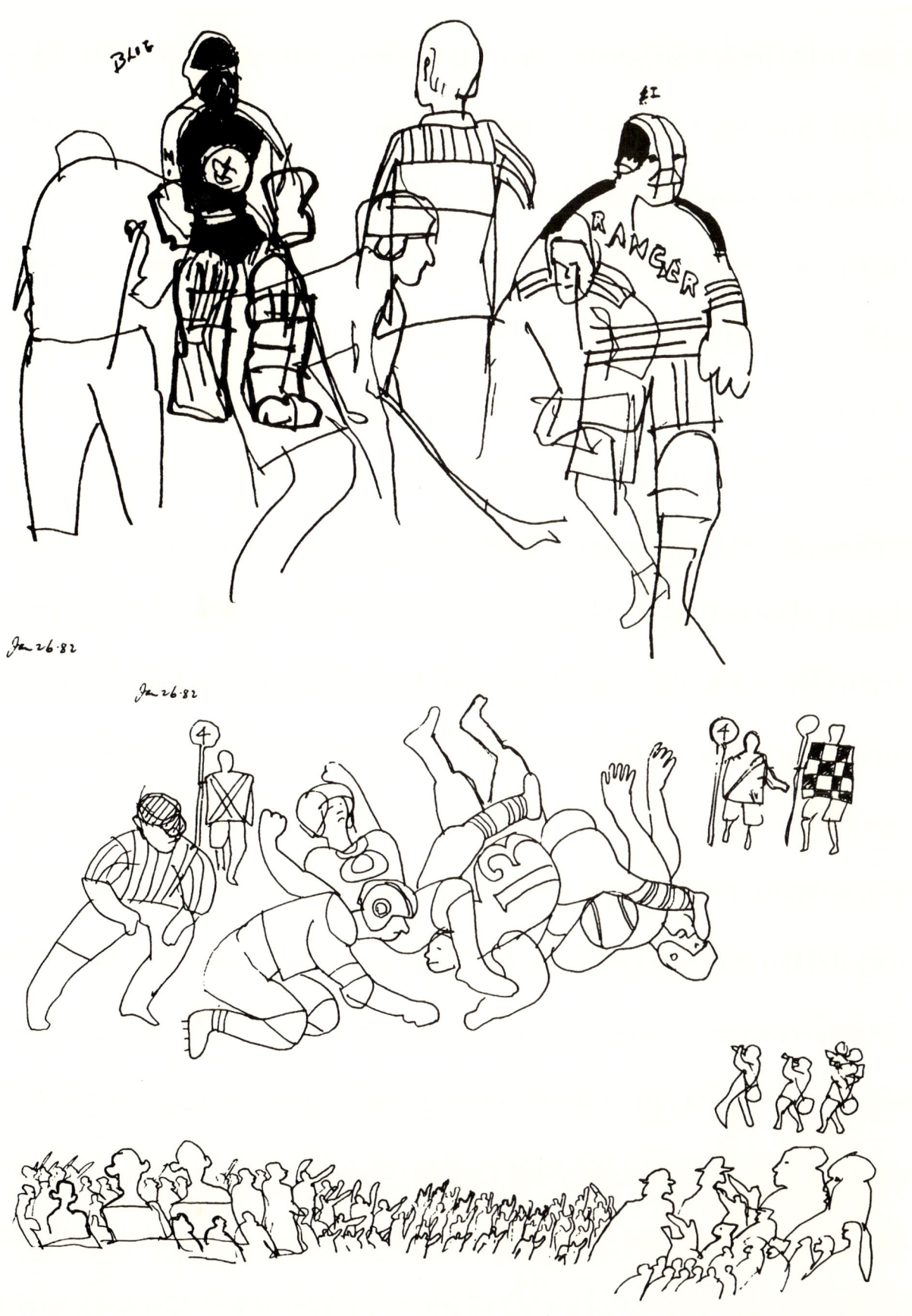

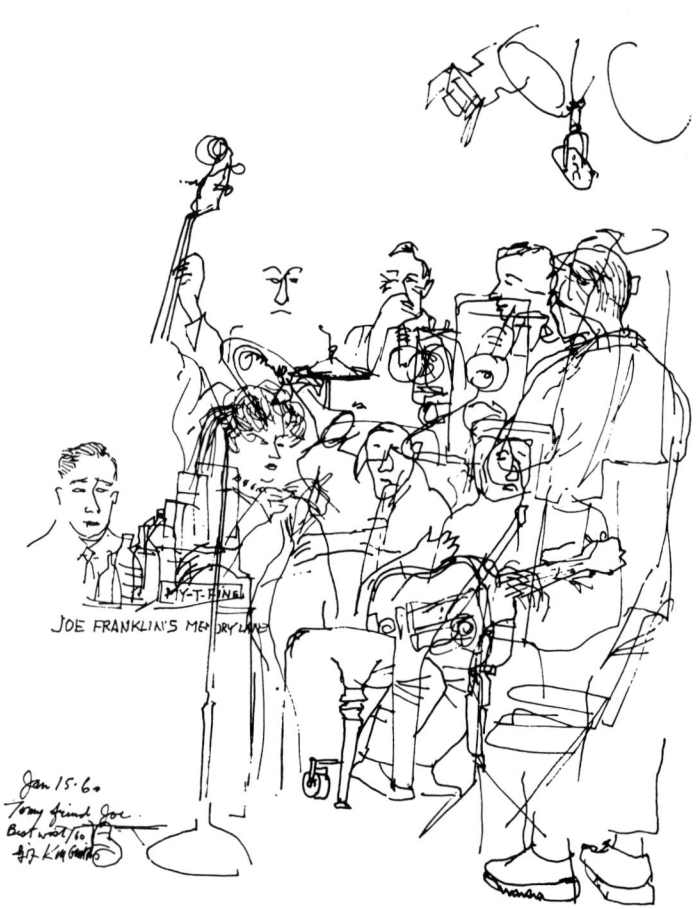

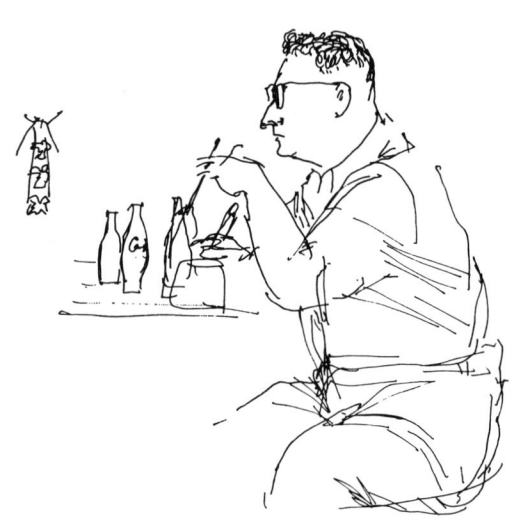

The journalist, Art Buchwald, caught in the web of Dong's penetrating line

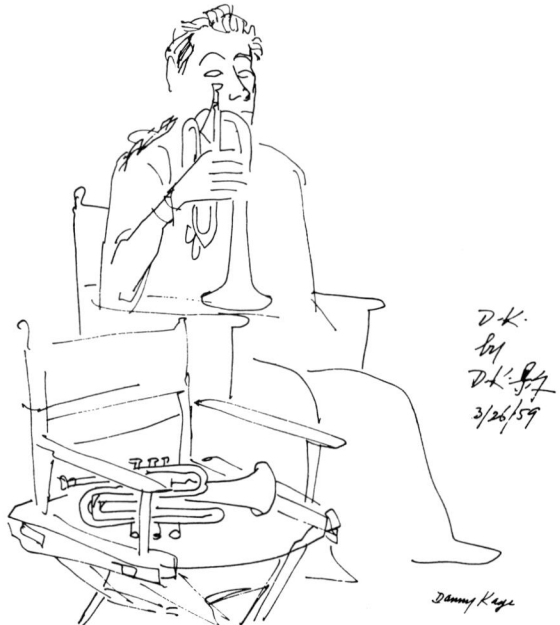

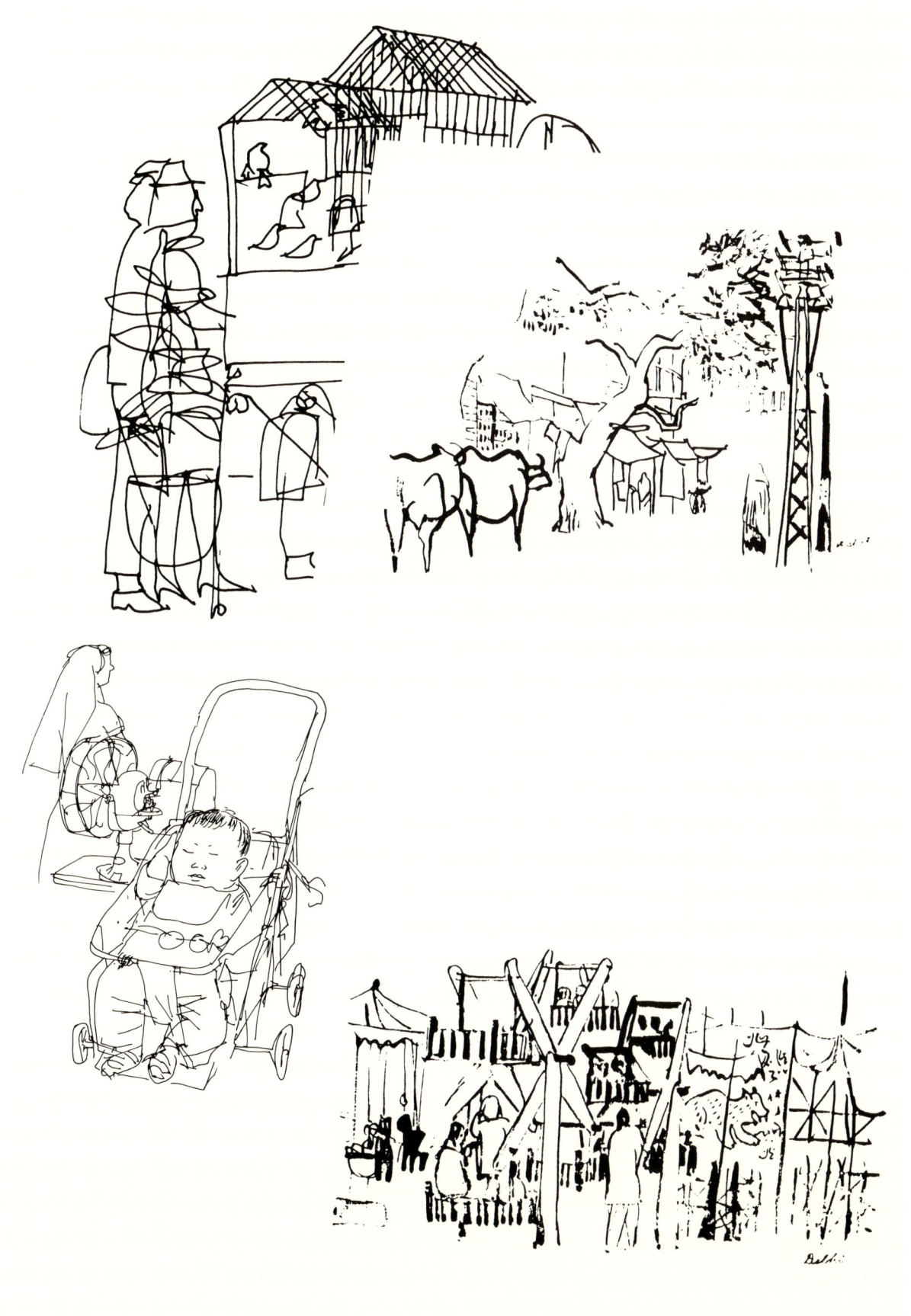

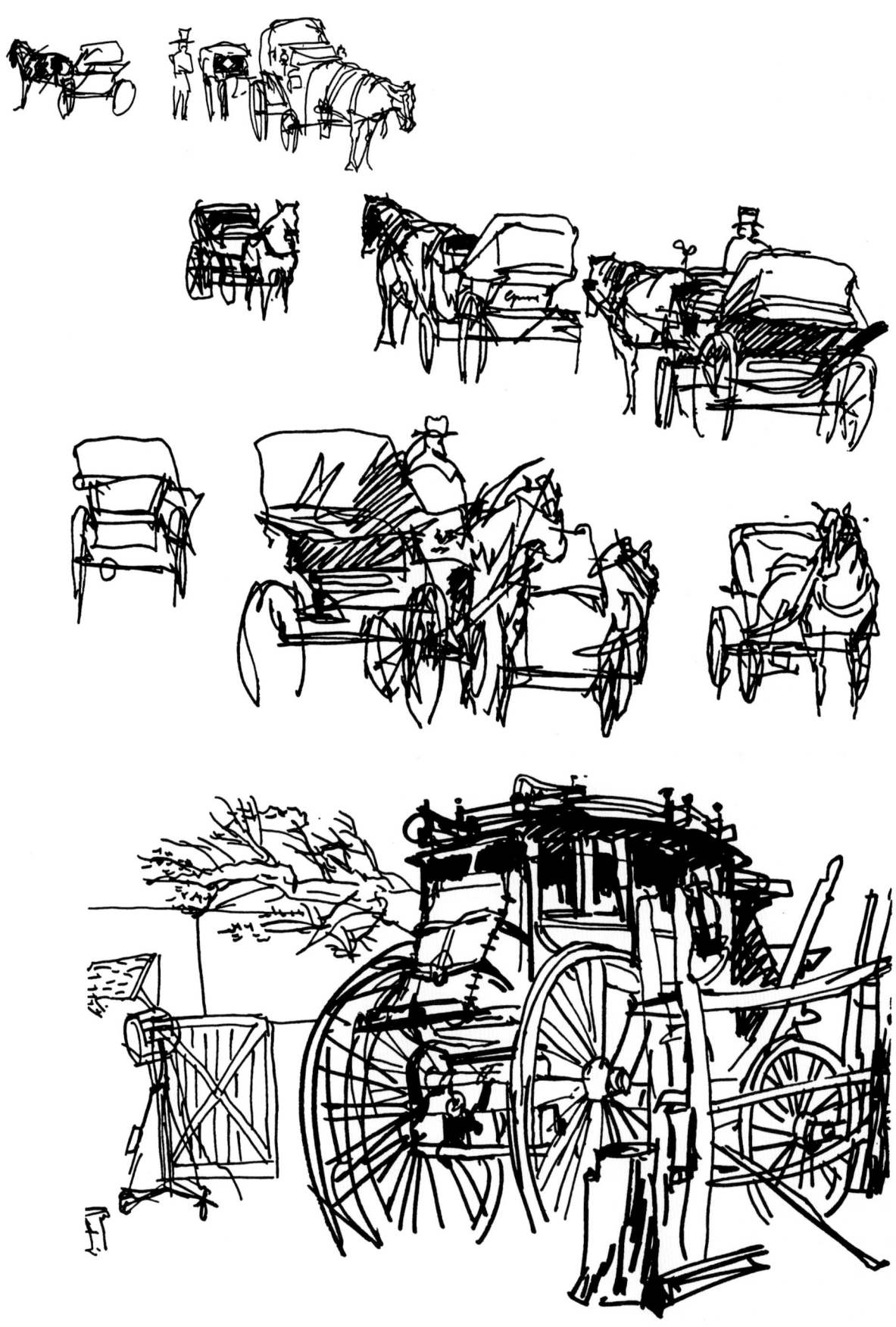

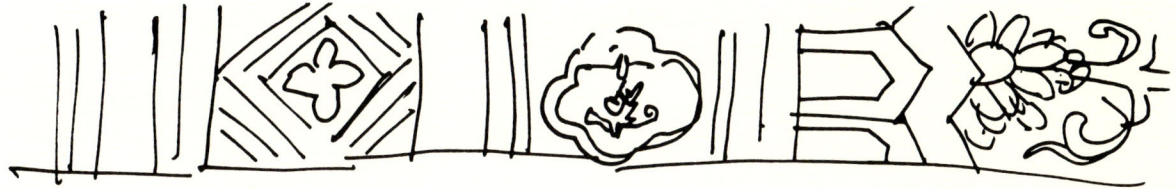

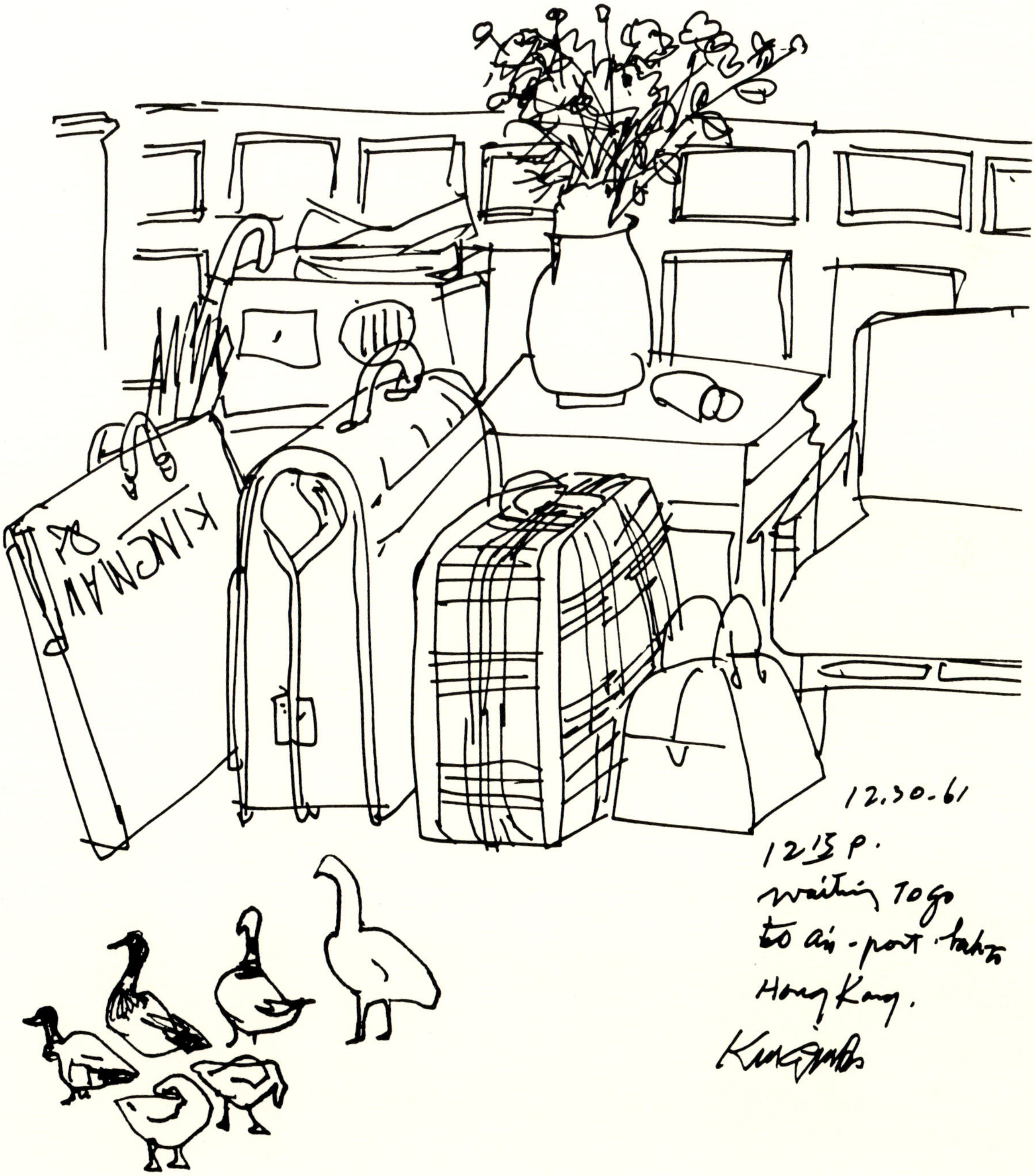

12.30.61
12:15 P.
waiting to go
to air-port taking
Hong Kong.
Kim Gumbs

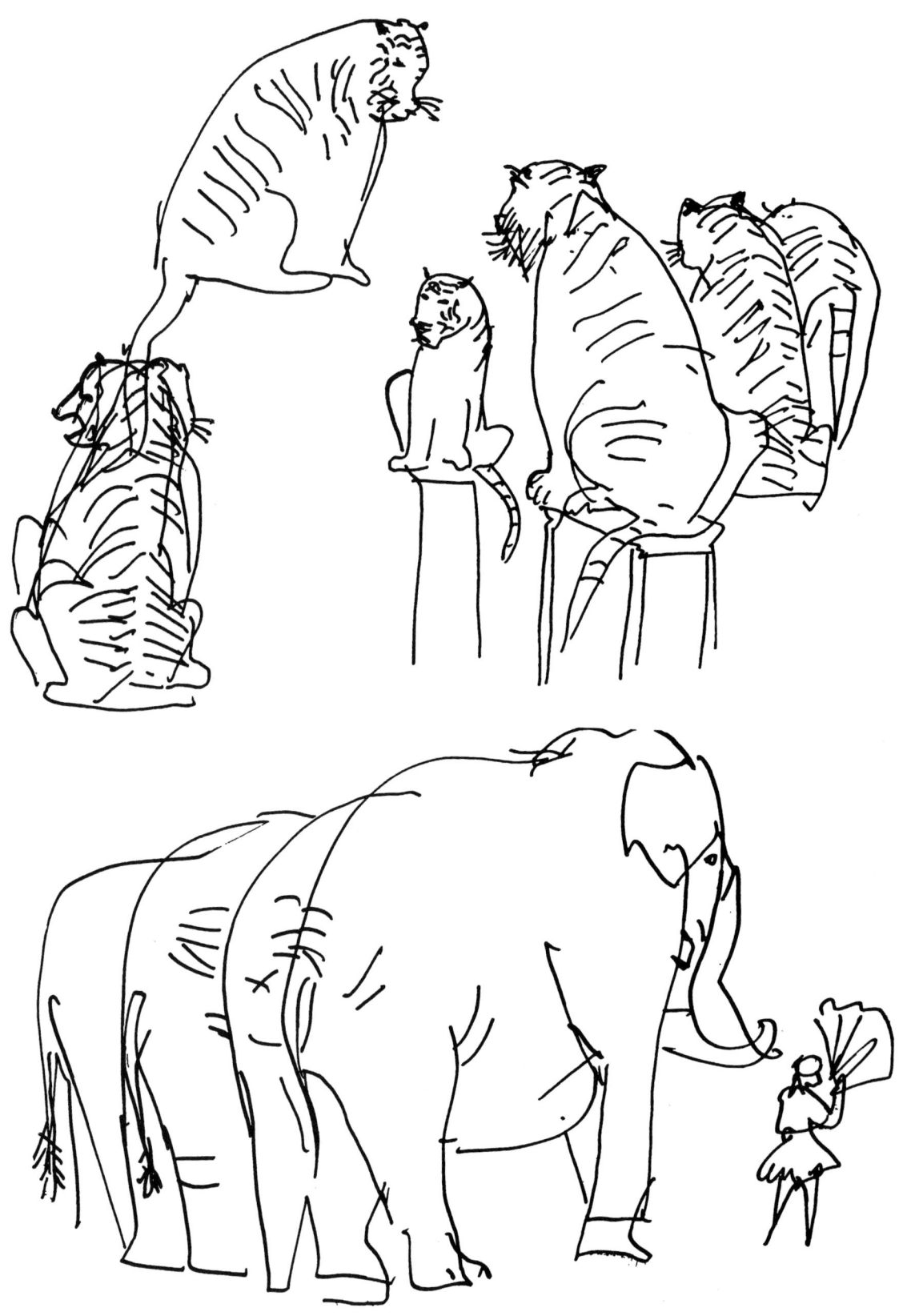

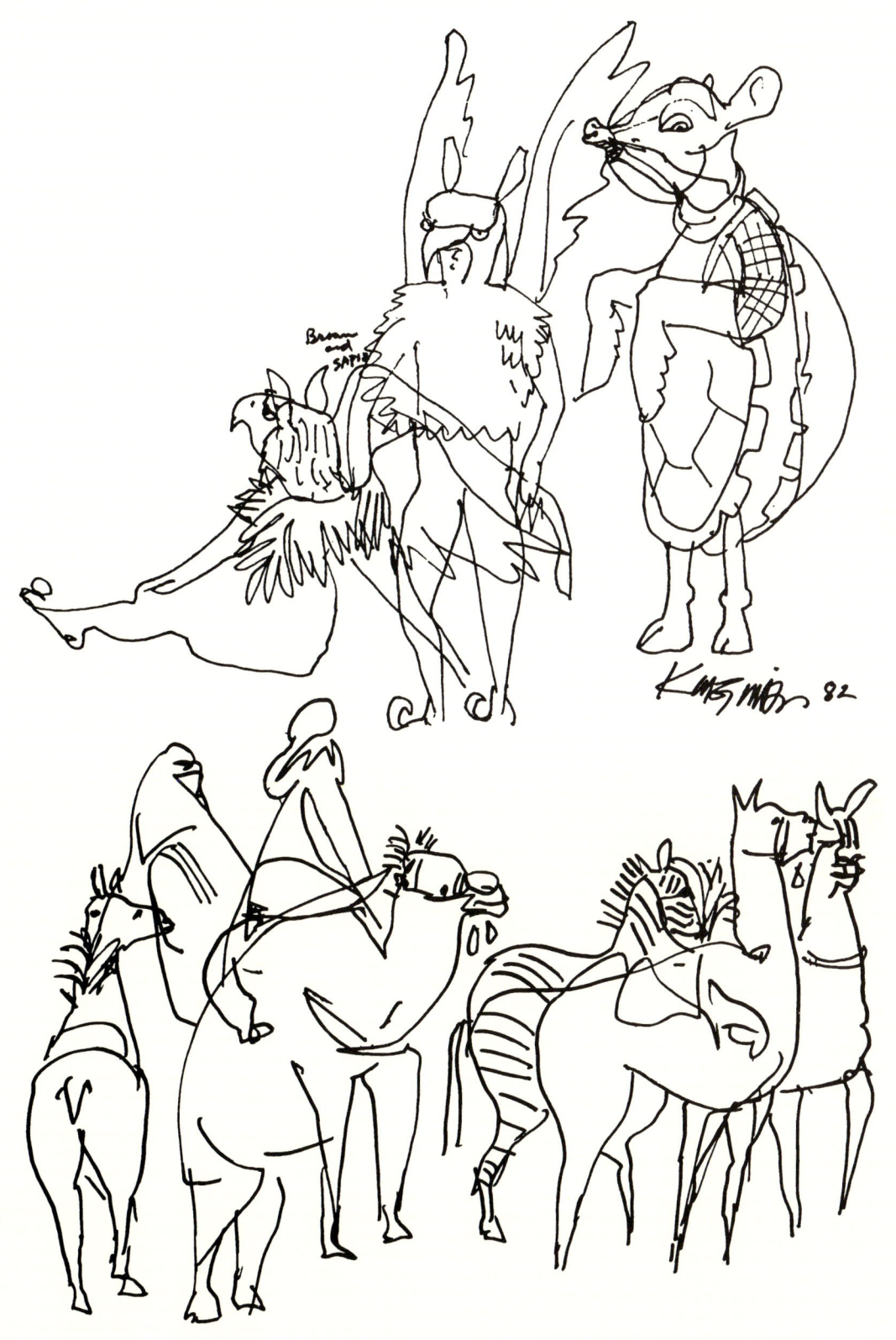

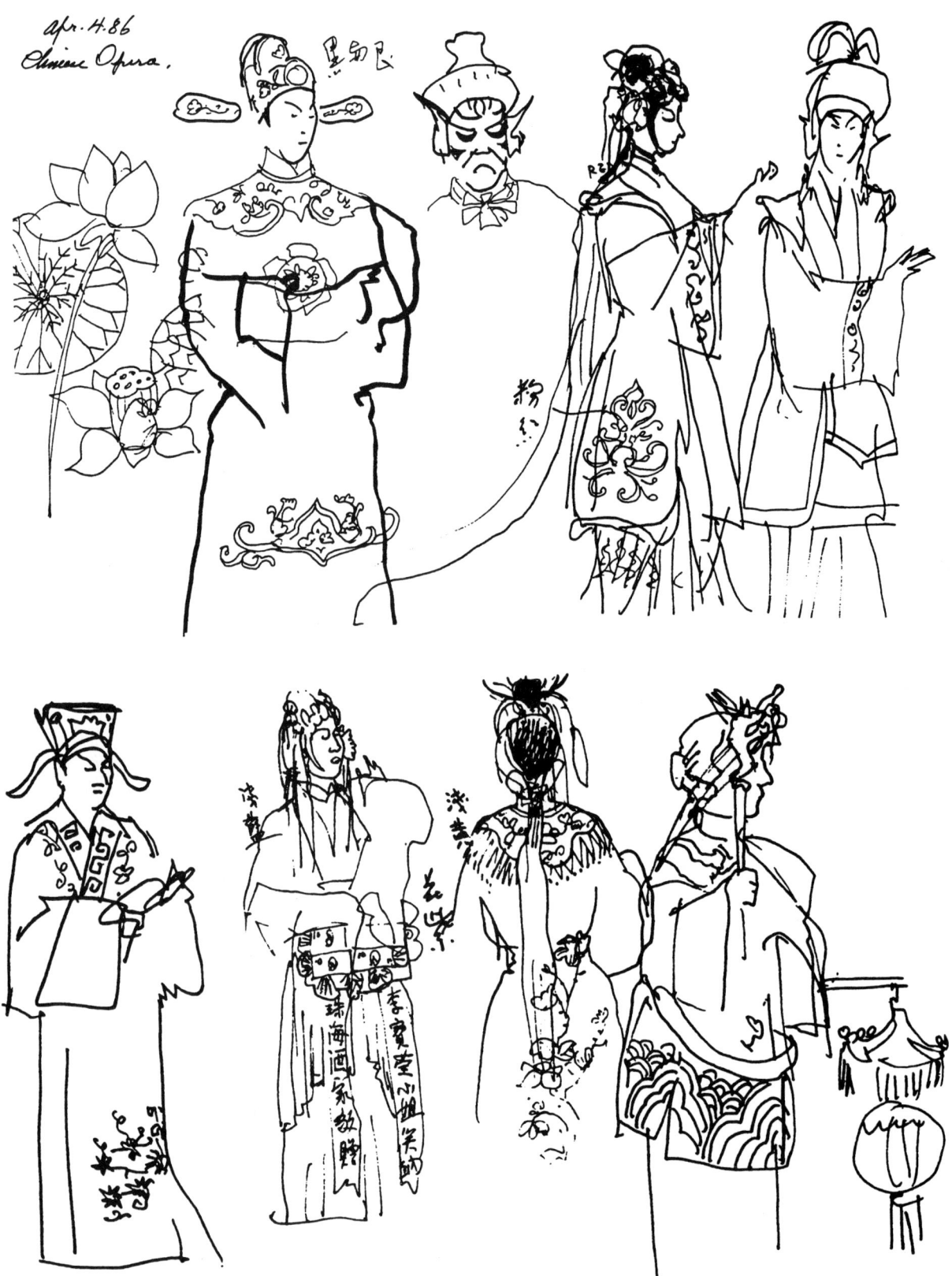

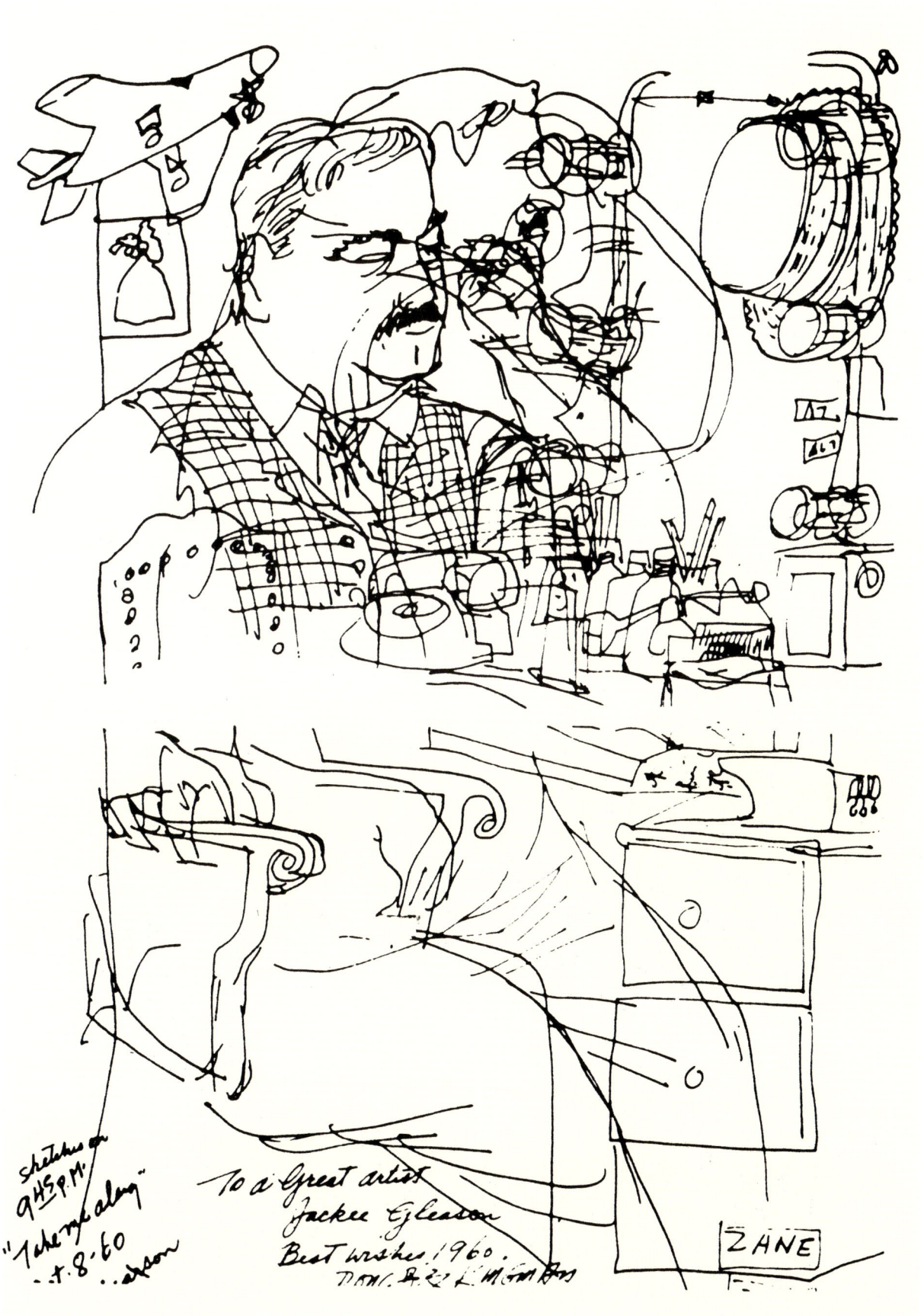

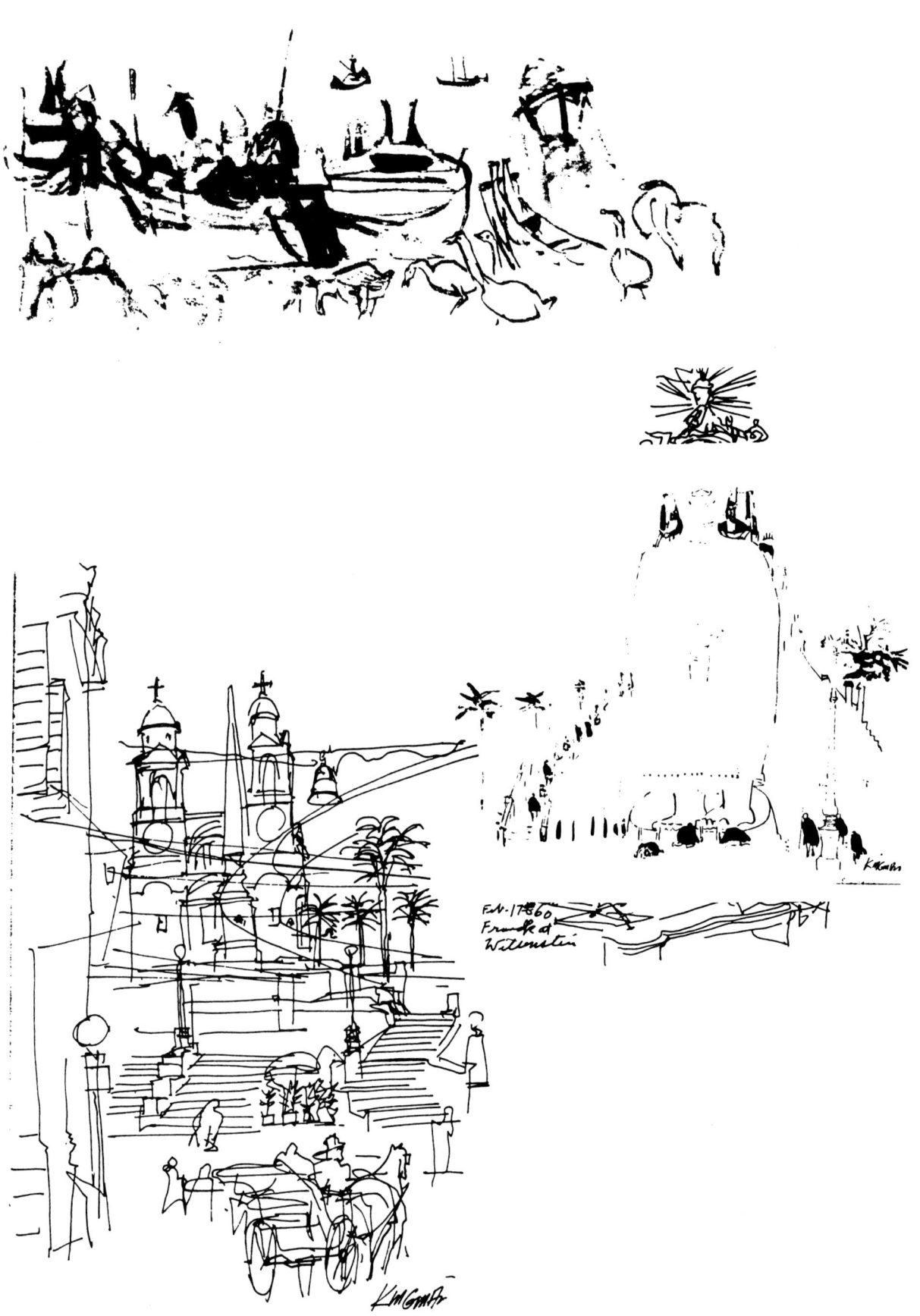

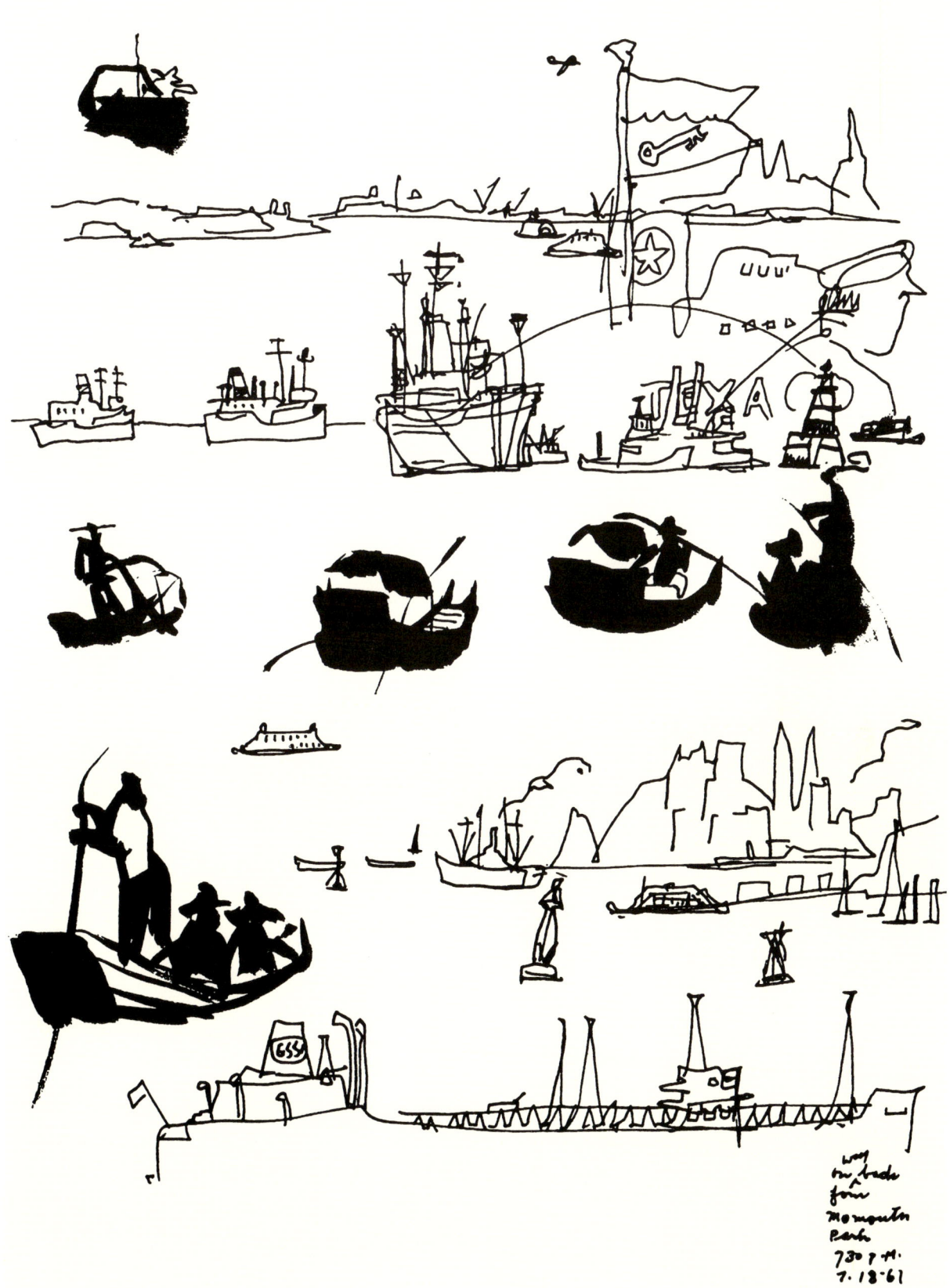

Artist's Magazine

This article was written specially for Artist's Magazine, 6 April, 1995. I painted four pictures using the same Army Plaza location which is near my studio on 5th Avenue in New York. These four pictures are: Plaza in Action, Yellow Taxicab, Plaza Sitter, and Four Men on a Bicycle. I have painted this subject many times in many years, but I used a different concept each time I painted it.

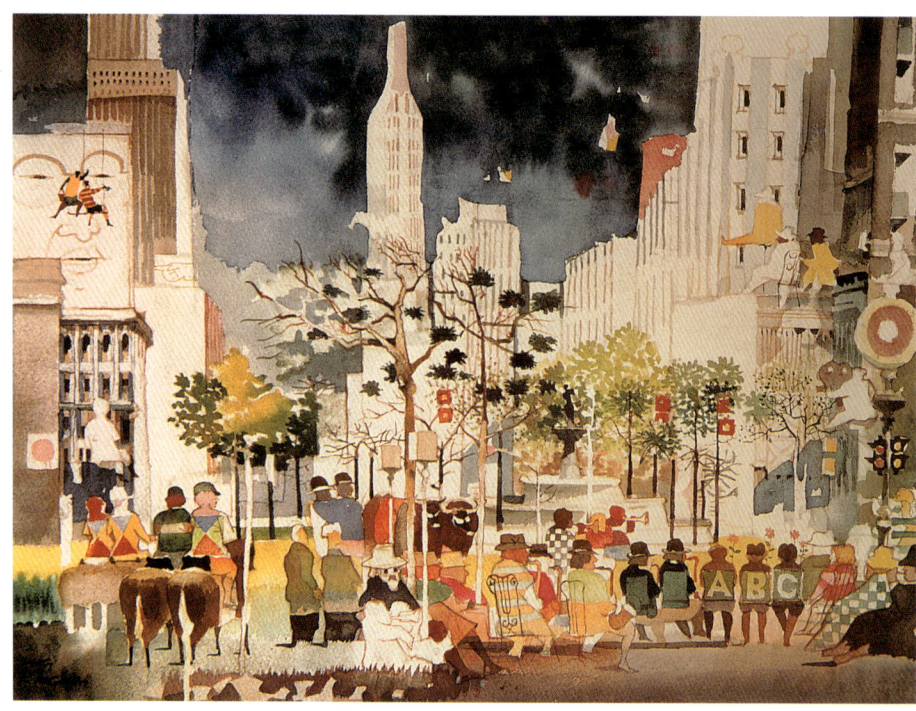

Staging Brilliant Watercolors
How quick sketches and whimsical imagination can set the stage for successful watercolors.
by dong kingman

I like to begin my painting on location, then complete the work later in my studio. Most often, I begin this process with an on-site sketch, which gives me necessary design information and helps me firm up my compositional ideas. I find such sketches particulary helpful for locking into the overall patterns of the abstract shapes that are so important to my paintings.

Since the characters that appear in my finished work come from my imagination, it isn't necessary to include them in the initial sketch. Instead, I let the sketch examine perspective and value, in effect creating an abstract stage on whcih my characters can act out their story.

I limit my on site painting to the completion of the stage setting process. My primary goal is to establish some of the basic colours and the general atmosphere of this backdrop. Once the composition's firmly rooted in my mind, I simply hope for the best and dive into the painting without giving the sketch any more thought.

BRINGING LIFE TO PAPER
I approach color in terms of Chinese watercolor painting, which is built around a limited palette and suble gradations of value. When sketching, I sometimes use shades of gray to illustrate different values, much likeChinese monochromatic ink painting.

I don't like colors that shock the eye, so I rarely use colors like yellow and orange. When I do use bright colors, I carefully choose them to bring life and a sense of happiness to a scene. To me, color is a feeling. When I started painting, I didn't use as much color as I do now-I've built up my feeling for color overtime.

I like to paint wet-on-wet, and I don't want my painting surface to buckle. To avoid thses potential problems, I use Arches 300-lb. paper when I'm doing full (22x30)" paintings, and Arches 140-lb. paper for half-size works. There are four paintings featured in this article. Three of them-*Plaza in Action, Plaza Stiier,* and *Yellow Taxicab*–use normal perspective, with compositional elements sprinkled over the foreground, middle ground and bvackground. The fourth picture, *Four Men on a Bicycle,* takes a very different approach. In this painting, I tried to tell a story with one, high-impact look, concentrating most of the activity in the foreground and leaving the background more or less empty.

Notice that while these

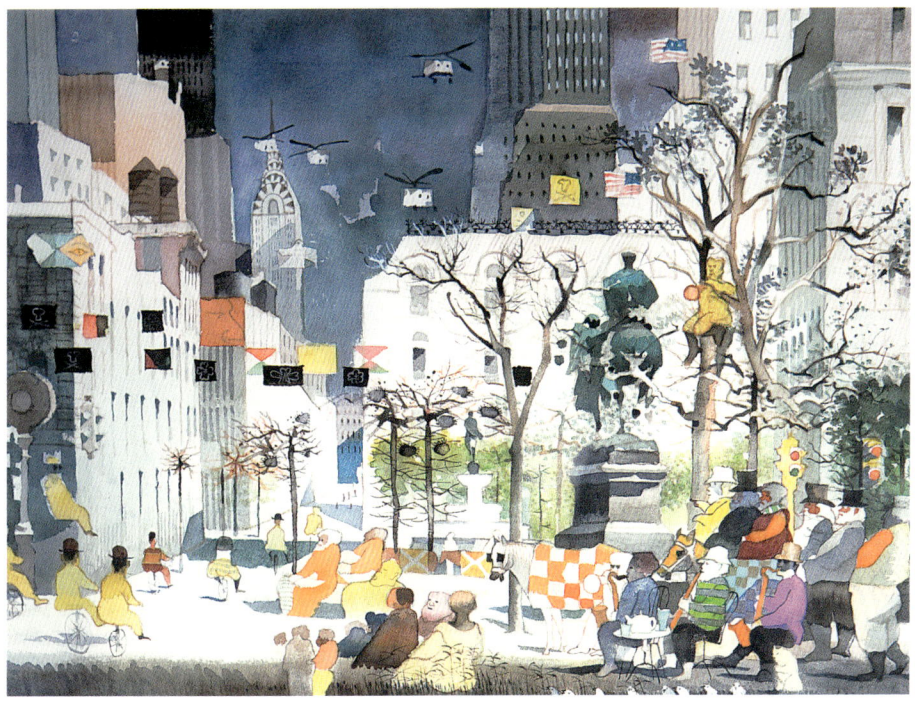

paintings all involve the same site-the *Grand Army Plaza* in New York City-the composition varies from painting to painting. I freely move buildings and other elements to suit the design I have in mind. This freedom is key to understanding the way I paint: I allow my imagination to play with all the elements in a painting in an effort to capture my mood, then project it onto paper.

DEFINING DARK & LIGHT
For *Plaza in Action*, I began with my compositional line drawing, then blocked in simple, abstract areas of light and dark. When the composition was in place, I began to paint the sky. I mixed blue and brown pigment and dappled the mixture to the top of the sky area using a wet-on wet technique. Before the sky dried, I added a little water to make the color thinner near the buildings. Then I added a blue/sepia mixture to make the sky dark and strong, creating the feeling of an approaching storm.

In this picture, I tried to create the feeling of late fall, when the yellow and orange leaves are falling and the bird's nests are bare and unprotected. I painted the trees wet-on wet, using a medium-size Winsor & Newton sable brush. I used a mixture of yellow and gree pigment for the sunny portions of the trees, and before the color dried, I added darker green along the bottom of the trees to create contrasting areas of light and shadow. When the paint was dry, I used a smaller sable brush to add dark green, blue/green or brown/green. These colors helped create a three-dimensional effect.

The people and animals give movement to this composition.Bit by bit, I put together a story. It"s like working out a jigsaw puzzle or a chess problem-and I proceed largely on instinct. I begin randomly placing the people and objects, making necessary changes to make the painting come out right.

COMBINING IMAGERY WITH ABSTRACTION
I began Plaza Sitter by making a light color line drawing to set up my composition. Then I used ight and datk grays to sketch in the main values. Again, I began my painting with the sky, eventually settling on a mixture of blue, sepia and black to create the desired darkness. I then added a few1x2-inch white dots that would later become flags and would later become flags and helicopters, and darkened the tops of all the buildings except the Empire State

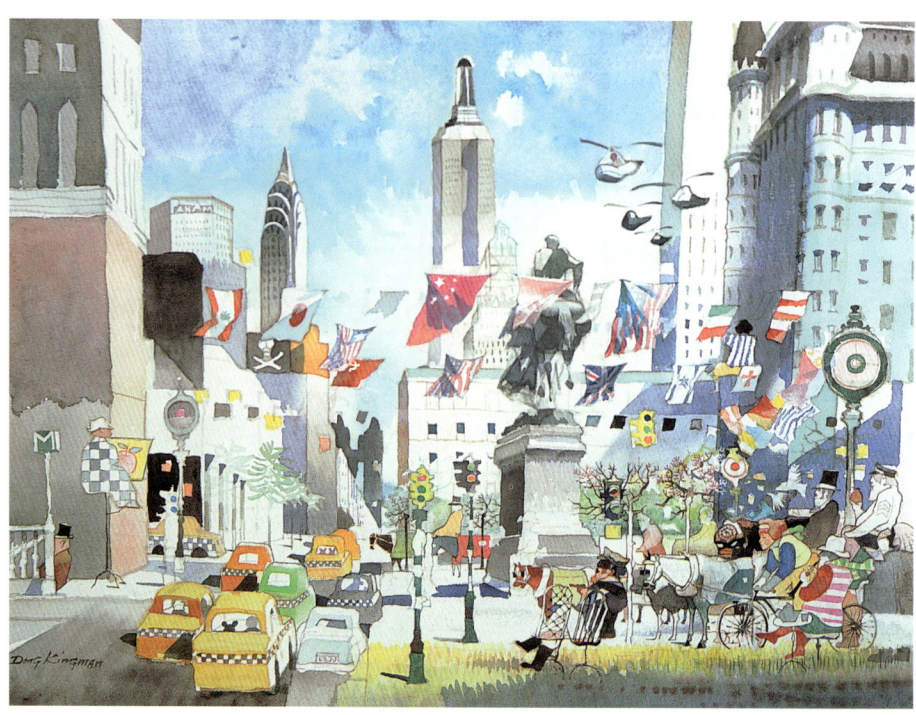

Building.

At this point, I began to focus on individual elements of the piece, but my approach remained abstract. For example, I knew that banners, flags, birds and helicopters often fill the air around Grand Army Plaza. My solution was to mix dark blue as 1x1-inch or 1x2-inch dots, about three or four inches apart in the center of the picture.

I include some of these dots in my original sketch, lining them up as abstract forms. Later, I added more dots– both light & dark– some of which became helicopters, flags and kites, and others whcih simply reminded unidentifiable dots. Finally, I enlivened the activity in the plaza by adding my imaginary cast of characters-men in the trees, musicians and men riding unicycles.

BUILDING A PORTABLE SKYLINE

In *Yellow Taxicab*, I built my composition around four buildings–the Plaza Hotel, the Chrysler Building, the Pan Am Building and the Empire State Building. If you are familiar with New York City, you know that all these buildings aren't visible from my vantage point in Grand Army Plaza. In my sketch, I took the liberty of rearranging the skyline to suit my compositional needs, even moving the Plaza Hotel right onto the square, near the statue of General William Tecumseh Sherman. In order to create a three-dimensional look for these buildings, I combined wet-on-wet techniques with hard and soft edges. Here's a look at how I handle this:

- Using a medium-sized brush, I painted wet-on wet to create the shadowy side of the Plaza Hotel. I employed hard edges for the contrasting shadows on the sunny side of the building.
- I created the sunny and shadowd portions of the Chrysler Building by employing a combination of hard and soft edges.
- I defined the play of light on the Empire State Building with hard-edged techniques, adding a little dark color near the top to make the skyscraper appear big and tall.
- The Pan-Am Building is surrounded by heavily shadowed buildings, so I decided to make it lighter. I'm always looking for abstract patterns of darks and lights to weave into my paintings.

Colorful yellow taxicabs are common site on New York streets, but I decided to create variety and whimsy by painting cabs in various colours and adding passengers that suggest Mickey Mouse and Donald Duck. I placed the flags over the street in the center of the picture, which gave me the opportunity to play the light and dark values against the movement of the wind. I used both small and medium brushes here, depending on what each flag demanded.

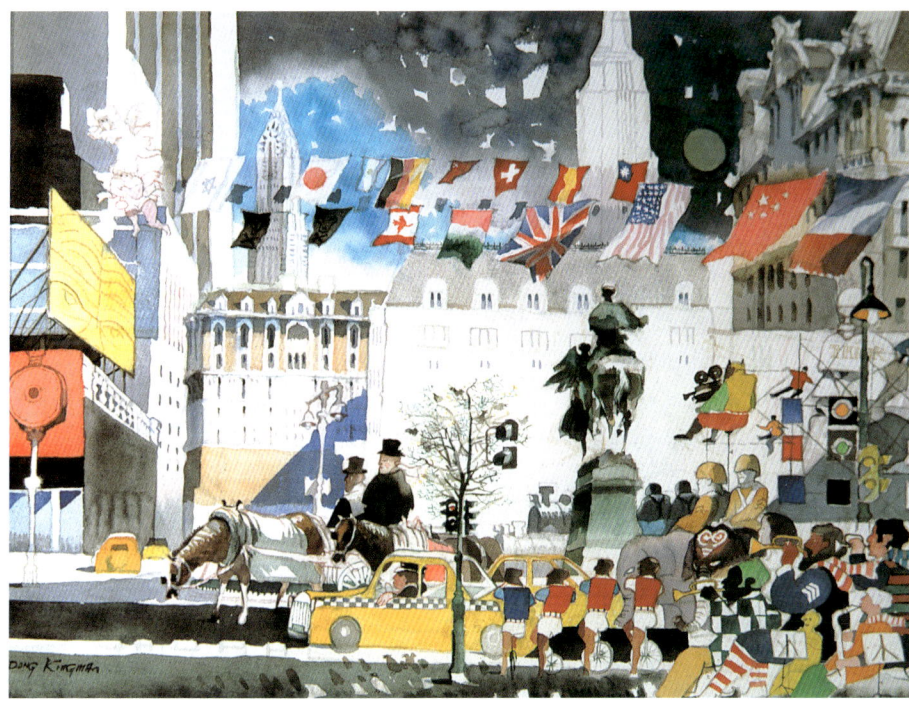

DIVIDING THE PAINTING SURFACE

I started *Four Men on a Bicycle* by sketching the general outline with light gray. I drew a straight, horizontal gray line to indicate how much of the paper I was using for the foreground and how much I was using for the background. Then, I made diagonal lines to indicate where the buildings were going to be.

It took about two hours to do the sketch on location. Back in the studio, I used a small sable brush and a light gray color to draw in elements such as the horse-drawn carriage, the man looking out the front window of a yellow taxicab, a soldier on an elephant and the rest.

Next, I applied color to the sky. I used clear water to set the sky areas, then applied a mixture of dark gray, sepia and blue. When I painted the sky halfway down, I washed the colors off the brush and dipped it in clear water to wash off the edges of the dark clouds, allowing the white paper to shine through.

While painting the sky, I began to think about the rest of the composition. I used a small brush to apply a gray/green color to the light side of General Sherman's statue, adding a dark green color to define the shadowy side. Then I added other elements—horse-drawn carriages, two soldiers mounted on elephants and a locomotive. When I got ready to paint the horses legs, I substituted a yellow taxicab instead. Last, I decided to add four men on bicycles.

BLENDING PHILOSOPHY AND TECHNIQUE

As you can see, my paintings evolve from a simple idea and a basic abstract composition. Once the composition is in place, my imaginary characters take the stage. Be aware of the surprising ideas coming out of your subconscious mind. Bringing these ideas to the surface takes persistence and hard work. Sometimes they come; sometimes not. The important thing is to keep trying.

I've found that a limited palette provides a perfect complement to this philosophy, allowing me to achieve spontaneity without letting my colors get out of control. And starting with a design/value sketch assures a satisfying underlying structure for the embellishments that bring each scene to life.

Magazine Assignments

In 1960, I met a gentleman called Major Stanley, Chief of Hong Kong Tourist Bureau, on the movie set of *The World of Susie Wong* for which I was doing a painting assignment in Hong Kong. Major Stanley asked me to do six watercolor paintings to advertise and promote his city. These paintings were used in many international magazines.

From then on, I had done many covers for magazines like Time, Holiday, Reporter, etc., and posters for Universal Studio Tour, 100th Anniversary of the Statue of Liberty, Anniversary of the Shrine of Democracy of Mount Rushmore, the Sarajevo Winter Olympics, the offical poster for the 1996 World Olympic Games, etc.

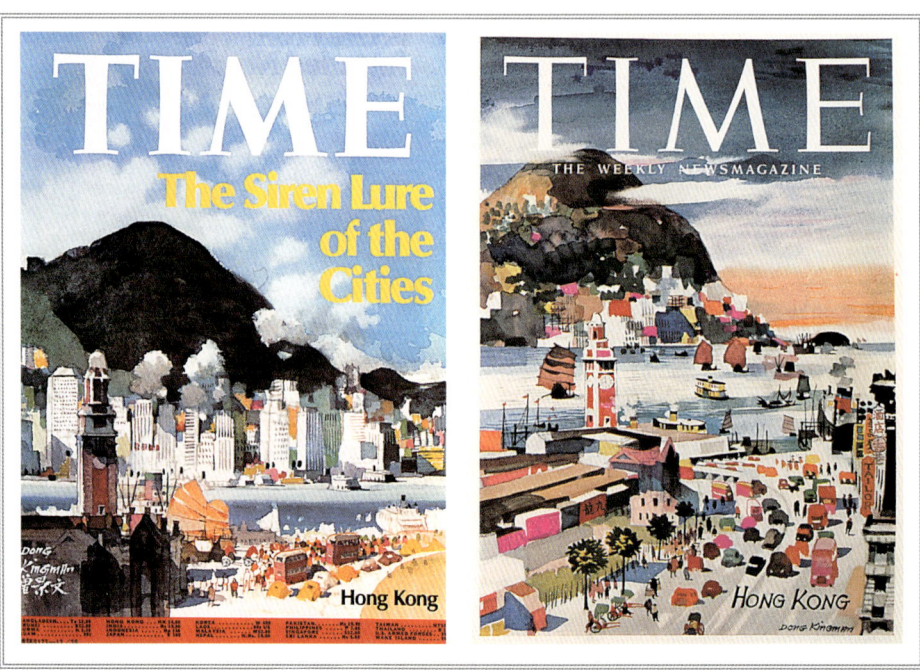

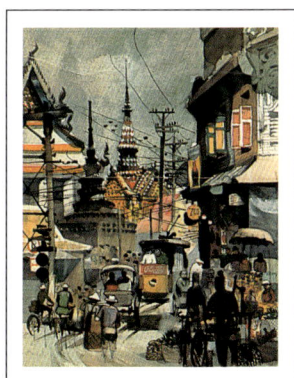

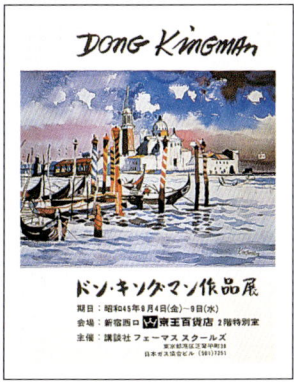

Olympics 1996

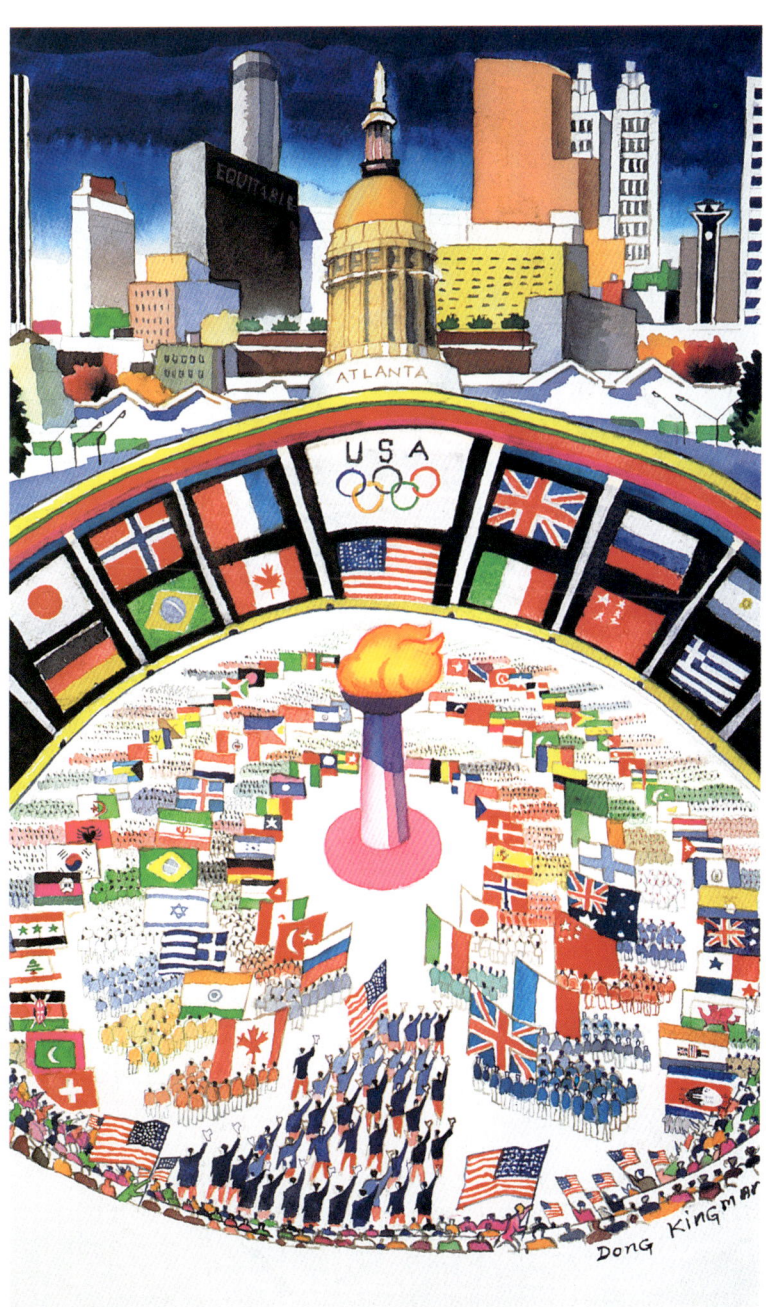

Magazine Assignment

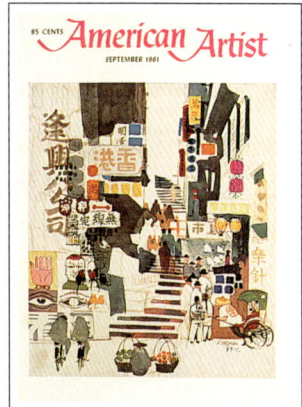 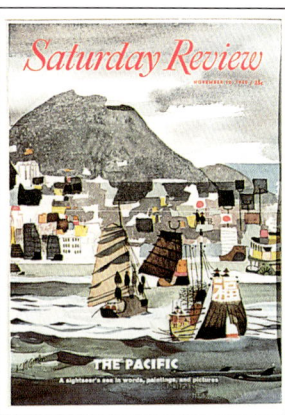 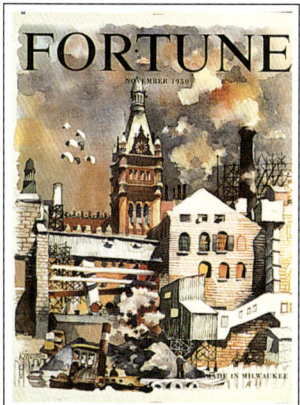 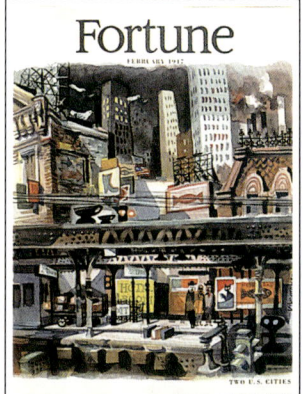

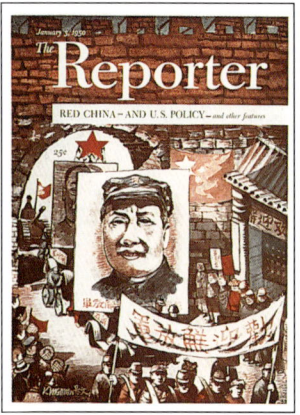 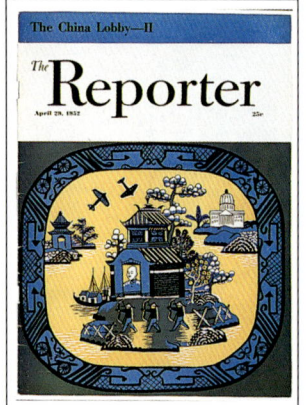 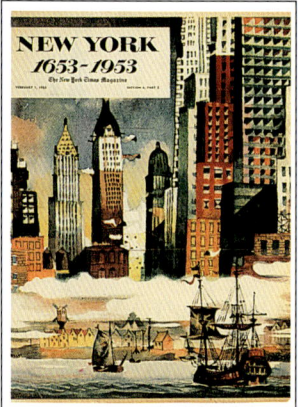 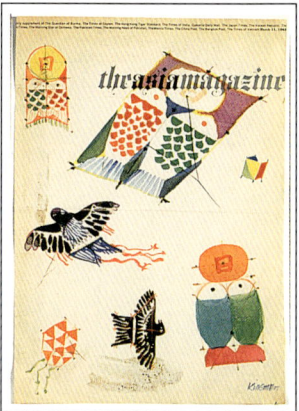

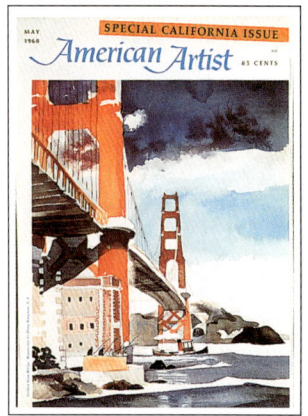 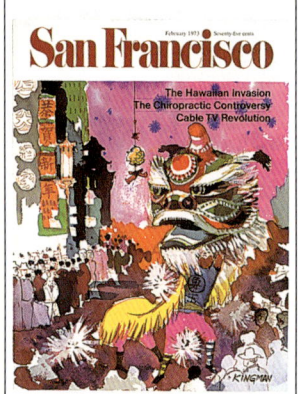 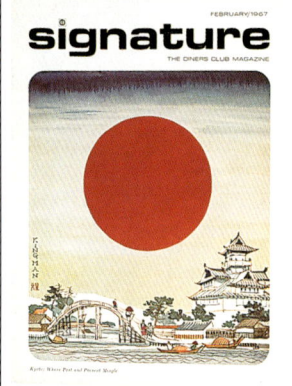 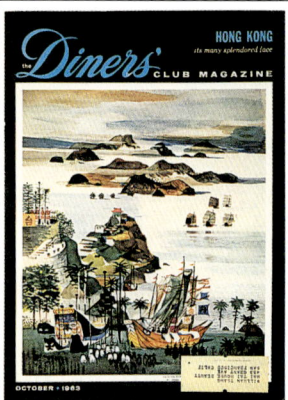

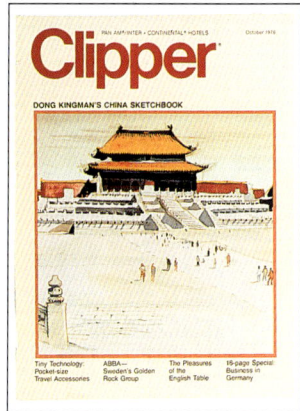 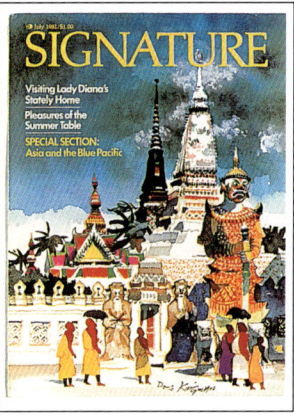 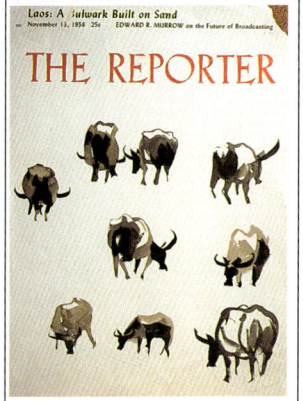 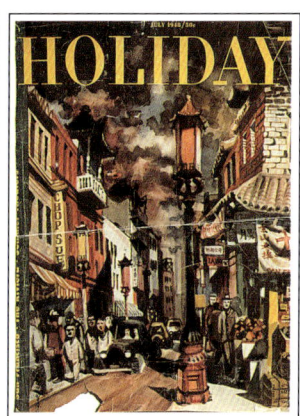
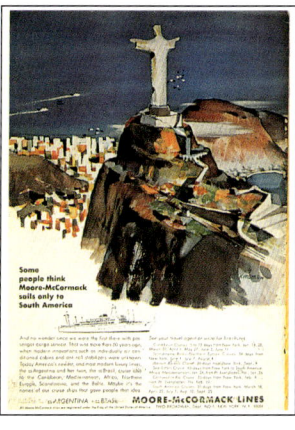 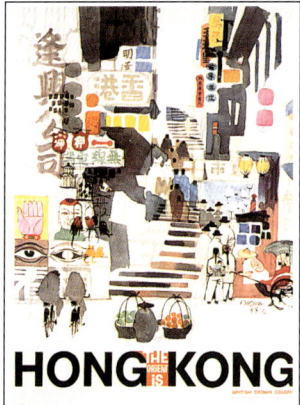 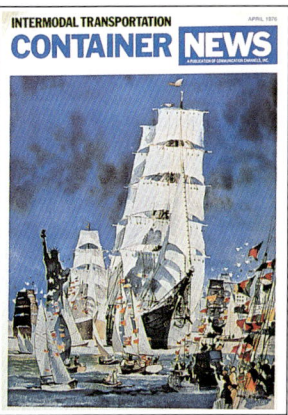 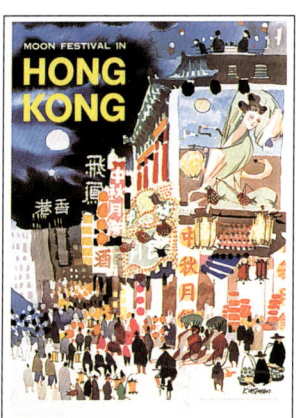
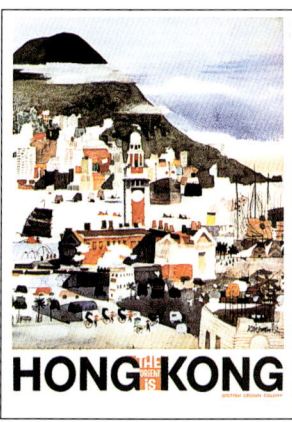 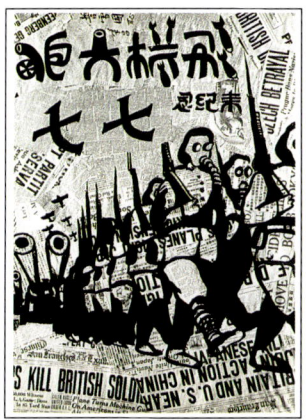 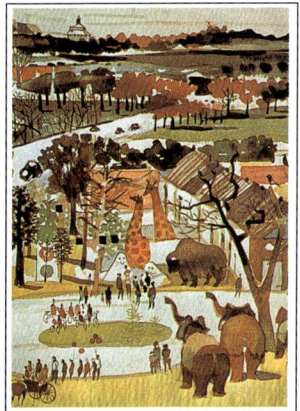 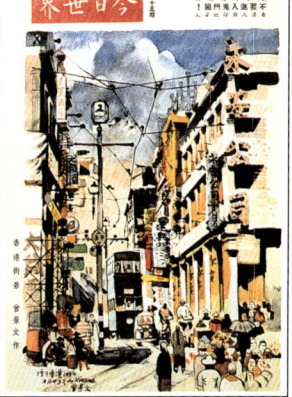

Pan-Am First Class Menus

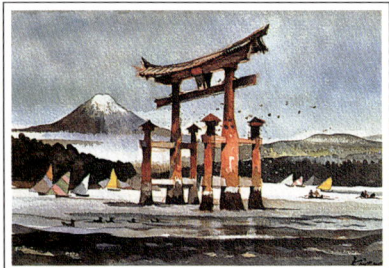
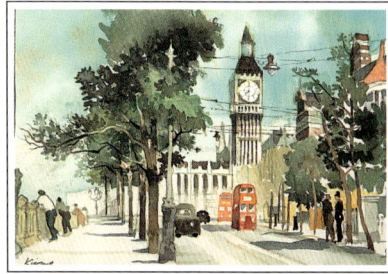
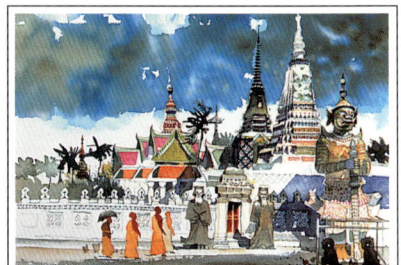

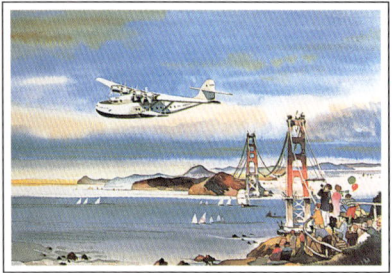
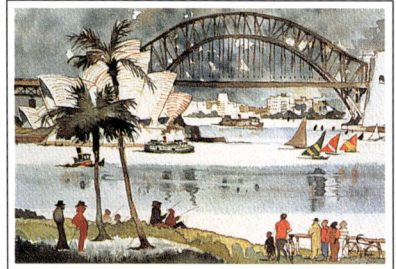
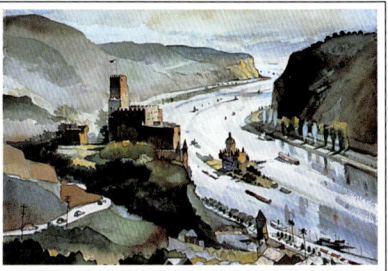

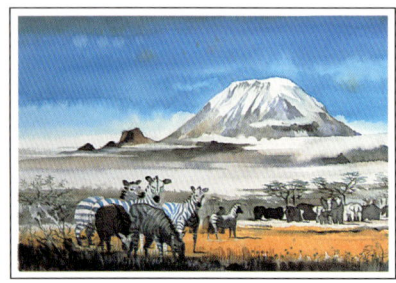
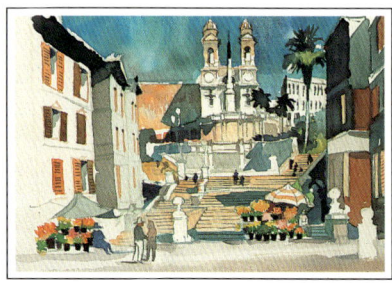
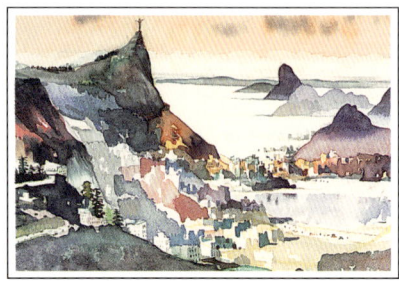

ABOUT PAN-AM
(Pan-American Airways, generally known as Pan-Am, or PAA)

I have been exhibiting all over the world, except China. In 1981, I was the first Chinese-American artist invited by the Chinese Government to give a travelling exhibition. Sponsoring the event, Pan-Am hauled 50 big wooden boxes of my work and a contingent of my press corp and related personnel to and back from the U.S.
On the gala evening honoring me in Beijing, a funny thing happened when I was called upon to give a speech. I spoke only English and Cantonese. I spoke no Mandarin which modern day Chinese called the Common Language. Fortunately, a gentleman from the American Embassy stood up to volunteer to do the translation. So I, a black-haired Chinese speaking in English, translated by a blue-eyed squire into perfect Common Language so all could understand.
I did various jobs for PAA through the years. One of the most significant ones was to paint 24 international PAA's Ports-of-call for their First Class menu covers which took us from Taj Mahal to Kilimanjaro, and which have become collector's items.
Another important assignment was for Helena my wife to write, and I to illustrate, 10 important American cities feature stories for their CLIPPER Magazine, and for which we received commendation from the U.S. Department of Commerce.

Pan Am

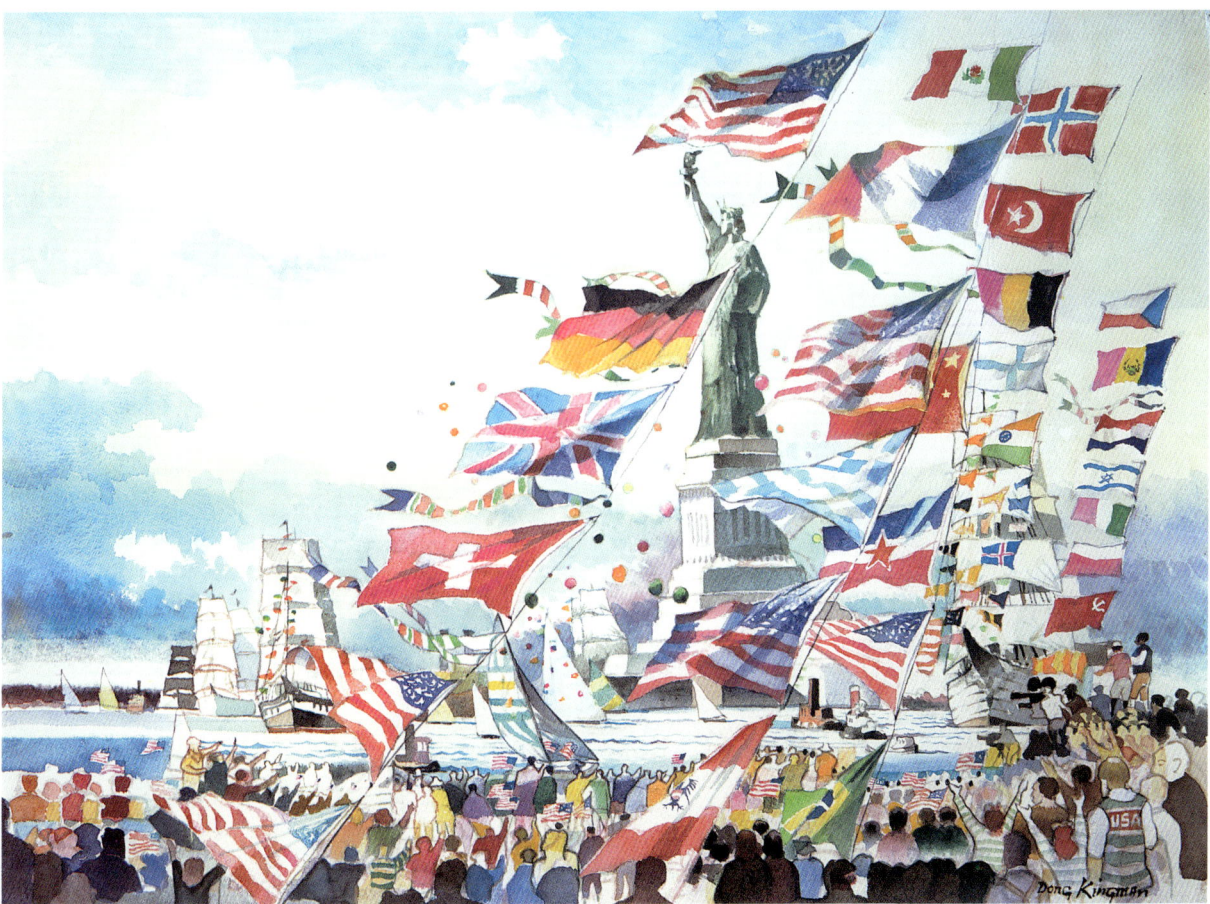

The New Hong Kong Airport

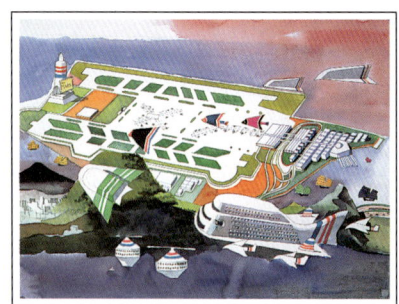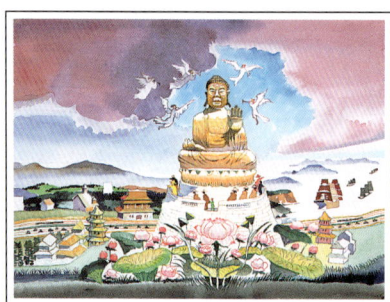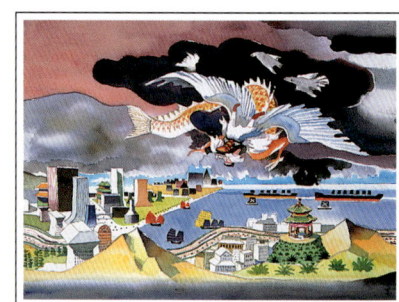

128

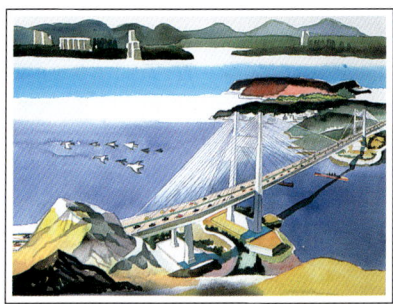 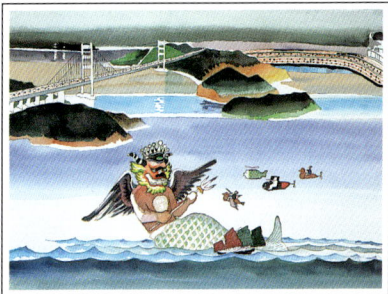 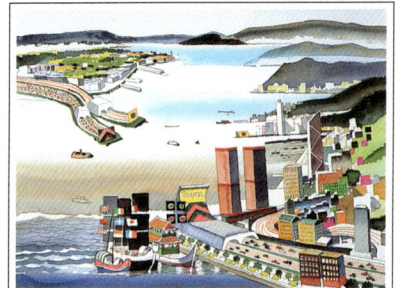

Not long ago when the new Hongkong Airport was still in the planning stage, my friend Charles Wang, President of Salon Films Ltd., asked if I would create a series of large watercolor paintings for the occasion. I said I would. I tossed around a few ideas after I returned to my New York studio. Finally I settled down on a fantasy of how and what will the new Hongkong Airport be like in circa 3001.

Things to come in circa 3001 will feature mainly on speed. People living or working in busy downtown Hongkong Island can take a new kind of helicopter to the new airport in Chek Lap Kok in ten minutes, which make the specially built 100-mile long highway and tunnel instantly obsolete.

Size of the future airplanes will have a seating capacity of 2,000 or more, with a speed of 1,000-mile per hour. You can have breakfast in New York, lunch in Hongkong, and dinner back home in New York again. They do not need runways, for they can land and take-off straight up and down, and sometimes landing on the rooftop of a large building.

For those adventurous enough, wanting to spend a honeymoon on a fantastic journey, they can take a rocket from this airport to the Moon, Mars, or Venus.

Life of a Mural

An Incredible Story by Dong Kingman

To Brooklyn Public Library from Mr and Mrs. Gene Gamiel January, 1997

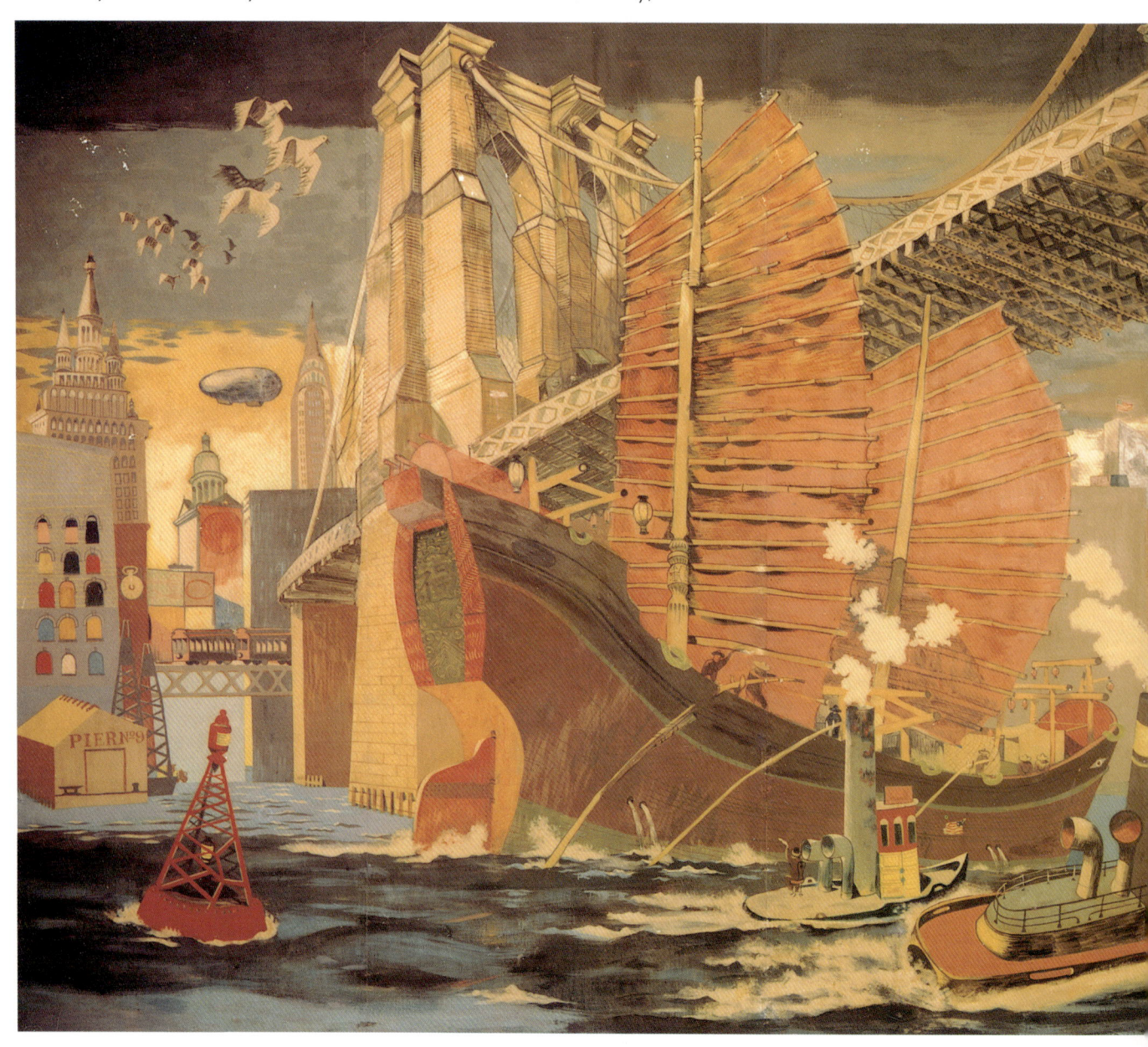

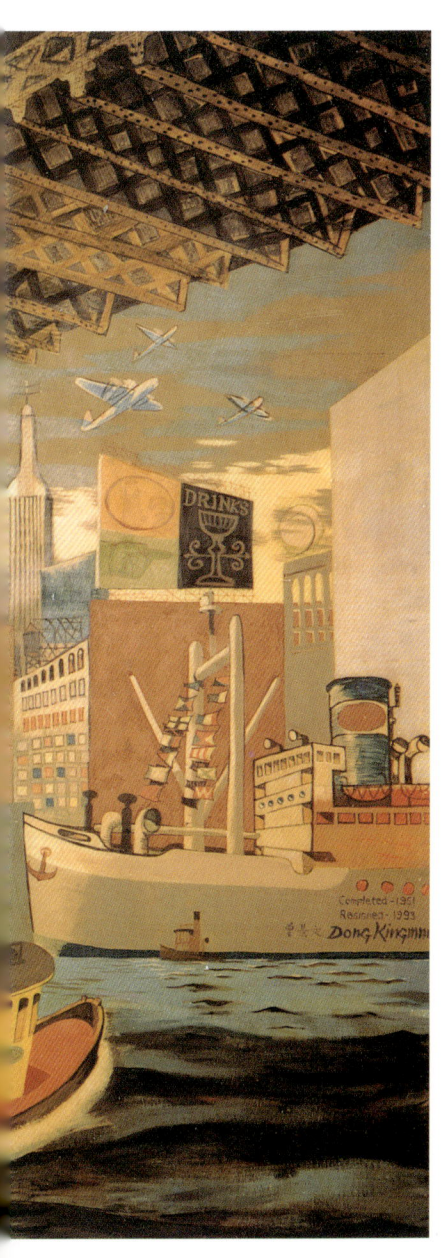

I painted a large mural for a restaurant called Lingnan on Broadway, corner of 90th Street in New York City in 1952. The remuneration was nil, but the owner said I could eat there as long and as much as I wished. Life magazine did a story on this. Sometime later, I told the Life magazine reporter that I had eaten the worth of most part of the mural, and he laughed. Subject of the mural was the Brooklyn Bridge,

The restaurant closed. The mural, taken down in sections, was piled with other garbage in the backyard waiting to be towed.

Roslyn, a former art student of mine in the Hunter College, heard about this, and went to ask the restaurant if she could buy it. She stored it in her basement, and then, she was married to a wonderful musician and conductor, Eugene Gamiel, and raised a family.

In the meantime, my dear friend Herbert Holzmann who owned a huge carpenter shop and factory gave permission to Roslyn to move her mural to his factory if she wished to touch up the cracks and damages. The mural looked like new, She sent word around she wanted to sell, but too large for regular normal accommodations.

40 years since I painted the mural.

Consequently, Roslyn and Eugene wrote me a letter saying they had decided to donate the mural to the Brooklyn Public Library so thousands of students and visitors from all over, including ourselves, could come see it.

The mural will have a long life after all. Brooklyn Bridge going back to the Brooklyn Library.

An incredible story indeed!

God bless the Gamiels.

ALL ABOUT DONG KINGMAN

Dong Kingman loves his work. So do I, and thousands of others whose walls have been brigntened and whose lives have been enriched by his artistry. But what I mean about Dong Kingman loving his work is this: in the thirty years that we have been friends, I have never seen him without his large notebook and India ink pen. As we chat in Chinatown restaurant or walk the streets of Telegraph Hill, he is constantly sketching, sketching, sketching—in lightning, shorthand strokes that capture a landscape in a line, a likeness in a flash, a hidden corner that is suddenly illuminated and captured a landscape in a line, a likeness in a flash, a hidden corner that is suddenly illuminated and captured by the eternal freshness of his vision.

His friends call him Dong, but to himself, he is "Kingman." The phone will ring and there will be that chirpy voice: "Hello, this is Kingman." The phone rings quite often, for although Dong lives in Manhattan, just around the corner from the Plaza Hotel, he is constantly on the move. To San Francisco. To Hong Kong, Hollywood, Europe— and always with his big notebook and busy pen, recording the wonderful world of Kingman, a happy world of bright scenes and hopeful people.

In his artistic outlook, he is only being true to himself, for Dong is one of the happiest people I know. His bright eyes dance, he speaks in chuckles, and he seems never to be bored, the true mark of the person who is not a bore. I have never asked him his age, for he shows no signs of any. He must be somewhere between fifty or sixty, but he still seems as young, trim, and bouncy as the day I met him, in 1936. At that time, he was painting for the WPA, and even then, knowledgeable San Franciscans were buying Kingmans as fast as he painted them.

Today, the fame of this dapper little man—he must be the best-dressed of artists—is established and secure. He is represented in the permanent collections of the country's leading museums and universities—among them the Metropolitan Museum, Whitney Museum, American Academy of Arts and Letters, Museum of Modern Art, Boston Museum, Art Institute of Chicago, and the San Francisco Museum. His awards include two Guggenheim fellowships, the $500 first award of the Metropolitan Museum in 1953, both the Philadelphia Watercolor Prize and the Pennell medal at the Pennsylvania Academy, three prizes of the American Watercolor Society Annuals, and the Audubon Gold Medal of Honor.

Herb Caen

Dong and I have been married more than 40 years. For better or for worse, we have been living together happily and quietly together, working together, facing problems together, travelling together for a greater part of our lives. We have travelled all over the world for Dong's assignments. One of the interesting and colorful episodes is having friends in every corner of the globe, the thought alone was enough to warm our hearts specially in cold miserable days.

Dong is a decisive and responsible person. Decisive because he cares for nothing else but to make a true artist of himself. Responsible because he never sleeps on a job, He delivers and always on time. That is why he is so much on demand, specially for major assignments like 100th Anniversary of the Statue of Liberty, Winter Olympic Games in Sarajevo, Universal Studio Tours, First Class menu covers of city stops of Pan-American Airways, Shrine of Democracy for Mount Rushmore, official poster for 1996 World Olympic Games, to name a few. Dong is going strong, and stronger than ever in spite of his advanced years besides the enormous number of books he has published, and the short subject films he produced. A wonder worker he is indeed. When you speak of an insatiable workaholic, he is one.

I am blessed with just such a man. When he sits in front of a blank piece of watercolor paper, he is not loafing, he is thinking hard trying to work out a composition so he could turn it into a brilliant colorful story-telling happy picture with humor, sometimes with satire or pathos.

When I was a little girl, I was taught a little Chinese poem which had meaning to me except its beautiful cadence and rhythm. Now that I am older, the meaning sinks deeply into my true life. Translation of the poem reads:

> "A glass of green wine, a round of songs,
> Again I bow to make my three wishes:
>
> First, I wish my love to live a thousand years,
> Secondly, I in constant good health;
>
> Thirdly, to be like the swallows on the beam
> Together always, year out year in."

The original Chinese version goes like this:

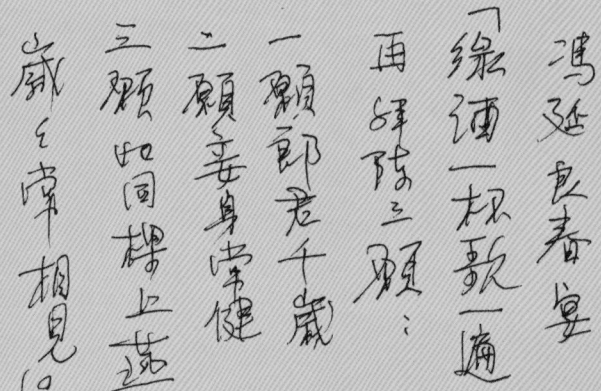

-HELENA KINGMAN

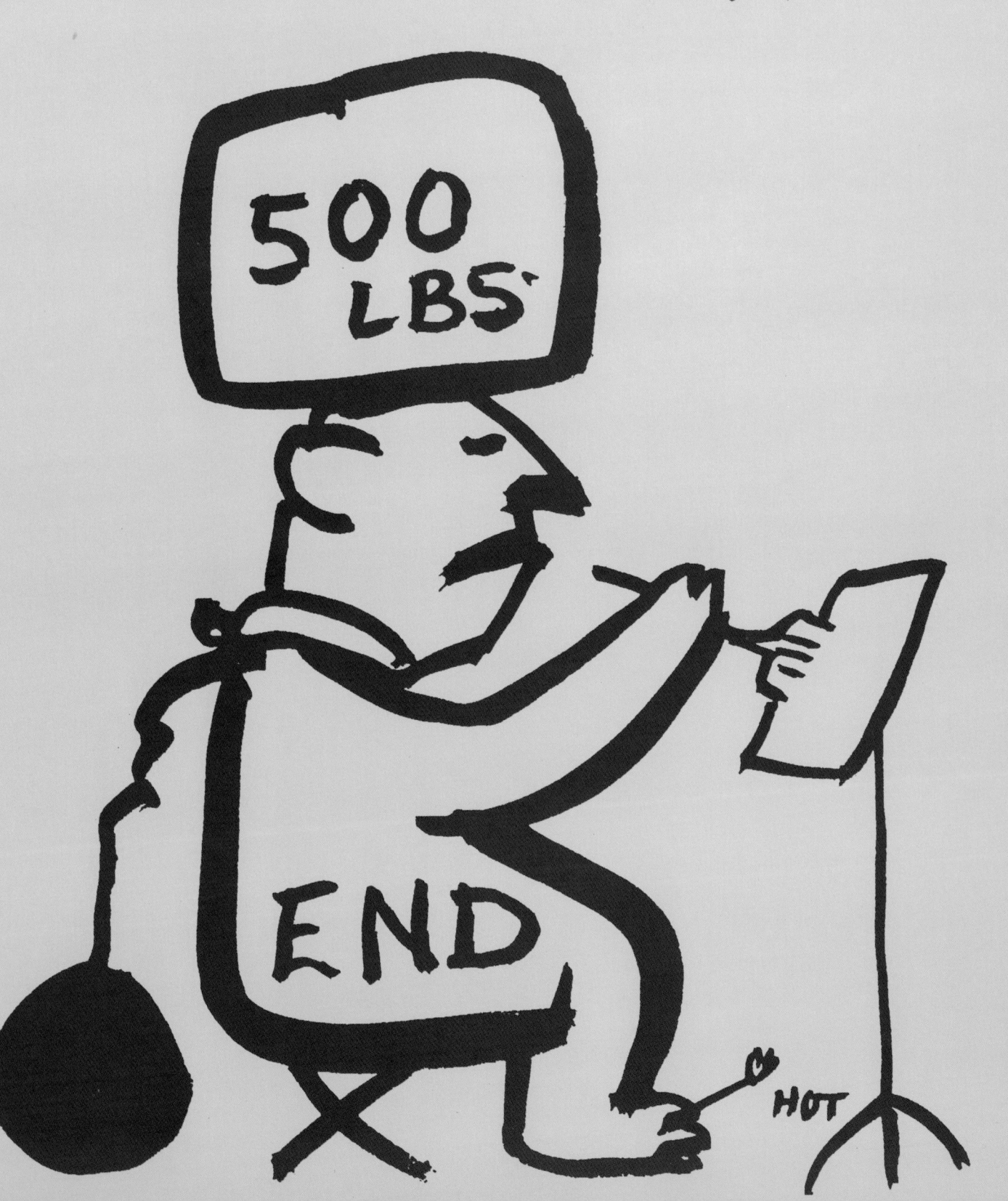

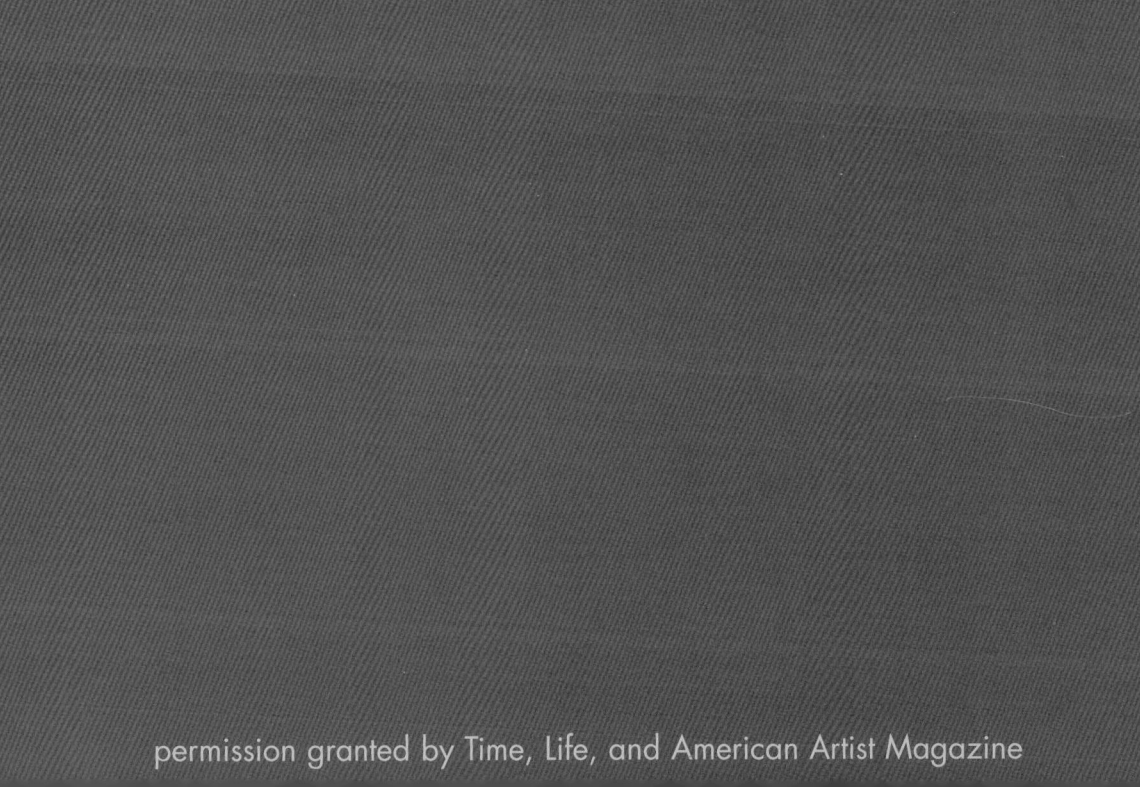

permission granted by Time, Life, and American Artist Magazine

PORTRAITS OF CITIES